TARGETING SCHOOLS

Woburn Education Series

General Series Editor: Professor Peter Gordon
ISSN 1462-2076

For over 20 years this series on the history, development and policy of education, under the distinguished editorship of Peter Gordon, has been evolving into a comprehensive and balanced survey of important trends in teaching and educational policy. The series is intended to reflect the changing nature of education in present-day society. The books are divided into four sections – educational policy studies, educational practice, the history of education and social history – and reflect the continuing interest in this area.

For a full series listing, please visit our website: www.woburnpress.com

History of Education
The Victorian School Manager: A Study in the Management of Education 1800–1902
Peter Gordon

Selection for Secondary Education
Peter Gordon

The Study of Education: Inaugural Lectures
Volume I: Early and Modern
Volume II: The Last Decade
Volume III: The Changing Scene
Volume IV: End of an Era?
edited by Peter Gordon

History of Education: The Making of a Discipline
edited by Peter Gordon and Richard Szreter

Educating the Respectable: A Study of Fleet Road Board School, Hampstead, 1879–1903
W.E. Marsden

In History and in Education: Essays Presented to Peter Gordon
edited by Richard Aldrich

An Anglo-Welsh Teaching Dynasty: The Adams Family from the 1840s to the 1930s
W.E. Marsden

Dictionary of British Educationists
Richard Aldrich and Peter Gordon

Biographical Dictionary of North American and European Educationists
Peter Gordon and Richard Aldrich

TARGETING SCHOOLS

Drill, Militarism and Imperialism

ALAN PENN

WOBURN PRESS
LONDON • PORTLAND, OR

First published in 1999 in Great Britain by
WOBURN PRESS
Newbury House
900 Eastern Avenue
London IG2 7HH

and in the United States of America by
WOBURN PRESS
c/o ISBS
5804 N.E. Hassalo Street
Portland, Oregon 97213-3644

Website: http://www.woburnpress.com

Copyright © 1999 Alan Penn

British Library Cataloguing in Publication Data
Penn, Alan
Targeting schools: drill, militarism and imperialism.
(The Woburn education series)
1. Drill and minor tactics – Study and teaching (Elementary)
– Great Britain – History – 19th century 2. Drill and minor
tactics – Study and teaching (Elementary) – Great Britain –
History – 20th century 3. Education and state – Great
Britain – History – 19th century 4. Education and state –
Great Britain – History – 20th century
I. Title
372.8'6'042'0941

ISBN 0-7130-0217-4 (cloth)
ISBN 0-7130-4038-6 (paper)

Library of Congress Cataloging in Publication Data
Penn, Alan, 1926–
    Targeting schools: drill, militarism, and imperialism /
Alan Penn.
        p.   cm. – (Woburn education series)
    Includes bibliographical references (p.   ) and index.
    ISBN 0-7130-0217-4 (cloth). –
    ISBN 0-7130-4038-6 (paper)
    1. Physical education for children – Great Britain –
History. 2. Drill and minor tactics – History. 3. Militarism
– Great Britain – History. 4. Education, Elementary –
Great Britain – History.
    I. Title. II. Series.
GV443.P388   1999
372.86'044'0941 – dc21   98–46124
                                                       CIP

Printed in Great Britain by
Creative Print and Design (Wales), Ebbw Vale

Contents

To Carol

Acknowledgements

I am particularly indebted to the library staffs of the following: Birmingham University, Bradford University, Huddersfield Polytechnic (now University), Leeds University and the Museum of the History of Education; the Public Libraries and Archive Departments of Birmingham, Bradford, Dewsbury, Halifax, Huddersfield and Leeds.

Preface

This study focuses attention on the elementary schools in England from 1870 to 1914, and on the impact of militarism and imperialism on those schools, particularly through the teaching of drill and physical training.

My own experience in schools and teacher-training has extended from the Black Country to Lincolnshire and West Yorkshire, and it was in the latter area that much of the research into local authorities and schools was carried out.

Official records consulted include parliamentary debates (Hansard), reports of the Committee of Council on Education and later, the reports of the Board of Education, Her/His Majesty's Inspectors' reports, Commissions and Interdepartmental inquiries, Codes of Regulations, School Board and Local Education Authority records and school log-books.

For the general situation, I have drawn particularly on *The Times*, the *School Board Chronicle*, and the *School Government Chronicle*.

The influential status of the London School Board is recognized, as its policies and programmes provided a model for others to follow. Independent societies and organizations have traditionally emerged to press specific issues and here the Society of Arts was prominent in its efforts to promote military drill. Individuals, including Lord Roberts, the Earl of Meath and Sir Lauder Brunton, were also active in attempting to secure military drill, and even rifle shooting, in the elementary schools.

Abbreviations

CCE	Committee of Council on Education
DDM	Duty and Discipline Movement
EDM	Empire Day Movement
HMI	Her/His Majesty's Inspectorate
IAAM	Incorporated Association of Assistant Masters
ILP	Independent Labour Party
LDA	Lads' Drill Association
LEA	Local Education Authority
NSL	National Service League
NUT	National Union of Teachers
OTC	Officers' Training Corps
Society of Arts	Society for the Encouragement of Arts, Commerce and Manufactures in Great Britain
TUC	Trades Union Congress
WO	War Office

'... one of the explicit criteria of national education after 1870 in most Western European countries was to produce generations physically fit for and psychologically attuned to war. It was a necessary part of citizenship. The history of one's country was depicted by writers both of school text-books and of popular works as the history of its military triumphs.'

(Michael Howard, inaugural lecture, 'War and the Nation-State', University of Oxford, 18 November 1977).

'School drill in military and naval exercises, besides their educational value in discipline and united action, sow the seed of national strength in an economical way.'

(Lyon Playfair, lecture to the National Association for the Promotion of Social Science, 1870).

Introduction

The period from 1870 to 1914 is an interesting one, both politically and in the field of education for the masses. The year 1870 marked 'the end of the great formative movements which created the German Empire, the Kingdom of Italy, the Third Republic, and the "Dual Monarchy"' [of Austria-Hungary].[1] It was an era to which the term 'New Imperialism' is often attached, when

> exclusive claims to territory by European powers and their attempts to assert effective control, as well as other forms of European intervention and influence overseas, proliferated more quickly than they had done since the eighteenth century and attracted an unusual degree of attention.[2]

IMPERIAL EXPANSION

Once a nation had embarked upon a course of imperial expansion, a sense of destiny and even of divine purpose tended to accompany the process. Joseph Chamberlain, Colonial Secretary, described by Fenner Brockway as 'the arch-imperialist of the age'[3] claimed in 1897: 'It seems to me that the tendency of the time is to throw all power into the hands of the greater empires, and the minor kingdoms – those which are non-progressive – seem to be destined to fall into a secondary and subordinate place.'[4] For imperialism to function it is, then, necessary to distinguish between states whose arrogated role is to dominate and those 'non-progressive' states whose function is to be submissive to the will of the former. Imperialists may, however, prefer to present it otherwise, referring, as did Chamberlain, to the sense of greatness of empire, believing that 'a nation like an individual, is the better for having great responsibilities and great obligations'.[5] At least as early as 1775 reference was made to the supposedly divine nature of imperialism. On

1

22 of March of that year Edmund Burke spoke of 'a great empire' which 'went ill with little minds', and declaimed: 'We ought to elevate our minds to the greatness of that task to which the order of Providence has called us.'[6] Many orators were to echo those sentiments during the closing decades of the nineteenth century. Typical of them was a speech delivered by Lord Curzon to a Birmingham audience exhorting them to be true to the imperial mission, which he described as 'an instrument through which God speaks to mankind'.[7]

Disraeli had seized upon the idea of enhancing Britain's imperial status as 'the obvious, indeed, the only, way of confirming Britain's position as a great power in a rapidly changing world'.[8] His policy of imperial consolidation was outlined in a speech at the Lord Mayor's banquet in 1875 when he encouraged the development of bilateral relationships between the United Kingdom and her colonies, assimilating their sympathies to the mother country.[9] Perhaps the grandest gesture in this direction was the establishment of the Queen as Empress of India the following year, though the event was not universally acclaimed. It has been described as 'a sublimation prosaically achieved by a far from unanimous vote in the House of Commons, but rapturously received by the Queen'.[10] After her long period of seclusion following the death of her beloved Albert she emerged to open parliament and to adopt an increasingly ceremonial role. Monarchy was 'promoted as a national symbol, above class and party, a focus for patriotic loyalty, stability and tradition'.[11] Hobsbawm reminds us that much 'tradition' was invented in subsequent decades.[12] The year 1876 was also marked by a sabre-rattling venture: the despatch of a British fleet to Turkish waters as a deterrent to any Russian penetration to the east. Supporters of that initiative earned for themselves the name 'jingoes', a term featured in a contemporary music-hall ditty. Ashmead Bartlett set up the Patriotic Association in 1878 in an attempt to bring together jingoistic elements, but the movement made only a marginal political impact.[13] Jingoism was to outlast that incident and to survive as a label associated with intense national pride and patriotism well into the twentieth century, as demonstrated during the Falklands War in 1982 and the Gulf War (1990–91).

If the Conservatives under Disraeli aspired to the title of champions of empire, the Liberal contention was that the Empire tended to hinder rather than to help Britain's status and position in the world. Gladstone, a reluctant imperialist, attacked the Conservatives in 1877 as a party 'striving to cajole or drive us into Imperialism',[14] yet the following year wrote that:

The sentiment of empire may be called innate in every Briton... It is part of our patrimony: born with our birth, dying only with our death; incorporating itself in the first elements of our knowledge, and interwoven with all our habits of mental action upon public affairs.[15]

On the eve of the Liberal election victory in 1880 Gladstone tabled 'six right principles' of foreign policy. He saw the strength of the empire nurtured by 'just legislation and economy at home' and by concentration abroad on 'great and worthy occasions', avoiding adventures or 'needless and entangling engagements'.[16] Those principles were easier to enunciate than to execute when Britain's rivals were also in search of 'great and worthy occasions'.

Pride in empire was the constant theme of many publications, public and parliamentary speeches and orations, and of pageants and celebrations. Among the most influential authors to address the imperial theme were Charles Dilke, J. R. Seeley and J. A. Froude, who shared a common concern for the white-settled colonies, though India was often accorded a special place. Dilke wrote of his conception of 'the grandeur of our race, already girdling the earth, which it is destined, perhaps, to overspread'.[17] Seeley, however, struck a note of caution when he suggested that Britain faced '... the largest of all political questions, for if our Empire is capable of further development, we have the problem of discovering what direction that development should take, and if it is a mischievous incumbrance, we have the still more anxious problem of getting rid of it'.[18] But Britain was riding a wave of history, and could believe 'without necessary hypocrisy, that God [was] on their side'.[19]

The emergence of a popular, mass-circulation press provided opportunities for imperialist policies to be presented non-intellectually, and for national patriotism to be encouraged. Harmsworth's *Daily Mail* (1896) and Pearson's *Daily Express* (1900) voiced their imperial messages to large reading publics, the latter proclaiming: 'Our policy is patriotic; our policy is the British Empire.' A whole tapestry of novels and poems, both for children and adults, was woven around imperial themes. Kipling became the poet of empire, though he felt it necessary to warn against 'frantic boast and foolish word'.[20] At a more lowly level, mundane children's readers and textbooks drew the attention of their young readers to the glorious empire on which the sun never set, and to the heroic qualities of the 'servants of empire', whether military or civil, who devoted their energies and even their lives to its cause.

Pageants and displays, whether expressed in the splendour of state

3

occasions associated with royal jubilees or in humble street or classroom, added their colourful contribution to the celebration of imperialism. For many years children in London and the provinces attended vast displays in which they drilled and paraded to the martial accompaniment of school bands before representatives of royalty and privilege. Under the banner 'One King, One Flag, One Fleet, One Empire' the Empire Day Movement, conceived by the Earl of Meath in 1896, and constantly spurred to fresh action by his unfailing enthusiasm, encouraged schools to celebrate Empire Day.[21] Meath's efforts to encourage the flying of the Union Jack flag on schools and public buildings marked another initiative of his, the appropriateness of which was hotly debated.[22] His initiatives contributed to the 'invention of tradition' noted above, in which the values associated with the upper middle classes and the public schools were presented to a wider public.[23]

THEORIES OF RACE AND NATION

In a chapter on 'Nationality' in his *Representative Government*, J. S. Mill referred to the common sympathies which bound together members of a nation and separated them from outsiders. He instanced identity of race and descent, community of language and religion, and the significance of geographical boundaries, but he insisted that the main factor was 'identity of political antecedents, the possession of a national history and consequent community of recollections, collective pride and humiliation, pleasure and regret, connected with the incidents in the past'.[24] Many writers did not differentiate between the genetic concept 'race' and 'nation', offering generalizations which treated them as virtual synonyms.[25] National institutions, including state and private sectors of education, were seen to have well-defined responsibilities in arousing appropriate sentiments and in teaching about those incidents and characters in the nation's history which contributed most forcefully to her status and to the cohesion of her people. C. E. Fayle stressed the need to foster and to encourage 'whatever is truly expressive of national qualities in our educational system, in our social institutions, in our literature and fine arts, in our general intellectual outlook'.[26] If that history was biased in the interests of militarism so that from childhood 'the main outlines of their country's history of war, the history of the gains achieved by victorious campaigns and of the stern and bitter consequences of lost battles'[27] were taught, so too were the seeds of conflict and strife. Prince von Bülow claimed that therein lay the difference between Prussia and other states. He believed that conflict among nations was inevitable, and consequently militarism had a necessary contribution to make in the context of a nation's education. The argument was to engage the close attention of those interested in, and responsible for, the education of children in Britain, as well as in Germany.

GERMAN IMPERIALISM

After Bismarck lost power in Germany in 1890, German foreign policy shifted its direction; efforts to keep France in an isolated position did not prevent that country from forming an alliance with Russia. Germany itself embarked upon a global policy (*Weltpolitik*). No longer was German foreign policy to concern itself primarily with the continent of Europe. The move was to form 'part of that strong tide of evolution which irresistibly bore the German State out beyond the bounds of its earlier policy'.[28]

Bülow commented that it was the application of modern industrial, commercial and trading techniques to German industry which carried the German Empire beyond the political limits which Bismarck had set for it.[29] New, unrestricted markets had to be sought, and this meant that Germany joined its European rivals in the seizure and exploitation of colonies. It was, however, somewhat late in the day, and the colonial opportunities left proved to be of little economic significance and, if anything, tended to demonstrate Germany's inability to compete with Britain and France. Thus thwarted, Germany turned to the east, seeking to inject its influence, economic and military, into Turkey, and beyond to the Persian Gulf. The 'Eastern Question', dormant for some 30 years after the Congress of Berlin (1878), was reopened by this interest and by internal problems endemic to the Balkans, which engaged the attention of Russia and Austria-Hungary. It raised the question as to whether Britain would remain a spectator, particularly if the strategic interest in the route to India was threatened.

Britain and France found it expedient to seek common accord in the early years of the twentieth century, acknowledging the respective interests of the former in Egypt, and of the latter in Morocco. An *entente* was agreed in 1904, to which Russia was admitted three years later,[30] but its bonds were much looser than those which bound the Triple Alliance of Germany, Austria-Hungary and Italy of 1882. Europe was fast dividing into the two power blocs which would embark upon open hostilities once the spark was kindled in 1914. Mindful of the dangers of an irrevocable split between Britain and Germany, the prime minister, Asquith, stated in December 1911: 'We do not desire to stand in the light of any Power which wants to find a place in the sun.'[31] Opportunities for such expansion were limited, as he well knew. Germany had turned its eyes to the East and, it appeared, was prepared to go to war. K. H. Janssen writes that Germany's political and military leaders did not seek a world war at any cost but were consciously prepared to risk it. 'They were not overwhelmed by catastrophe: they made political events develop to the brink of catastrophe.'[32] Of that time, Gerhard Ritter maintains:

> There was a certain fatalism, a belief that a great war was inevitable, as well as a belief in strong national prestige and a desire to be accepted in the world, both of which could lead to political blindness. This was certainly not the case in Vienna and Berlin alone, but it was especially disastrous there because of the threat to the Central Powers' position … .[33]

Thus Germany's quest for 'a place in the sun' amongst the imperialist nations was based unashamedly on militarism. Prince von Bülow wrote:

> The German nation can assert before the whole world that its greatest strength, which has stood the test of the past and of the present, is to be found in that which in the hour of direst need and danger saved the life of Germany: German militarism.[34]

However, the 20 years preceding the major army Bills of 1912 and 1913 marked a period in which there was little if any expansion of the German army. Berghahn suggests that neither the war minister nor the Reich Chancellor, Bethmann Hollweg, was prepared to risk diluting the quality and character of the officer corps through the admission of 'undesirable elements'.[35]

IMPERIALISM AND MILITARISM

In 1886, Herbert Spencer had referred to militarism as 'a military type of society', in which the process of regimentation, although most prominent in the army, affected the whole of society.[36] Alfred Vagts has drawn an interesting distinction between an army 'maintained in a military way' and one operating in a militaristic way. The former concentrates on winning particular military objectives in the most

6

efficient manner, both in terms of men and of financial cost. In contrast, militarism 'presents a vast array of customs, interests, prestige, actions and thoughts associated with armies and wars and yet transcending the true military purposes'.[37] In the latter, the military mentality as well as its modes of action and decision-making intrude into the civilian sector of society.

Military sentiments were certainly spreading in English society, as in the presence of army bands with their ceremony and colour at local fêtes and other occasions, the emergence of uniformed and semi-uniformed youth organizations, and the employment of members of the Militia to train boys in military drill in elementary schools. The Salvation Army (1865) and the Church Army (1882) both adopted military models, and perhaps the most popular hymn of the time was *Onward Christian Soldiers*.

Clearly, militarism was widely practised by imperial states, and Britain, in spite of its protests to the contrary, must be counted among them. She had her active militarists, in civilian circles as in the armed services, many of them in positions of influence and authority. The qualities which were most admired and worthy of emulation were set out by General Lord Wolseley. Writing in the *United Services Magazine* (March 1897), he asserted:

> War with all its evil calls out and puts to the proof of the highest and best qualities of man. Fearlessness, daring, contempt of death, self-sacrifice, readiness to die for country or some other sacred cause ... . The training involved in all this preparation for war is an invigorating antidote against that luxury and effeminacy which destroys nations, as well as individuals.[38]

Wolseley was writing at a time when the British army had for many years been engaged in imperial skirmishes and punitive expeditions; it had yet to be tested by the Boer irregulars, let alone the military might of the German army on European soil.

The training to which Wolseley referred was not to be confined to army volunteers: it was considered by many to be appropriate for the population at large, including those still at school, both in the private sector and in the state system of education. As will appear in subsequent chapters, the provision was not necessarily confined to boys, and it extended even down into infant schools. The training of school children, whether in the form of military drill or of physical training, was encouraged by militarists on the one hand and by those primarily concerned for the physical well-being of the country's youth on the

7

other. Perhaps of all aspects of imperialism which impinged upon education, this was the one most fiercely debated and most tenaciously defended.

A. J. Marder sees militarism as 'a conspicuous element in pre-1914 European thought', more responsible for the outbreak of a major war than '"incidents" and assassinations, telegrams and ultimata'.[39] It provided the culture that could legitimize aggressive action when a spark was kindled by some 'incident' or stance which appeared threatening to a nation's esteem or its ambitions.

Naval power, or 'navalism', as it has often been dubbed, was an essential aspect of the general phenomenon of militarism which attracted its own adherents and supporters. Writing of the two decades after 1875, when the Suez Canal shares were acquired, James Morris claims: 'British military supremacy was scarcely tested, and the Royal Navy sailed the world, convoying its expeditionary forces, showing the Queen's flag, as though its admirals owned the oceans.' He suggests that the effect of this on the general public was to give them a growing sense of national pride to the extent that 'for the first and probably the last time in their history, the British people acquired a taste for drums, guns and glory'.[40] (The reader is left to wonder whether Morris would have written that had his book been published after the Falklands War instead of anticipating it by a mere three years.)

THE BALANCE OF POWER

The situation at the turn of the century was that in Europe the power balance was in Germany's favour, and worldwide the balance was in favour of Britain. As Thomson puts it: 'In comparison with Germany's position of concentrated power in central Europe, the British Empire was peripheral and diffused.'[41] According to Berghahn, many Germans were of the opinion that Bismarck's failure to secure colonies in the 1870s and 1880s could be compensated to some extent by a strong naval programme providing the political leverage by which territorial concessions might be gained. Such an advantage would be a bonus to the navy's role in protecting existing German colonies.[42] In Germany and Britain, huge capital investment in ever more sophisticated and powerful warships was accompanied by propaganda measures aimed at enlisting public support. Both countries founded Navy Leagues to co-ordinate these efforts. They evoked images of a hostile world and heightened international tension in their bid to intensify loyalty to the nation. The policy of the British organization was to appeal to both adults and schoolchildren. Evidence of these promotional activities is found in many school log-books which recorded visits by representatives of the Navy League and lectures and other activities organized by schools using materials supplied by the League.

IMPERIALISTIC ORGANIZATIONS

A number of other organizations of an imperialistic kind emerged in Britain to encourage support for expansionist policies among the populace. One of the earliest was the Primrose League, which was set up in 1884 in honour of Disraeli, with the motto '*Imperium et libertas*'. It was founded both to draw attention to Conservative principles in home and foreign policies and to further the cause of imperialism. The importance of imbuing young citizens with a patriotic understanding of, and respect for, imperial principles was not forgotten. Many such organizations recognized the opportunities within the schools for their concerns to be developed among the generations who would themselves in due course don the imperial mantle. The Navy League, the Empire Day Movement, and the Duty and Discipline movement were of that band. Beyond the school gates the semi-uniformed brigades such as the Boys' Brigade, the Church Lads' Brigade, and later the Boy Scouts, beckoned, along with their sister organizations.

INDUSTRIALIZATION

Industrialism was also a major factor in stimulating national rivalries, with the United States and Germany rapidly overtaking Britain in many key areas of production. Ramsay Muir suggests that industrialism and commercialism, instead of making for peace, appeared to be major contributors to international jealousy and friction: 'War and industry were not, it seemed, incompatible, as Cobden had believed: war could lay the foundations of industrial success; and industry, in its turn, could supply the materials of war.'[43] Paul Kennedy also draws attention to this relationship:

> Far-reaching industrial and technological developments were under way, changing global economic balances more swiftly than ever before. And it would not be too long before those alterations

9

in the productive/industrial base would have their impacts upon the military capacities and external policies of the great Powers.[44]

During the age of the new imperialism perceptions of traditional social and political norms were challenged. Power was to reside no longer exclusively with an elite aristocracy and an influential middle class: increasingly the proletariat demanded to be heard as it reaped the benefits of successive measures to extend the electorate. Robert Lowe, Vice-President of the Committee of Council on Education from 1859 to 1864, was a lively participant in the debates for reform, which he fiercely opposed, in the years 1866 and 1887. However, when the Reform Bill of 1867 became law, he realized that if a democracy was becoming a reality, there was a need for it to be educated. The Elementary Education Act of 1870 began that process.

This study is concerned with one aspect of life in imperial England between 1870 and 1914 – the endeavours of a politically influential and powerful group of individuals to incorporate the teaching of military drill in the curriculum of the nation's elementary schools. A smaller number wished to extend that provision so as to include the handling of weapons, such as carbines discarded by the army, and shooting at targets with 'rabbit guns'. In opposition to the militarists were ranged those who expressed political objections to the practice which they saw as acting against the interests of the working classes, those who had religious and ethical objections to the teaching of methods of war to schoolchildren, and the growing number of educationalists who favoured 'ordinary' drill or physical exercises on strictly health and educational grounds.

THE ELEMENTARY EDUCATION ACT OF 1870

Educationally, 1870 was a milestone in the field of elementary provision, marking as it did the time when a serious effort was set in train to provide schooling on a compulsory basis for all children. The Elementary Education Act of that year was a compromise measure – it did not create a new national system, nor a completely compulsory system, nor a free system, accepting as it did the principles of voluntary effort, of school fees and of private endowments. Local authorities known as School Boards were set up on an *ad hoc* basis where denominational provision was inadequate or insufficient, which tended to be concentrated in urban areas of growing population. Membership of the controlling School Boards carried no property qualification (as was the case for Town Councils and Boards of Guardians), which meant that working men could be elected, as could women. This marked a significant advance in the democratic process: the parents of children who would attend the schools could anticipate that some at least of their representatives on the Boards would have their perceived interests at heart. The presence of women on School Boards provided them with the opportunity to effect a tenuous entrance into official public life and for male domination to be challenged.

Under the terms of the Act the curriculum of the elementary schools was destined to serve the twin criteria of social utility and cheapness of operation. Ambitious schemes were compiled by many enthusiastic School Boards which were quite inappropriate until the compulsory clauses were enforced so that regular attendance of children could be secured. In many schools the sheer novelty of schooling or the inadequacy of any previous experience of schooling meant that the curriculum had to be confined initially to the three Rs (reading, writing and arithmetic). This was the situation in a Dudley school where it was not until September 1875 that a visiting Inspector advised the managers to add sewing to the reading, writing and arithmetic which until then had been the only subjects taught, besides religious instruction.[45]

INTRODUCTION OF DRILL

In industrial towns and cities space was at a premium: miserable houses crowded back-to-back in the shadow of factories and mills, and space for schools was not readily available. The consequence was that children often had little space for recreation when allowed a break from the strict regime of the classroom. As drill was introduced into the curriculum the lack of available space for classes of 50 or 60 children was a serious handicap.[46] Some schools which had flat roofs drilled the children there; others made do with arm exercises in the aisles between rows of desks or forms in the classrooms.

It was in this climate that one of the major educational controversies was played out. What form of drill should be adopted into the curriculum – military drill or physical exercises? The debate engaged the attention of both Houses of Parliament, of School Boards and the managers of voluntary schools, of parents, of trade unionists, of the members of associations which had allied themselves to one side or the other, and of individuals who engaged in the fray with much enthusiasm. There was to be argument and counter-argument which persisted throughout this period and, indeed, was to continue for some time thereafter.

While some advocates of military drill adopted an unashamed militaristic stance others attempted to avoid association with militarism by stressing the other advantages of the practice. Thus military drill was presented as a manly, masculine activity. Increasingly, the need to prepare the nation's youth to serve the imperial cause and to protect England against her potential enemies loomed. These were powerful claims and they were advanced by men who exercised influence themselves or who had easy access to those who occupied the corridors of power. Themselves the products of public school education, it is not surprising that they wished to inculcate the manly virtues of such schools. The term 'Christian manliness' epitomizes the qualities which would mark the ideal individual to whom the future of the empire could be trusted. It was certainly a man's world, with every aspect of governance and the judiciary within their control. Masculinity, with its concomitant qualities of bravery, honour, moral courage and glory, was enshrined in the form of the male warrior. If in its highest form it would be sought in the officer class, it could perhaps be engendered to some degree at least among the common soldiery, if the appropriate means of instilling it were pursued. It seemed to many that an early start could be made in the schools, through military drill and other patriotic pursuits.

To appreciate the sweep of events and the flow of argument and counter-argument it is necessary to follow the respective courses of both physical exercises and military drill. Particular attention is drawn to the provisions made by the London School Board, whose prestige and influence guided other bodies as they attempted to meet local requirements and to make judgements as to the direction of policies.

The Boer War was to sharpen perceptions and harden attitudes. In 1902 the National Service League was formed in reaction to the shortcomings of the army in South Africa and to demand universal military training and a more disciplined society. Although the NSL extended its appeal for support across the whole spectrum of society it was in essence a right-wing organization.[47] Attention in the first decade of the twentieth century focused on measures to reform the army and the cadet units, and on the training of youths for potential service to their country. Organizations and individuals were actively involved in the process, and if interest appeared sometimes to fluctuate, there was never a time when the question of the military training of elementary school children failed to attract English people at all levels of society and to arouse their passions.

Introduction

NOTES

1. E. Lipson, *Europe in the Nineteenth Century, 1815–1914* (London: A. & C. Black, 1948), p. 247.
2. Andrew Porter, *European Imperialism, 1860–1914* (London: Macmillan, 1994), p. 2.
3. Fenner Brockway, *The Colonial Revolution* (London: Hart-Davis/MacGibbon, 1973), p. 28.
4. Charles W. Boyd, *Mr Chamberlain's Speeches*, Vol. II (London: Constable, 1914), p. 5.
5. Cited by A. J. Marder, *The Anatomy of British Sea Power* (London: Frank Cass, 1972), p. 11.
6. Cited by Edward Grierson, *The Imperial Dream: The British Commonwealth and Empire, 1775–1969* (London: Collins, 1972), p. 24.
7. Lord Curzon, cited by G. Bennett, *The Concept of Empire, Burke to Attlee, 1774–1947* (London: A. & C. Black, 1953), pp. 354–7.
8. Freda Harcourt, 'Disraeli's Imperialism 1866–1868: A Question of Timing', *Historical Journal*, 23, 1 (March 1980): 87–109.
9. Julius Vogel, 'Greater or Lesser Britain', *The Nineteenth Century* (July 1877): 811.
10. James Morris, *Heaven's Command: An Imperial Progress* (Harmondsworth: Penguin Books, 1979), p. 329.
11. J. Richards, *Happiest Days: The Public Schools in English Fiction* (Manchester: Manchester University Press, 1988), p. 299.
12. Eric Hobsbawm and Terence Ranger (eds), *The Invention of Tradition* (Cambridge: Cambridge University Press, 1983). In 'The Context, Performance and Meaning of Ritual: the British Monarchy and the "Invention of Tradition"' (p. 124), David Cannadine points out that, prior to 1877, when the Queen was made Empress of India, no royal ceremony was an imperial event, whereas subsequently every great royal occasion, including her Jubilees, was also an imperial occasion. Throughout the land schoolchildren celebrated Jubilees and royal birthdays.
13. Hugh Cunningham, 'Jingoism in 1877–78', *Victorian Studies*, 14 (June 1971): 429–53.
14. G. Kitson Clark, *An Expanding Society, Britain 1830–1900* (Cambridge: Cambridge University Press, 1967), p. 52.
15. W. E. Gladstone, 'England's Mission', *The Nineteenth Century* (September 1878): 569–73.
16. R. Shannon, *The Crisis of Imperialism, 1865–1915* (St Albans: Paladin, 1976), p. 140.
17. Charles Dilke, cited in H. Gollwitzer, *Europe in the Age of Imperialism, 1880–1914* (London: Thames & Hudson, 1969), p. 50.
18. J. R. Seeley, *The Expansion of England* (London: Macmillan, 1883; 1901), p. 299.
19. G. Woodcock, *The British in the Far East* (1969), cited in A. P. Thornton, *Imperialism in the Twentieth Century* (London: Macmillan, 1978), p. 86.
20. Rudyard Kipling, *Recessional*, cited in C. E. Carrington, *The British Overseas: Exploits of a Nation of Shopkeepers* (Cambridge: Cambridge University Press, 1950), p. 675.
21. The Earl of Meath wrote to the editor of the *School Government Chronicle* in May 1909 drawing attention to the enormous numbers of children participating in outdoor demonstrations on Empire Day. He stressed the need for perfect discipline and the ability to move rapidly at the word of command – in the interests of safety. *School Government Chronicle* (29 May 1909): 483.
22. Meath wrote in his *Memories of the Nineteenth Century* (London: John Murray, 1923), p. 328, that he had offered £50 to the London School Board to purchase Union Jacks, adding

    it is curious to recall the outcry which my offer produced in some quarters. At that time (1892–3) indeed there was no officially recognized national flag, and it was several years before Mr H. O. Arnold-Forster, MP, and I could induce Parliament and Mr Gladstone's Government to permit the Union Jack to be flown over the Houses of Parliament.

    (On 16 April 1995 the *Observer* newspaper reported that a Labour MP had drawn attention to the late Education Minister John Patten's 'patriotic call for more flag-flying' and asked how many schools had responded to Patten's request. The answer by a Junior Minister was a curt 'None'.)

23. J. A. Mangan, '"The Grit of our Forefathers". Invented Traditions, Propaganda and

Imperialism', in John M. Mackenzie (ed.), *Imperialism and Popular Culture* (Manchester: Manchester University Press, 1986), p. 135.

24. John Stuart Mill, 'Representative Government' (1861), in his *Utilitarianism, Liberty and Representative Government* (London: Everyman, J. M. Dent, 1910), p. 89; John Stuart Mill, *Essays on Politics and Society* (Toronto: University of Toronto Press, 1977), Vol. XIX of the Collected Works, Chapter 16, 'Of Nationality, as Connected with Representative Government', p. 546.

25. E. J. Hobsbawm, *Nations and Nationalism since 1780: Programme, Myth, Reality* (Cambridge: Cambridge University Press, 1992), p. 108.

26. C. E. Fayle, *The New Patriotism: A Study in Social Obligations* (London: Harrison & Sons, 1914), p. 70. Fayle did, however, also point to the danger of insularity, and stressed the need for a free exchange of ideas and for contacts with neighbouring countries.

27. Prince von Bülow, cited in Sir R. A. Falconer, *Idealism in National Character: Essays and Addresses* (London: Hodder & Stoughton, 1920), p. 46.

28. H. Oncken, 'The German Empire', in *Cambridge Modern History*, Vol. XII (Cambridge: Cambridge University Press, 1910), p. 168.

29. Prince von Bülow, *Deutsche Politik* (1913), trans. Marie A. Lewenz, as *Imperial Germany* (London: Cassell, 1914), p. 15.

30. France and Russia had formed a Dual Alliance in 1895. Kiernan suggests that 'the three old imperialists were not burying the hatchet, but turning its edge against Germany'. See V. G. Kiernan, *From Conquest to Collapse: European Empires from 1815–1960* (New York: Pantheon, 1982), p. 180.

31. E. Lipson, *Europe in the Nineteenth Century*, p. 292.

32. K. H. Janssen, 'A Patriotic Historian's Justification', in H. W. Koch, *The Origins of the First World War: Great Power Rivalry and German War Aims* (London: Macmillan, 1972), p. 261. Janssen claims that his assessment is supported by the research of Fritz Fischer and others, and from the diaries of Kurt Riezler, private secretary to Bethmann Hollweg, the Imperial Chancellor.

33. Ibid., p. 261.

34. Prince von Bülow, cited in R. Falconer, *Idealism in National Character*, pp. 43–4.

35. V. R. Berghahn, *Germany and the Approach of War in 1914* (London: Macmillan, 1973), pp. 6–7.

36. Herbert Spencer, *The Principles of Sociology*, Vol. III/2 (1886), pp. 568–602. Cited in V. R. Berghahn, *Militarism: The History of an International Debate, 1861–1979* (Leamington Spa: Berg, 1981), p. 11.

37. Alfred Vagts, *A History of Militarism* (1938), cited in Berghahn, *Militarism*, p. 39.

38. A. J. Marder, *The Anatomy of British Sea Power*, p. 19.

39. Geoffrey Best, 'Militarism and the Victorian Public School', in Brian Simon and Ian Bradley (eds), *The Victorian Public School* (Dublin: Gill & Macmillan, 1975), p. 130.

40. James Morris, *Farewell the Trumpets: An Imperial Retreat* (Harmondsworth: Penguin, 1979), p. 421.

41. David Thomson, *Europe since Napoleon* (Harmondsworth: Penguin, 1966), p. 532.

42. V. R. Berghahn, *Germany and the Approach of War*, p. 20.

43. Ramsay Muir, *A Short History of the British Commonwealth*, Vol. II (London: George Philip, 1927), p. 607. The author cites the example of Germany, drawing attention to her exploitation of the rich iron deposits of Lorraine and the thriving textile factories of Alsace, territories won from France in the Franco-Prussian War.

44. Paul Kennedy, *The Rise and Fall of the Great Powers: Economic Change and Military Conflict from 1500 to 2000* (London: Collins/Fontana, 1989), p. 248.

45. A Scheme of Education was drawn up by the Dudley School Board in August 1872. The first HMI reports on the initial three schools of the Dudley School Board were received in October 1873. Very few scholars were presented for examination, only 17 out of 113 present at Dudley Wood school, where boys, girls and infants were taught the three Rs and religious instruction in one room. Such inauspicious beginnings were not confined to that school board; much depended on what voluntary provision already existed and on the quality of that provision. A. Penn, 'A Historical Survey of Curricular Development in the Elementary

Schools of Dudley' (unpublished dissertation, Birmingham University, 1963), pp. 36–8, 42–3, 44.

46. The numbers of children taught by individual teachers varied greatly. Indeed, when the North of England Education Conference discussed 'Staffing in Primary Schools' in 1906 reference was drawn to a 'census' of about 1,200 classes in suburban East London which had been reported in *The Class Teacher* (1 July 1904). The survey had been conducted two or three weeks before the end of the school year 'when upper classes are at their lowest ebb'. Out of 1,200 classes only 170 had 40 or fewer children, and one class of 114 Standard 1 girls was being taught by a certificated mistress with the help of a pupil teacher. In all:

299	classes comprised	41–50 children
362		51–60
280		61–70
52		71–75
35		76–80

and some classes were even larger. There were 'babies' classes of 71, 80, 81, 94, and 98 children. A. R. Pickles, Chairman of the Education Committee of the National Union of Teachers Executive, in presenting this example of under-staffing also gave the national numbers of certificated teachers (including head teachers) as 74,720; 40,715 uncertificated teachers who were 'partially and often very partially' qualified; 18,296 supplementary teachers; and 24,833 pupil-teachers or apprentices. These were collectively responsible for the education of over 6,000,000 children in 20,619 'common' schools. On average, the head teacher of an elementary school was likely to have fewer qualified or 'certificated' teachers than those who were partly qualified or apprentices (*School Government Chronicle*, 75 (13 January 1906): 52). Such large classes presented difficulties whatever subject was to be taught. (Class size continues to be an issue in the years approaching the millennium, though the problem is of a significantly different order when compared with the statistical evidence presented here.)

47. Anne Summers, 'Militarism in Britain before the Great War', *History Workshop Journal*, 2 (Autumn 1976): 114.

PART I

Drill in the Late Victorian/Early Edwardian Era, 1870–1902

'Drill in its varied forms is spreading rapidly through the schools that I visit. The large ones almost all show me some form of Swedish, musical, or other exercises, and in the smaller ones different variations find favour. The children like the exercise and it is a refreshment to them from their lessons.'

(from report of the Revd C. F. Johnstone, HMI)

1

Drill in Elementary Schools, 1870–75

The period 1870–75 was one in which the teaching of drill and, in particular, military drill, became an accepted practice in the nation's elementary schools. It was sanctioned by the Department of Education and encouraged by members of Her Majesty's Inspectorate. It was at that time, too, that the Society for the Encouragement of Arts, Commerce and Manufactures in Great Britain (hereafter referred to as the Society of Arts) involved itself in the issue. Drill, whether 'military' or 'ordinary' was accorded a place in the curriculum of most elementary schools. Whilst the subject itself found few to criticize its inclusion there was to be sustained discussion and argument as to the form it should take.

OFFICIAL ARRANGEMENTS FOR THE TEACHING OF DRILL

After the tabling of the Elementary Education Act of 1870 the Code was amended so that 'attendance at drill under a competent instructor, for not more than two hours a week, and twenty weeks in the year' could be counted as school attendance for grant purposes.[1] The accompanying *Instructions on the Administration of the New Code* (1871) pointed out that Article 24 referred to drill which was taken as part of the ordinary school routine, and therefore 'falling within the ordinary school hours'. It added, however, that a school meeting could be held on Saturday mornings for drill purposes. It advised that not more than an hour at any one time should be devoted to drill.[2] In practice, teachers were to find that shorter periods than that were preferable to prevent children from becoming over-tired.[3] There was initially no attempt to enforce the teaching of drill; the inducement to School Boards and the managers of voluntary schools was that it could be taken into account when the grant awarded to the school was being reckoned. An attempt was made to render drill compulsory for boys over the age of 8 years in all rate-aided and state-aided schools in March 1871. Mr Torrens MP moved a resolution in the House of Commons to that effect, drawing attention to the fact that such provisions were made in Switzerland, for example, and pointing to the importance of military drill as an aid to national defence. In reply, Forster referred to the Code of 1871 'which acknowledged for the first time the usefulness of drill', but he concluded by saying that he could not consent to its being made compulsory.[4] The harsh realities encountered by many School Boards merely in establishing the teaching of reading, writing and arithmetic has been touched upon in the Introduction. At that early time other subjects, however worthy, could only be acknowledged and perhaps encouraged. Article 24 was amended the following year restricting the provision to boys only, and again in 1873 when the phrase 'twenty weeks in the year' was replaced by 'forty hours in the year'. Some School Boards and managers, however, continued to treat girls on an equal footing, accepting the responsibility and meeting the cost themselves.

The decision to exclude girls from recognition for grant purposes did not pass unchallenged. Matthew Arnold, HMI, in his general report for 1872 pressed for the teaching of drill or callisthenics, when regularly and properly taught, to count as part of school time for girls, as drill did for boys.[5] At the same time, E.H. Brodie, HMI for the County of Lancaster, reminded their Lordships of the Committee of Council on Education (to whom Inspectors' Reports were addressed) that where drill had been introduced into mixed schools, some of the girls had also been drilled, and 'Why not?' he added in conclusion.[6] The formal nature of drill, whether termed military drill or not, was more easily related to the instruction of boys than girls. The official answer to that situation was to ignore the needs of girls for some form of physical exercise rather than to seek a style more suitable to the feminine physique and demeanour. As the Civil Service, the school Inspectorate and parliament were strictly male preserves at that time such a solution was probably reached without difficulty.

Since 1840 the Church had enjoyed the privilege of nominating individuals as inspectors of its schools, as had the non-conformists. Clerics were usually appointed, and many continued to serve after Board schools were added to existing denominational ones. It was to be some considerable time before women were considered eligible for the responsibility of school inspection. Consequently the onus of addressing the educational needs of girls rested with the more enlightened of the male inspectors and, at a local level, the female members of School Boards. As a consequence, there were many men in positions of influence and authority to further the cause of military drill, but few women to advocate appropriate forms of drill or physical exercise for girls in elementary schools.

REPORTS OF HMIs

The general reports of HMIs, published annually, showed that a number of them were anxious to encourage the teaching of military drill in the elementary schools under their jurisdiction. In his last report to deal exclusively with Church of England schools the Revd H. W. Bellairs commented:

> The drill in our schools is generally bad; I should like to see a regular system of military drill introduced, with marching tunes and, where practicable, with drum and fife bands. Arrangements with the adjutants of the militia and volunteers for providing the necessary teaching might easily be made, and the expense of it by employing drill sergeants would not be great.[7]

This latter suggestion bore fruit, as a letter from the War Office to F. R. Sandford, Secretary to the Committee of Council on Education, demonstrated. It was agreed that there would be no objection to 'the employment, with the approval of their commanding officers, of sergeants of the permanent staff of Militia and Volunteers, in the vicinity of schools on the terms proposed'.[8] Already a few schools had established school bands, examples being at Colchester and Ossett in the Revd Nevill Gream's Essex District, and at Puddletown in Dorset where the children at Wyke Regis school 'are taught to march in step', and where 'the band helps to bring old and present pupils together in a common amusement'.

The suggestion that a number of schools in well-populated districts might 'usefully and economically' arrange for their boys to participate in corporate drilling was made by Mr Coward, HMI for the Warrington District of Lancashire.[9] As will be demonstrated in due course, the useful and economic advantages he envisaged carried with them other characteristics the value of which was not universally acknowledged.

HMIs did not shrink from general observations of a political rather than an educational nature. Part of the Revd H. R. Sandford's general report fell into this category:

> The importance in a national point of view of having the youth of a country subjected to a system of good discipline cannot be

overestimated. Surely not the least of the advantages which in the late war Germany has possessed over her antagonist has been the superiority of her people in regard to discipline, and in regard to the habit of self control and the power of acting in concert in obedience to orders, which discipline gives. Nor can it be doubted that this superiority is in great measure owing to the educational training to which, especially in Protestant Germany, the mass of the youthful population is subjected.[10]

There were to be many similar references to the German model of national efficiency and discipline in the years to come; for some it engendered respect, for others apprehension. Dr J. D. Morell, reporting on the City of London and the Metropolitan Division of Greenwich, enthused on the military drill as taught in schools such as St John's National School and St Joseph's Roman Catholic School, Deptford. He opined that if generally applied it could make a significant contribution in three ways: by improving health and physical development; by training good habits and obedience to orders; and by 'laying the foundation for rendering an aptitude for military service almost universal amongst the English people'.[11] There would be no lack of supporters for the last-named objective, as will emerge in due course.

AIDS FOR TEACHERS

The War Office recommended that school drill should be drawn from Part One and some of Part Two of the *Field Exercise Book* (1870), comprising squad, or recruit, and company drill. The frequency with which the terms 'squad' and 'company' occur in accounts of school drill suggests that the War Office publication was well-used. Schools could also purchase a short *Manual of Elementary Military Exercise and Drill*, which had been adopted in army schools catering for soldiers' children, and which was available from the Stationery Office for twopence.

Elementary school teachers who undertook the teaching of military drill provided a new market for commercially produced drill instruction manuals. One such aid was *Browne's Position Drill: A Practical Guide to Squad and Setting-Up Drill*, first published in 1871 and addressed to a wide readership. It claimed to be specially adapted 'for the use of recruits, rifle volunteers, the militia, police force, schools and families'. The drill it contained was based on the first part of *Field Exercise of the Army*, and contained '68 illustrations of back-stick and club exercise, extension motions, and sword exercise positions'.[12] The adaptation would appear to be more suitable for use by the military and police units than by schools or families. A similar publication, the title of which was at least a more appropriate one, was *The Schoolmaster's Drill Assistant: A manual for Elementary Schools*, by Commander F. M. Norman, RN.[13] This author also introduced *Dual Desk Drill* as a supplement to the above work. It was intended for use in schoolrooms where 'Moss's patent School Board desks and other desks on the same plan' were in use. Pupils were arranged in double files between the desks for the purpose of drill, thus catering for those schools where outdoor facilities could not be provided. The author claimed that the manual was intended for use in boys', girls' or mixed departments; it contained appropriate words of command and full descriptions of the 'manœuvres', however restricted they must have been.[14]

The Committee of the Home and Colonial School Society produced its own manual of *School Drill* for the use of its teachers, compiled by an ex-adjutant of infantry. It went into its third edition, being reviewed in the *School Board Chronicle* of 30 June 1877.[15] No doubt the third edition, which was revised and enlarged by W. S. Glover, drill master to the Home and Colonial schools, benefited from the latter's knowledge and experience of teaching drill to children. It is interesting to note that the first section of the book describes gallery exercises for infants, which may appear a somewhat hazardous undertaking to the present-day reader.[16] The opening lesson had as its purpose: 'to ensure that the pupils know once and for ever, without an instant's hesitation, their right hand from their left'. One can only conjecture how many repetitions of that lesson were found to be necessary in practice before the infants' mistress could move bravely on to lesson two. The author reassured his more apprehensive readers with the observation that: 'The infant drill is happily adapted to amuse and interest the class while it trains them in obedience and develops their physical system.' Gallery exercises were followed by 'imitative exercises' and 'geometrical exercises' to develop the idea of form, and by marching. The programme for 'juvenile classes' included forming, opening and closing ranks, followed by 'flexions, callisthenic movements, and combinations of exercises, etc., for girls and for boys'. A complete chapter was devoted to military drill for boys: 'extension motions, saluting, balance motions and combined motions'. Remaining sections of the manual covered marching, the formation of squads, wheeling, formation of fours, company drill, battalion drill, and so on.

The military element seems to have been accepted from the outset in all these manuals, it dominated the whole programme of exercises whether directed towards infants, young children of either sex, or older boys. For the latter it must often have been but a short step to the intricacies of army drill proper, and where serving or ex-army personnel were engaged to conduct the drill the demarcation line between school drill and army drill would have been very close indeed.

DIFFICULTIES IN PROVIDING FOR MILITARY DRILL

A major difficulty facing many town schools was the serious lack of playground space where children could be drilled. This question had certainly not engaged the attention of School Boards and their architects when some of the early Board schools were planned. In some instances ground space was at such a premium that a minimal play area was created on the flat roof of the school building. Prominent among those who persistently drew attention to the lack of playground space was the Revd T. W. Sharpe, HMI for the Lambeth Division of London. He claimed that it was the principal reason why many schools did not attempt to teach military drill; it was, he claimed, 'an insuperable barrier'.[17]

An appendix to Mr Hernaman's General Report on the Worcestershire schools was penned by Mr J. Pember, his assistant. Pember reported that military drill was taught in 21 of the 271 departments visited, and was, on the whole, satisfactory. However, he attached great importance to the 'ordinary school drill' which in his judgement did not disturb the general school arrangements. 'Military drill', he claimed, 'can only be practised in a limited number of schools and under certain circumstances.'[18] If visiting instructors were employed they would have to be accommodated within timetable arrangements with potential disruption; in mixed schools where girls were not drilled, alternative arrangements would need to be made for them. Planning could be further complicated if boys from a number of classes were grouped together for drill lessons, provided of course that sufficient space was available for that to be done.

There were other reasons too for not providing instruction in military drill. In Wiltshire two reasons were given, firstly there were difficulties in engaging suitably qualified instructors, and secondly, it was considered that 'the usual school drill' was 'adequate to the maintenance of order and cultivation of habits of discipline'.[19] Here the requirement appeared to be a form of drill which was effective in instilling and maintaining good order and the habits of discipline. Finding that ordinary drill met this criterion there was perhaps little enthusiasm for a search to be made for instructors well versed in military drill. Elsewhere, other factors entered the reckoning, such as physical and general educative effects, or the possible advantages or disadvantages associated with the teaching of the rudiments of military drill *per se*. In the latter case the perceived advantages were twofold; the children would be imbued with a spirit of militarism and they would receive a basic drilling programme on which Volunteer or Regular Army training units could capitalize in due course.

In rural districts the position was very different from that which commonly obtained in the towns. Many country children travelled considerable distances on foot every day to and from school, so they did not lack physical exercise. They also enjoyed space and opportunities for play which were not available to many urban children; if school playgrounds were not adequate, alternatives were likely to be found close at hand. Many rural schools were small, with few teachers and less adequate funding than town schools. A schoolmistress, perhaps mature in years, would experience difficulty in drilling a large class of children, and the prospect of mastering the intricacies of military drill would be daunting indeed. Nevertheless, there were arguments in favour of the encouragement of military drill in rural districts. Military considerations were applicable there as in urban areas, while for Mr Gream, HMI for the County of Essex, military drill offered distinct advantages for country children who were 'naturally dull and slow in their movements'.[20]

The early years of the School Board era were demanding ones. To the burden of building new schools and furnishing them, appointing teaching staff and officials, and ensuring that children did attend school, was added the need to establish curricula and effective teaching such as would satisfy Her Majesty's Inspectors and so qualify for the receipt of grant aid. Voluntary schools often struggled to keep abreast of developments, their finances coming under pressure in the face of ever-increasing demands made upon them. All schools depended on such grants and allowances as were available to them. This gave the Education Department, and any independent body seeking to influence the course of education, an effective lever by which to encourage schools to adopt measures and policies. The intervention of the Society of Arts in this respect is considered later on, in Chapter 3.

NOTES

1. *Report of the Committee of Council on Education (CCE), 1870–71*, England and Wales (C.-406-I), New Code, Article 24, p. cix.
2. Ibid., p. cxxxiii.
3. There was abundant evidence to show that many children attended elementary schools without receiving sufficient nutritious food to sustain them during the day. Some of them reached school after walking long distances and without having had any breakfast at all. Others were half-timers spending half a day at school and half a day in mill or factory. Teachers were wise not to impose too much additional physical exertion on such children.
4. *House of Commons Debates* (Hansard), Third Series, vol. CCIV, col. 1559 (7 March 1871).
5. *Report of CCE, 1872–73* (C.-812-I), p. 26.
6. Ibid., p. 52.
7. *Report of CCE, 1870–71* (C.-406-I), p. 26.
8. The letter from the War Office was dated 19 May 1871, and was in reply to a Memorandum from the Committee of Council on Education of 15th ultimo. It was printed as an Appendix of Notes to the Code, on p. 214 of the Code for 1896–97.

   This Appendix also carried a copy of the Memorandum of the Education Department which is set out here in view of its clear description of potential teaching arrangements:

   > In the vicinity of a great number of schools throughout England, there are now detachments of volunteers drilled once or twice a week, during at least six months of the year, by Government instructors. These drills take place in the evening, and the instructors have little to do in the day time. By going to the villages a few hours earlier they would be able to drill the boys in the afternoon and be ready for the volunteers in the evening. Except in thinly inhabited districts, where the villages lie far apart, an instructor could drill five or six schools, each once a week. The elementary drill which would be suitable for boys is capable of being imparted by instructors of either Artillery, Engineers, or Rifle Volunteers, and would be sufficient to teach the boys habits of sharp obedience, smartness, order, and cleanliness.
   >
   > In some districts there are many schoolmasters among the Volunteers who frequently rise to be Non-commissioned Officers. If the Government instructors were employed in the first instance, the schoolmasters who passed a sergeant's examination before an Adjutant of Volunteers, might, after the first year, be made drill instructors of their schools.
   >
   > Where the demand for instructors was great the permanent staff of the Militia might also give assistance, as during the greater part of the year they have not much to do.

9. *Report of CCE, 1870–71* (C.-406-I), p. 177.
10. Ibid., p. 177. The Revd H. R. Sandford was, of course, referring to the Franco-German war of 1870, which ended in a crushing defeat for the French after a campaign of less than two months.

    Lyon Playfair, professor of chemistry at Edinburgh (1858–69), and Liberal MP for the Scottish Universities, had already made this point in the course of a lecture to the National Association for the Promotion of Social Science in 1870. He commented that two belligerents were not fairly matched if one, as in the case of France, had 28 per cent of its soldiers illiterate, while the other, as with Germany, had less than 3 per cent illiterate. He claimed that: 'School drill in military and naval exercises, besides their educational value in discipline and united action, sow the seed of national strength in an economical way', and suggested that since European countries such as Germany, Holland, Switzerland and France had incorporated physical training into their school curricula, Britain would be advised to follow suit. D. A. Reeder (ed.), *Educating our Masters* (Leicester: Leicester University Press, 1980), pp. 127–49.
11. *Report of CCE, 1871–72* (C.-601-I), p. 63.
12. *School Board Chronicle* (18 April 1874): 350.
13. Advertised in *School Board Chronicle* (18 April 1874): 410.
14. *School Board Chronicle* (15 July 1876): 68.

15. *School Board Chronicle* (30 June 1877): 660.
16. Infant schoolrooms were commonly provided with tiered benches, or galleries, so that those children who were accommodated on the rows furthest from the teacher were at a considerable height from the floor of the classroom.
17. *Report of CCE, 1873–74* (C.-1019-I), p. 193. Twenty years later Revd Sharpe, HMI, was still critical – *Report of CCE, 1893–94* (C.-7437-I), p. 92, and *Report of CCE, 1895–96* (C.-8249), p. 134. In the latter report Sharpe complained that 'within a radius of a mile from Charing Cross there are 25,000 children for whom no playground is provided', and 'in most parts of London there are very few playgrounds worthy of the name'. (Sharpe was promoted to Senior Chief Inspector in 1890, retiring in 1897. He was principal of Queen's College, London, from 1898 to 1905.)
18. *Report of CCE, 1874–75* (C.-1265-I), p. 105.
19. *Report of CCE, 1873–74* (C.-1019-I), p. 104.
20. *Report of CCE, 1874–75* (C.-1265-I), pp. 94–5.

2

Drill and Physical Training:
Debate and Decisions, 1875–99

In the last quarter of the nineteenth century the debate on the relative merits of military drill versus physical training on the Swedish model gained momentum. Drill, in whatever form, was associated with the maintenance of good order and discipline, ensuring its place at the heart of the elementary school curriculum.

DEBATES ON MILITARY DRILL AND PHYSICAL EDUCATION

On 19 April 1875, when the members of the House of Lords debated military training, the Earl of Lauderdale suggested that the matter needed to be considered while Britain was still at peace.[1] He supported the teaching of military drill in schools and pointed to its beneficial effects with respect to the promotion of order, regularity and cleanliness. An official reaction was provided by the Duke of Richmond who stated that the Government was 'well aware of the necessity of giving proper facilities for school drill'.[2] Other members gave general support to the practice of military drill in the nation's elementary schools, the Marquess of Lansdowne claiming that it could do much 'to diffuse a military spirit among the people'.[3] This debate drew attention to the general concern of the ruling classes that the common people should be prepared from an early age for an orderly and compliant role in society, and be ready to participate in the defence of that society as occasion might demand.

A very different view was presented by Mr Butler-Johnstone MP, in the Commons during the course of a debate on physical education in July 1875. He called attention to the desirability of introducing physical education into public elementary schools. Admitting that there was some confusion between drill and physical education, he said that his concept of the latter referred to 'the inculcation of some sound, though elementary principles of hygiene, combined with the practice of simple,

28

though scientifically devised, exercises founded on sound physiological and anatomical principles'. He referred to the teaching of Ling in Sweden,[4] whose principles in respect of physical training had been appreciated in Prussia, Germany, Italy, Hungary and Russia. Here in England, Dr Roth, who had been a student at the Kungl Gymnastika Central Institutet in Stockholm, had undertaken to provide free instruction based on Ling's methods to women teachers, which in turn, claimed Butler-Johnstone, was benefiting some 400–500 girl pupils. In reply, Viscount Sandon, Vice-President of the Committee of Council on Education, stated that he could not promise that any further steps would be taken, although he accepted that the introduction of military drill was 'very advantageous'.[5] Butler-Johnstone's definition of physical education is a useful one; unfortunately many of his contemporaries were not so accurate in their use of terms. Physical education, physical instruction, physical training, physical exercises and drill were terms freely used and often interchanged, making it necessary for the reader to seek contextual clues to qualify the actual terms employed.

Support for the physical education lobby came from Mr Jolly HMI, who read a paper to the Economic Section of the British Association on 'Physical Education and Hygiene in Schools' in 1876. As a result of this, the Association's General Committee was recommended to 'press on the Government the view of fostering physical education by giving grants for its teaching and of making physical training and hygiene necessary elements in the professional training of teachers'.[6] This association of physical training and hygiene by Jolly and by Butler-Johnstone was a significant pointer to the time when more attention would be focused on the general health of the nation's youth.

DISCIPLINE AND ORGANIZATION GRANTS

A clause introduced into the New Code of 1875 was to make an immediate, if indirect, contribution towards a strengthening of the case for the encouragement of drill. Article 19 A3 allowed a special grant of one shilling per scholar to be paid if the visiting HMI judged the discipline and organization of the school to be satisfactory. Already there were a number of HMIs whose recent reports directly associated drill, whether 'ordinary' or 'military' in character, with good order and discipline.[7] Unfortunately, HMIs did not always specify which type of drill they were referring to in their reports. Military drill followed the recommendations set out in the *Field Exercise Book* (1870) published by the War Office,[8] but 'ordinary' drill was less clearly defined. The Revd C. H. Parez commented that ordinary drill, as practised in his district in the northwest, comprised 'a few arm exercises and simple extension movements'. With a view to propriety, he thought it desirable that girls should not be required to carry out the stooping exercises.[9]

An indication of the very rudimentary nature of the exercises which constituted 'the usual school drill' in some schools can be gleaned from E. H. Brodie's report on his Worcestershire schools. The drill consisted of 'some twelve to twenty movements of the arms, facings, and getting in and out of desks'. The rows of heavy iron-framed desks and benches in school classrooms restricted the movements of children so that little if any movement other than that carried out in unison was practicable. Hence the front, left and right 'facing' drill, and the stepping (or perhaps stumbling) into aisles, which, with the limited arm movements, made up the class drill.[10] As late as 1898–99, Mr W. E. Currey, HMI for the East Division, could present the alarming observation that: 'It is too common to find children being drilled standing on forms in a close schoolroom.'[11] Surprisingly he did not condemn the practice nor comment on the potential dangers should a child fall or obstruct another child.

The Report of the Committee of Council on Education for the year 1875–76 stated that there were 1,001 school departments in which boys were receiving training in military drill, but there was no indication at that time of the number of schools or departments teaching physical exercises.[12]

At a time when government grants and inducements were fragmented, and to a significant extent dependent on attendance and individual performance within specified curricular areas, a new grant related to school discipline and organization offered additional funding which no school managers or School Boards could afford to ignore. Favourable comments from HMIs linking drill and discipline would have carried considerable weight and influence.[13] Concern at the interpretation of Article 19A which, since 1875, had made available discipline and organization grants, was expressed by H. W. G. Markheim HMI, in his report for 1878.

> That this humanizing discipline and the mere external order mechanically enforced in schools morally uncared for by their managers should be pecuniarily recognised by the same rate of grant, seems an anomaly contrary to the spirit and intention of your Lordships' instructions, and suggests the question whether a graduation of the grant under Article 19A would not be the best

means of impressing upon all the importance which your Lordships attach to the maintenance of a high moral standard in our national education.[14]

His criticism of the current system was not to pass unnoticed.

For a short period inspectors' reports on schools were available separately under the title *What Her Majesty's Inspectors Say, Being their Reports*, and published by the North of England School Furnishing Company of Newcastle-on-Tyne. The first such issue carried reports for the year 1879–80 without mention of either drill or physical exercises; however, this omission was rectified the following year. The final issue of *What Her Majesty's Inspectors Say* was that for 1885–86, after which its readers had to resort again to the appendices of the annual Reports of the Committee of Council on Education.

The Revd W. Campbell, reporting on the Chelsea schools, reiterated the Revd Sharpe's concern at the lack of space available to London schools. The problem which Campbell drew attention to was the encroachment of playgrounds to accommodate enlargements and additions to buildings. As a consequence, 'small numbers only can be exercised at one time, while in many schools military drill is dropped altogether. Many of the voluntary schools have only a very small playground or yard, and movement of numbers for drill is impossible.'[15]

VARIABLE GRANTS INTRODUCED

Certainly, from the written comments of a number of inspectors it appeared that very few schools failed to meet the minimum standards of discipline and organization necessary in order to qualify for the original shilling-per-scholar grant.[16] Markheim's critical observations (see above) were endorsed by the Cross Commission on Elementary Education which issued its final report in 1888. The Code of 1890 confirmed that the Committee of Council on Education was prepared to remedy the situation, and the Revised Instructions to Her Majesty's Inspectors drew attention to the proposed change in grant structure. The latter stated:

The report of the Royal Commissioners rightly calls attention to the importance of moral training and discipline in a school, and Article 101b is designed to give effect to their recommendations on this point, by establishing for the first time a variable grant for discipline and organisation.[17]

The outcome was that from 1890 schools qualified for either a higher grant of 1s 6d per head or a lower grant of 1s per head, depending upon the assessment made by the local inspector.

In 1890 Mr Howard, HMI for the Southwest Division, observed that 'In the New Code attention is drawn, and not before its time, to physical exercises. What has hitherto gone by that name is a series of simultaneous movements of little or no value.'[18] It is remarkable that there appears to be no mention of this innovation in the actual Report of the Committee of Council on Education for 1889–90, nor in the Minute modifying certain provisions of the New Code, nor yet in the Revised Instructions to Her Majesty's Inspectors. Previously Article 12(f) had read: 'For boys, military drill under a competent instructor for not more than two hours in any week or forty hours in any school year, and for girls lessons in practical cookery.'[19] As amended the following year, Article 12(f) read:

> In making up the minimum time constituting an attendance there may be reckoned time occupied by instruction in any of the following subjects,whether or not it is given in the school premises or by the ordinary teachers of the school, provided that special and appropriate provision approved by the Inspector is made for such instruction, and the times for giving it are entered in the approved Time Table:–
> Drawing
> Manual Instruction
> Science
> Suitable physical exercises
> Military drill (for boys)
> Practical cookery or laundry work (for girls above Standard III).[20]

This provision was part of a more general easing of curricular control subsequent to the Cross Commission recommendations by which a grant for class subjects replaced the system of grants based on percentage passes in elementary subjects. The significance of Article 12(f) in respect of physical exercises can be appreciated, particularly in respect of girls; as a school subject it was now accorded equal status with military drill. One consequence of the introduction of lessons in cookery or laundry work, manual instruction, and other subjects noted above, was the need for special rooms, the building of which would eat into existing playground space. Sharpe's General Report for the Metropolitan Division of 1887–88 continued to express his concern at the cramped playground spaces or 'yards' in central London but gave credit to teachers who persisted in the teaching of drill which 'produces at once a marked improvement in discipline and in physical health and bearing'.[21]

MUSICAL DRILL

Some HMIs had already been referring warmly to the value of school bands, an example being the Revd J. W. D. Hernaman's Report of 1878–79 in which he stressed their value in maintaining good discipline and 'a healthy tone' in schools. He referred to schools which also kept a connection with their old scholars through their bands, but did not elaborate. At one of his schools, South Lambeth Road Board School, 'the older boys, dressed in uniform, led the marching capitally to the music of a brass band'.[22] It would be interesting to know how the uniforms and band instruments were obtained for the boys. A few years later four Manchester Board schools were credited with having 'excellent drum and fife bands'. At the inspection conducted by Mr H. E. Oakeley, 'the little musicians presented a very smart appearance with military caps just come from Woolwich'.[23] Here we learn that the school was able to obtain military caps from Woolwich, from which it may be inferred that the supplier was the military academy. If uniforms, including caps, were available for school cadet corps, there would be little reason why elementary schools could not place orders with that supplier.

In 1889 Mr Waddington of the Southeast Division reported with enthusiasm:

> School drill has been enormously improved by the introduction of musical drill; this is becoming more and more common with the best results; in some cases where there is no musical instrument in the schools the scholars sing the tunes while doing the exercises. Military drill is taught in only a *very* small proportion of schools.

He singled out the Guildford Holy Trinity National School as an example of a school in which military drill was competently taught. There the headmaster brought his long experience as a Volunteer to bear on the situation, with the result that the whole school was exercised in regular army drill, including battalion drill and signalling.[24]

Where large numbers of children were participating in marching drill the advantages of music in supplying a steady rhythmic beat were appreciated. The practice was best demonstrated in the mass displays orchestrated by the Society of Arts where schools marched to the music of accompanying bands. Mr Waddington's report suggests that musical drill was of a less militant nature than was the case when a band was formed with the express purpose of assisting military drill.

THE TRADES UNION CONGRESS REGISTERS ITS OPPOSITION

A few years earlier in 1885, the Trades Union Congress (TUC), meeting at Southport for its annual conference, passed a resolution deprecating the continuing practice of teaching military drill in the elementary schools:

> Seeing that military drill was introduced into Board schools professedly for its physical advantages, and that it is now being followed up by the formation of cadet corps, the boys comprising which are to be dressed as soldiers, and supplied with rifles by the War Office, the Congress enters its emphatic protest against the cunningly devised scheme by which military authorities and a number of Board schools have been, step by step, preparing the way for the pernicious Continental system of conscription, and entreats the working class rate-payers to use every effort to frustrate the design of the promoters, and confine School Boards to the task for which they were designed – viz. to develop the intellectual and moral faculties of children committed to their care.[25]

The TUC was expressing a general concern of the labour movement and of anti-militarists with respect to the teaching of military drill in the nation's elementary schools. Fears lest the Continental practice of conscription spread to Britain were becoming more widespread and, as will be demonstrated in due course, many advocates of military drill found it necessary, or at least desirable, to distance themselves from the conscription lobby in England. Some of the cadet units referred to in the TUC resolution were based on working boys' clubs associated with public school missions or university settlements. In such cases the public schools or university colleges provided the officer cadre, whose members thereby enjoyed an early opportunity to exercise authoritative control over others.

In a lengthy article published in the *Journal* of the Society of Arts, Edwin Chadwick, chairman of that body's Education Committee, repudiated the claim and absolved the War Office from entertaining any designs such as the TUC levied against them. Chadwick claimed that his committee was responsible for initiating the movement for the introduction of military drill in elementary schools. He took advantage of the opportunity to reiterate all the well-rehearsed arguments in favour of military drill, adding the colourful claim that:

> Military drill improves his [the boy's] walk (he can move more quickly with the same effort) – drill makes him tread more evenly, and saves shoe leather. School teachers, who have been trained in the military drill, state that they find that they now save a pair of boots a year by not treading unevenly as they used to do. The even tread saves trousers by throwing up less mud upon them.

Chadwick was quick to add that this was much appreciated by the boys' mothers. In conclusion, he suggested that the TUC was wrong in expressing apprehension lest military drill should be a precursor to conscription. He said that, on the contrary, 'it will contribute, to an important extent, to the great volunteer movement, which comprises a large majority of the wage classes throughout the country'. His final comment, appearing almost as an afterthought, recalled Britain's role as a leading imperial power, which must, of necessity, defend and maintain its enviable position: 'In any case, whilst other nations are advancing with exercise of the military drill in their elementary schools, would it be for us to stay such exercise in ours?'[26] The temptation to add weight to his previous arguments by hinting at external threats was one which he could not resist.

CHANGES IN THE CODE FAVOUR PHYSICAL EXERCISES

According to Inspectors' returns there were 1,414 elementary schools teaching military drill in 1889, but the changes in the Code (already discussed) were to be responsible for a shift of emphasis from military drill to the teaching of physical exercises. From 1891, when schools were allowed to include either 'suitable physical exercises' or military drill (the latter for boys only) under Article 12(f) of the Code, the number of school departments teaching military drill doubled by 1899 to a total of 2,659 (from 1,365 in 1891). In comparison, 1,441 departments elected to introduce physical exercises in 1891, to increase six-fold to 9,115 by 1899. The rapid development of physical exercises as compared with the less spectacular increase in military drill is illustrated in Table 1.

TABLE 1

Year	Number of schools visited by HMI	Number of departments under separate head	Number teaching	
			Military drill	Physical exercises
1876	14,273	20,782	1,056	–
1890	19,419	29,339	1,414	–
1891	19,508	29,533	1,365	1,441
1982	19,515	29,672	1,352	1,703
1893	19,577	29,804	1,346	1,938
1894	19,709	30,033	1,343	2,259
1895	19,739	30,237	1,572	3,185
1896	19,848	30,521	1,903	5,333
1897	19,958	30,847	2,418	7,845
1898	19,937	30,911	2,555	8,569
1899	20,064	31,173	2,659	9,115

Source: CCE Reports for the years stated.

Within 12 months of the changes in the Code, the general report of the Revd C. F. Johnstone for the Southeast Division could state that

> Drill in its varied forms is spreading rapidly through the schools that I visit. The large ones almost all show me some form of Swedish, musical, or other exercises, and in the smaller ones different variations find favour. The children like the exercise, and it is a refreshment to them from their lessons. Under the competition of other systems military drill has become less prominent, but the increasing vigour and accuracy with which the present exercises are done make this to be the less regretted.[27]

It is interesting to note his observation that two of the qualities which had most clearly identified the teaching of military drill, namely vigour and accuracy, were now observed in the physical exercises practised by an increasing number of schools. Other aspects of military drill may have served the purpose of providing an early introduction to practices associated with the militia, but the physical training of school children could follow a more benign route.

Mr Rankine HMI, responsible for the West Ham schools under the Revd T. W. Sharpe (Senior Chief Inspector, Metropolitan Division), wrote of his schools:

> In the infant and girls' schools some kind of drill, Swedish or other, is systematically taught. In the boys' schools, although in most of

the playgrounds gymnastic apparatus is provided, there is no attempt to make gymnastics part of the school course, nor is military drill taught except in a few cases. On the other hand most schools have their cricket or football clubs. Those games should be encouraged; they are far superior to any artificial system of gymnastics for strengthening heart and lungs, and giving quickness and steadiness to eye and hand. Besides this they are an excellent preparation for civic life in accustoming boys to work together in conducting the business of a club and in the subordination, which they entail, they contain in themselves the first elements of moral training.[28]

These observations suggest that a considerable shift in both the philosophy and the practice of physical instruction was emerging. Reference to football and cricket clubs, and to their moral as well as their physical attributes, show how far some schools had progressed. The Inspector could now point to civic advantages in joint physical activities; at an earlier time the only advantages, other than the physical and military ones, related to preparation for future labouring employment. Encouragement also came through the pamphlets and tracts of the Fabian Society. For example, J. W. Martin in Tract 52, *State Education at Home and Abroad*, welcomed the encouragement of self-control associated with the playing of the national games of football and cricket.[29] Tract 55, drafted by Sidney Webb, demanded that 'a course of scientific physical training' should comprise daily lessons which were given as much care in preparation and execution as was accorded to the teaching of reading and writing.[30] That elevation of physical training to a par with reading and writing indicates the progress which was being made.

The public schools had demonstrated the supremacy of the games ethic over corps training, and their pupils had responded positively. J. A. Mangan has shown how qualities such as courage, endurance, assertion and self-control were fostered in the interests of future imperial service.[31] It was now being shown that similar arguments could be advanced on behalf of programmes which included games for elementary school children.

FURTHER ADVANCES

All these innovations were laudable enough, but Mr Fisher HMI was looking even further ahead. In his report for 1893–94 he said: 'I do not see why an account of the growth in weight, height, and size of muscle should not be chronicled for each child as well as his progress through the standards.'[32]

It was to require the pioneering efforts of the McMillan sisters and others in Bradford and elsewhere, and the setting up of the School Medical Service in 1907 before this proposal could be implemented. There is, however, clear evidence of a growing concern for the general health and welfare of schoolchildren, in contrast to the previous preoccupation with training them for some future role or service.

In response to a question with regard to swimming and physical training which Mr H. S. Foster MP addressed to the Vice-President of the Committee of Council on Education in January 1894, Mr Acland stated that swimming was already taught in some schools and physical exercises in many. He went so far as to agree that the latter should be part of the ordinary curriculum of every school and said that he was giving the matter further consideration in anticipation of the next year's Code.[33] The Code of 1895 was duly amended to make payment of the higher grant for discipline and organization conditional on satisfactory provision of 'Swedish or other drill'. Exemptions were allowed in respect of half-timers and those children for whom 'such instruction is unsuitable'.[34] It was anticipated that members of School Boards and school managers would respond positively to this condition and endeavour to meet the standards necessary to secure a higher level of grant. The Education Department's policy of rewarding compliance rather than enforcing practice continued.

REVISED INSTRUCTIONS FOR HMIs

Revised instructions to HMIs issued to assist their interpretation of the Code for 1896–97 certainly showed a shift from the official stance which had hitherto encouraged members of the Inspectorate to view military drill with enthusiasm. The instructions now directed that: 'When circumstances permit, the best form of physical exercise is a healthy game which will satisfy the conditions of the Code, and in country schools such games are almost always possible.' It was accepted that conditions in most towns made this impossible as a general rule, and so 'some scientific form of drill and gymnastics' was recommended. A warning was given not to over-tax half-timers or those children who faced a long daily walk to and from school.[35] HMIs and teachers alike must have been surprised at the rapidity with which the Education Department had turned from its advocacy of military drill to support of physical exercises and, where circumstances permitted, to 'healthy games'.

SHOULD BOYS HANDLE WEAPONS?

From this surge of interest in physical education and change in official policy it might be assumed that military drill had been superseded by other practices. The military drill lobby, however, was by no means exhausted, as future events will demonstrate. Before concluding this chapter mention must be made of the vexed question as to whether boys should be allowed, or encouraged, to handle actual weapons in the course of drill exercises. In the summer of 1893 Mr Cremer MP asked the Vice-President of the Committee of Council on Education whether the 1870 Education Act or any subsequent Code authorized instruction in the use of military weapons within elementary, industrial, or other rate-supported schools. In reply Mr Acland stated:

> Drill in the form of physical exercises is commonly taught in elementary schools. Since 1875 what is called military drill has been sanctioned by the Code. Particular methods of drill are left to the discretion of managers, but I do not find on an inquiry, made on very short notice, that any case is known to the Department in which actual weapons are used. Popguns [much laughter] are used in some infant schools for playing at soldiers; and I am told that many years ago boys were taught how to carry arms with pieces of wood shaped like gunstocks, but these are said to have gone out of use now. As regards industrial schools, these, even when set up and maintained by School Boards, are entirely under the jurisdiction of the Home Office, and are expressly excluded from the administration of the Education Department.[36]

Mr Acland was misinformed. As late as 1885 the Revd D. J. Stewart HMI had reported that the Abingdon National School's programme of military drill included 'skirmishing with dummy muskets'.[37] And within 12 months of Mr Acland's statement in the House of Commons, Mr Wilkinson HMI reported of the Ellacombe National School, Torquay, that:

> An enthusiastic school manager has presented the school with 100 dummy rifles, 100 solid leather belts with bayonets and leather sheets complete, etc., – as preliminaries, however, only to a more

real gun drill with actual carbines procured from the Horse Guards for the elder boys.[38]

Mr Cremer's fears were well founded, and the minister's ignorance of the evidence readily available in the reports of HMIs submitted to his department in 1885 cannot be condoned.

A major difficulty lay in the fact that there had been all too little knowledge or experience of physical instruction other than that directly associated with military drill. In accepting the military drill model, which often included the involvement of army personnel as instructors, many education authorities and individual schools found themselves committed to practices which had little relevance to the needs of children through a co-ordinated programme of physical instruction. Where, as in the case of the Ellacombe National School, an enthusiastic school manager provided carbines, belts and bayonets, or where a head teacher brought his own experience as a member of the local Volunteers to bear, the effect was to lose sight of the original objective, if indeed that objective related primarily to the well-being of the children and not to the encouragement of militarism.

THE CENTURY DRAWS TO A CLOSE

During the period from 1875 to 1899 parliamentary debates swung to and fro with the contest to determine what form of physical training should be provided for elementary school children. The Trades Union Congress (TUC) powerfully expressed its anxiety over the looming threat of conscription and the inherent dangers of military training when imposed on young children. Her Majesty's Inspectors reported favourably on one kind of drill or critically on another, or drew attention to the lack of proper facilities for any form of physical exercise to be practised effectively. The introduction of variable grants for discipline and organization and changes in the annual Codes accelerated the process by which physical training or military drill gained a permanent place in the curriculum. Gradually the Education Department moved towards the adoption of physical training of a non-military nature and the encouragement of games. The public schools had long accepted the 'games ethic' in preference to corps training, and now the elementary schools were beginning to follow that example.

A major development in administration occurred in 1899 with the establishment of a central authority. Powers previously exercised by the

Education Department, the Science and Art Department and the Charity Commission, as regards its educational work, were brought together in the Board of Education. As a Board it never met during its 45-year life-span; in practical terms it comprised a president, a Permanent secretary and senior administrative officials. That year was also marked by the first Peace Conference at The Hague and, in October, war against the Boers.

NOTES

1. Lauderdale pointed to the unpredictability of wars at that time. He said: 'War began now before one knew what he was about, and it was brought to an end before either side had time to train new lives' (*House of Lords Debates* (Hansard), Third Series, Vol. CCXXIII, cols. 1202–6, 19 April 1875). Kennedy compares the long drawn-out wars of the eighteenth century with the Austro-Prussian War (of seven weeks duration in 1866) and the Franco-Prussian War (five months in 1870–71) which were concluded within the space of a season's campaigning. Swift, knock-out victories were seen to be the pattern of future conflicts. Paul Kennedy, *The Rise and Fall of the Great Powers: Economic Change and Military Conflict from 1500 to 2000* (London: Collins/Fontana, 1989), p. 246. Reasons for such rapid victories by the Prussian forces are given by Fuller as the limited nature of both wars, the superiority of the Prussian General Staff, the speed of Prussian mobilization, and superior Prussian tactics. Major-General J. F. C. Fuller, *The Conduct of War* (London: Eyre Methuen, 1972), p. 116.
2. *House of Commons Debates*, Third series, Vol. CCXXIII, cols. 1202–6 (19 April 1875).
3. Ibid.
4. The Swedish system of Physical Exercises was introduced by Per Henrik Ling (1776–1839) in 1813. He believed that organized physical training should be accepted as an essential and integral component of general education, of national defence and of medical remedial treatment. He was the first director of the Kungl Gymnastika Central-Institutet in Stockholm. His son Hjalmar became the principal exponent of educational gymnastics as taught in Sweden.
5. *House of Commons Debates*, Third Series, Vol. CCXXV, cols. 794–9 (1 July 1875).
6. P. C. McIntosh, *Physical Education in England since 1800* (London: Bell, 1968), p. 112.
7. Mr Currey's General Report for 1875 said of his Northamptonshire schools: 'Drill is not so much cultivated as I think it might be. Where it is taught it usually improves the general discipline.' *Report of the CCE, 1875–76* (C.-1513-I), p. 297.
      Mr Danby, HMI for Suffolk and Essex, submitted that: 'Military drill is regularly taught in several schools … It would be well, if instruction in military drill were much more general than it is now … [it] promotes habits of smartness and discipline', ibid, p. 307. Writing of the Northumberland schools, Mr D. P. Pennethorne stated that he considered drill of great service to schools: 'Both at Berwick and Tynemouth the children are taught drill by a sergeant in the regular army, and the effect is very marked in conducting general movements in or dismissal from the school. It improves the posture of the children and it produces a certain kind of order' (ibid., p. 381). And with one eye on the children's future workplace and one on their present situation, A. G. Legard HMI reported that military drill was becoming very common in his schools within the Leeds district. He claimed that it had 'good effects in habituating boys to be obedient; as a physical exercise, especially for those whose life would be spent in the workshop or factory it is most useful, but as an aid to discipline it is invaluable'. Ibid., p. 346.
8. See Chapter 1.
9. *Report of CCE, 1876–77* (C.-1780-I), p. 535.
10. *Report of CCE, 1881–82* (C.-3312-I), p. 226.
11. *Report of CCE, 1898–99* (C.-9401), p. 179.
12. From the statistical tables in the Report it can be seen that almost one in 12 boys'

departments taught military drill at that time. *Report of CCE, 1875–76* (C.-1513-I), p. 381.

13. The Revd H. R. Sandford HMI, Sheffield District, drew attention in his General Report for 1876 to the initiative of the Clerk to the Barnsley School Board in bravely inviting both Board and voluntary schools to compete for drill prizes. It is not divulged whether the prizes were provided out of the rates. He wrote:

> Military drill in a school generally has a good effect on the discipline. Considering how many teachers have, as students, been members of the volunteer corps connected with their colleges, it is surprising that so few of them make any effort to introduce the system into their schools. Military drill has, however, been taught with excellent results in the Sheffield and Barnsley Board Schools by sergeants employed by the boards. In the latter town the clerk of the board has induced some of the voluntary schools as well as those under the board to adopt the drill by offering prizes for competition. To have the youth of the country trained in the practice of drill is a matter of such national importance that I certainly think a small annual grant might be given to encourage it in State-aided schools.

Report of CCE, 1876–77 (C.-1780-I), p. 555.
14. *Report of CCE, 1878–79* (C.-2342-I), pp. 646–7.
15. *Report of CCE, 1880–81* (C.-2948-I), p. 277.
16. The Revd J. W. D. Hernaman's Report for West Lambeth in 1883–84 included the observation that 188 out of the 216 he had visited rated 'good' in respect of discipline, and in no cases were the grants withheld. *Report of CCE, 1883–84* (C.-4091-I), p. 74.
17. *Report of CCE, 1890–91* (C.-4638-I), p. 196.
18. Ibid., p. 366.
19. *Report of CCE, 1888–89* (C.-5804-I), p. 117.
20. *Report of CCE, 1889–90* (C.6079-I), p. 118.
21. *Report of CCE, 1887–88* (C.-5467-I), p. 333.
22. *Report of CCE, 1878–79* (C.-2342-I), p. 586.
23. *Report of CCE, 1883–84* (C.-4091-I), p. 80.
24. *Report of CCE, 1889–90* (C.-6079-I), p. 347.
25. *The Times* (14 September 1885), p. 8.
26. *Society of Arts, Journal* (16 October 1885): 1069–72, 1086–8; *The Times* (25 September 1885), pp. 13–14.
27. *Report of CCE, 1891–92* (C.-6746-I), p. 411.
28. *Report of CCE, 1893–94* (C.-7437-I), p. 94.
29. Fabian Society Tract 52, *State Education at Home and Abroad* (1894), p. 5.
30. Fabian Society Tract 55, *The Workers' School Board Programme* (1894), p. 10.
31. J. A. Mangan, *The Games Ethic and Imperialism: Aspects of the Diffusion of an Ideal* (Harmondsworth: Viking, 1986), p. 18.
32. *Report of CCE, 1893–94* (C.-7437-I), p. 18.
33. *School Board Chronicle* (6 January 1894): 19.
34. Article 101 (b) (i) of the Code of 1895 read:

> For any school year beginning after 31 August 1895, the higher grant for discipline and organisation will not be paid to any school in which provision has not been made in the approved timetable for instruction in Swedish or other drill, as suitable physical exercises, but children employed in labour and attending school half-time, and children for whom such instruction is unsuitable, may be excepted. (*School Board Chronicle*, 2 March 1895: 240–3)

This provision met the objectives of the Earl of Meath's unsuccessful Bills of 1890 and 1891, so it can perhaps be claimed that his efforts at that time helped to prepare the way for the strong official encouragement of appropriate physical exercises some four years later.
35. *Report of CCE, 1896–97* (C.-8545-I), 'Revised Instructions issued to Her Majesty's Inspectors, and applicable to the Code of 1897', Appendix, Part 3, pp. 508–9.
36. *School Board Chronicle* (8 July 1893), p. 20.
37. *Report of CCE, 1885–86* (C.-4849-I), p. 322.
38. *Report of CCE, 1894–95* (C.-7776-I), p. 15.

3

The Society of Arts:
Its Advocacy of Military Drill

Few independent bodies could have exerted as much pressure on government and on local authorities in support of military drill as did the Society for the Encouragement of Arts, Commerce and Manufactures in Great Britain (hereafter referred to as the Society of Arts).[1] The Society (founded in 1754) had earlier concerned itself with Poor Law District Schools which had been set up under the Poor Law Amendment Act of 1844, with industrial schools and naval and military schools. Drill was introduced in those schools primarily in an effort to combat the indiscipline of the children attending the schools. Having demonstrated the beneficial effects of the drill programmes through the promotion of displays, the Society of Arts expanded its sights to embrace other elementary schools. The establishment of School Boards after 1870 stimulated their efforts.

HENRY COLE STATES THE SOCIETY'S POSITION

In the period immediately preceding the introduction of the Education Bill in 1870, a paper was delivered to the Society by Henry Cole[2] entitled *On the Efficiency and Economy of a National Army, in Connection with the Industry and Education of the People.* Cole argued that a more efficient military organization could be achieved at a cost some seven million pounds less than the current expenditure on the army. He proposed that drill should be encouraged as an essential component of the curriculum in all boys' schools, with military pensioners employed as instructors. On leaving school, the boys would be induced to become Volunteers or to join the reorganized militia. During the ensuing discussion Edwin Chadwick[3] suggested that if instruction began when the child was 5½ or 6 years old, instead of 10 as Cole proposed, by the time he reached the latter age he would be ready to practise with a light rifle.[4]

Cole's paper stimulated an active involvement by the Society in the related questions of the teaching of drill to schoolchildren in all elementary schools and of their preparation for future military service in the interests of their country. The association of these two considerations was to be fiercely debated, and there were many different opinions on the subject, as we have seen in the previous chapter. There were those, like many members of the Society of Arts, who unashamedly linked the teaching of drill with the encouragement of a military spirit, and who endeavoured to encourage others to support such teaching in the schools. Others were prepared to recognize that there were educational, in addition to physical, advantages in the teaching of military drill. Those who belonged to this category were probably aware that few alternatives to military drill existed at the time, but they were anxious to restrict the military influences as far as they could. A third group comprised those who were opposed to the incursion of military drill in the schools because of their revulsion to any attempts to introduce practices which were of a military character.

PHYSICAL INSTRUCTION AN AID TO EFFICIENCY

The Society of Arts pursued its interest in education, and particularly in physical instruction, through the publication of a supplement to its *Journal* in December 1869. This carried instructions to delegates attending meetings arranged for the consideration of an improved system of education. A prime tenet was that much would depend on the extent to which greater efficiency could be attained, and to this end the benefits of physical instruction were stressed. Indeed, it was suggested that so great would be the advantages to the pupils that the amount of time allocated to the elements of general instruction could be reduced by some one and a half to two years. In terms of organization it was proposed to achieve this saving through an extension of infant school teaching and the exploitation and development of the existing half-time principle. Employers of labour were advised of the potential advantages which would accrue if physical exercises had taught children how to move in unison and how to utilize their combined lifting capabilities. Appeals for the support of practices which carried with them the potential for financial and labour savings of no mean magnitude and for maintaining a submissive labour force were likely to gain the sympathy of middle-class industrial interests. The general tone of the statement was both confident and forceful:

> It is declared that by improving gymnastic exercises, superadded to the common military drill, the efficiency of five is given to three for all purposes of ordinary labour. The military drill is an exercise of mental habits, of visible and undoubted habits of attention, and of all that is implied in the word discipline – self-restraint, patience, silence when under orders, prompt and exact obedience, and highest respect for gradations of authority.[5]

The intention here was clearly enunciated, whether the future of elementary school children lay in the armed forces or in humble mill or workshop. Members of the lower orders of society needed to be well versed in their subservient role, and merit lay in such means as furthered that end. Those worthies who drew up the statement were appreciative of the fact that imperialism depended on firm hierarchical structures both at home and in the dependent colonies overseas.

A PUBLIC DEMONSTRATION OF DRILL PROFICIENCY

In March of the following year the *Journal* reported that the Society's Committee on Drill was to consider how drill could be introduced into all schools throughout the United Kingdom. Members appointed to serve on this committee held impressive qualifications, so that from the outset it was recognized as an influential and powerful body whose deliberations and recommendations would carry considerable weight.[6] The committee decision of 7 March 1870 was to make a pronounced impact on the teaching of drill in elementary schools, particularly in the metropolis. The resolution read:

> In order to direct public attention to this important branch of education, and to show with what success drill has been already introduced into some schools, and to show what proficiency can readily be obtained, the Committee decided to recommend to the Council (of the Society) to invite the managers of the various army, navy, marine, district, and other schools, in the neighbourhood of the metropolis, whose drill forms part of the system of education, to send their boys to take part in a review to be held at the Crystal Palace in June next.[7]

A subscription fund would provide prizes and cover the expense of staging the review, and it was hoped that representatives of the great public schools would support the event. The Council of the Society of

Arts confirmed the recommendations and directed that the necessary action be taken to set preparations in train for the review.

A brake to the generally enthusiastic response to the project was applied by Captain A. F. Lendy's letter to the editor of the Society's *Journal* of 18 March 1870. He referred to the work of the Drill Committee and tendered his own observations which he claimed were based on some 15 years' experience as headmaster of a military school. His letter read:

> Drilling does not make a soldier; nay, drilling may prevent a young man becoming a soldier. Although my pupils were exclusively military, and left me to join the army as ensigns and cornets, I had to give up drill; and my observations agree with those contained in the report of the Royal Commission on Military Education. This report recommends that the Sandhurst cadets should know as little drill as possible because the colonels of regiments found that the cadets had to learn it afresh on joining. At first young men like it, then they grow tired of it, and at last they hate it.[8]

The captain concluded by saying that if the Committee wanted to foster the military spirit, then it should encourage something besides drill; he suggested that 'drill and spade' should be combined on the Cheltenham College pattern, where fortifications and military drawing were included in the curriculum. His was a lone voice, however, from the military side of the debate.[9]

When the provisions of the Forster Education Bill became known, a petition to the House of Commons was prepared by Sir John Pakington on behalf of the Society. The introduction of the Bill was welcomed but regret was expressed that no Minister was proposed to shoulder the sole responsibility for education. Both the petition and a list of amendments which the full Council of the Society forwarded for consideration favoured the teaching of military drill.

On 21 June 1870 a drill review took place at the Crystal Palace before the guests of honour: the Prince of Teck and his wife, Princess Mary of Cambridge. Some 2,000–3,000 boys from 18 schools participated. About two-thirds were half-timers. Only a few were drawn from ordinary elementary schools; better represented were industrial schools and training establishments (such as the Schools of the Homeless Boys of London, the Royal Naval School of Greenwich and the Royal Military Asylum). The district schools mentioned were those set up under the Poor Law Amendment Act of 1844 where drill had been introduced to control noisy and indisciplined boys. A sergeant-major of the Guards was in charge of the parade and responsible for the direction of all the drill movements performed by the schools. There were swimming, gymnastics and drill competitions, though most attention was focused on the latter. Each school was led by its own drill instructor (who was expected to wear uniform if he had one in his possession), and either the school's own band or the band of the Royal Military Asylum played each contingent past the saluting point. The bearing and performance of the boys earned them 'the very highest commendations from the eminent officers of the Army and Navy who witnessed them', and the soldiers and Volunteers who were present were equally appreciative of the smartness with which the drill was carried out.[10]

A statement issued by the Society immediately following the Drill Review made a clear and unequivocal pronouncement of its objectives in organizing the event, and offered encouragement to other schools wishing to participate in the teaching of military drill:

> The special interest is military – to judge of how much economy of military force may be obtained by the transference of as much as possible of military training and exercise from the productive adult stages to the non-productive and school stages of life; how far a pre-disposition to a higher order of voluntary recruitment and of aptitude for the new arms of precision, which require more and more of intelligence and aptitude to wield them, may be diffused amongst the general population.[11]

Again the Society spoke in favour of 'graded half-time schools of mixed physical and mental training', estimating that such a policy would result in the saving of between two and three million pounds on the cost to the nation of elementary education. The money so saved could be redirected in the interests of 'the middle classes and those who could be kept at school to the fourteenth year'. The Society was also anxious to stress that the adoption of its proposals could result in 'the great bulk of the male population' forming 'an inexpensive reserve force for military purposes'.[12]

The statement was an honest one; the Society made no attempt to hide its purpose in advocating military drill and its inclusion in the curriculum of schools. It was to begin the teaching of military drill at as early an age as possible and to encourage an easy transfer to the Volunteers in due course. As new 'arms of precision' became available, so more intelligence and more intense training would be required, and the schools were seen to have a part to play in that training. Existing difficulties in recruiting to the regular army and to the Volunteers would be progressively eased as children reached school leaving age, having attained some elementary proficiency in martial exercises. Captain Lendy's warning that beginning drill training too early might prove to be counterproductive was ignored in the enthusiasm to extend the practice throughout the elementary schools.

DEPUTATIONS TO THE VICE-PRESIDENT OF THE EDUCATION DEPARTMENT

Drill and music were the two curricular subjects carried by deputations from the Society's Drill Committee and its Musical Education Committee which waited on W. E. Forster at the Privy Council Office in January 1871. Their joint purpose was to urge the compulsory teaching of both subjects in all state-aided schools. It is unlikely that music was encouraged merely as a recreative and artistic pursuit; its potential practical association with drill was one with which the Society was familiar. The drill delegation was led by Lord Henry Lennox MP, and included Major-General Lindsay, whom the War Office had deputed to attend on their behalf. Lennox spoke of the Society's long interest in the matter of military drill and of its efforts to publicize the advantages of gymnastics and physical training. E. C. Tufnell, Inspector of Industrial Schools, claimed that a system of drill had been adopted in all the large London industrial schools in his area of inspection, catering for some 8,000 pauper children. Every one of these schools had its own salaried drill master. The inference would seem to be that if such a scheme could be successfully implemented in the industrial schools then it should be possible to extend the practice to all schools which were in receipt of state aid.

By way of reply, Forster said that he had no doubt as to the advantage of drill. The Government was considering how far it was possible to provide facilities so as to enable drill to be practised in schools. He did not consider it very wise, however, 'to rely much on the purely military aspect of the question'.[13] In that Forster's observations were neither dismissive nor enthusiastic, they were familiar ministerial responses to controversial or sensitive issues. His apprehension regarding 'the purely military aspect of the question' of drill, should have warned the more forceful advocates of the teaching of military drill that their cause was unlikely to gain official support, at least from the current Government. In the event, Forster's successors at the Education Department showed no more enthusiasm than he did on this occasion.

FURTHER DRILL REVIEWS

A second Drill Review was held in July 1871, this time at the Horticultural Gardens, South Kensington, before Prince Arthur and the Prince of Teck. As in the previous year, the winner's banner was awarded to a military or naval training establishment. To overcome the built-in advantages of those schools it was decided that on future occasions there should be separate prizes for the different types of schools.

In preparation for the review in 1872, Captain O'Hea visited all the participating schools in the course of the year. His report to the Society drew attention to the need for standardizing the drill procedures, and continued: 'Wooden dummy rifles, as in use in the Hanwell and Brentwood schools, are of great service in rendering the boys steady in the ranks on parade, and an additional means of improving the setting-up of the boys.'[14]

By this time it could be claimed with justification that the Society of Arts was in effect staging a drill review on the lines of a full-scale military exercise. It was also engaging professional soldiers to conduct that operation and to visit schools to report upon the effectiveness of their teaching of military drill. Almost inevitably this led to a blurring of the distinction between what was acceptable as current army practice for men serving in the regular or Volunteer units, and what was appropriate for the exercising of elementary schoolboys.[15] O'Hea appreciated how the drill as such could be improved and developed in military terms, but he was not an educationalist. Had he been so, he might not have been so anxious to place dummy rifles into the hands of young children and to encourage them to perform as if they were grown-up soldiers.

THE SOCIETY FOCUSES ITS SIGHTS ON THE LONDON SCHOOL BOARD

In May 1875 the Society shifted its attention from the industrial and service schools towards the far more influential London School Board and its schools. A deputation waited on members of the School Board bearing a memorial which opened grandly: 'That the Society for many years has endeavoured to promote drill in schools as a necessary part of school training, and has caused several reviews of schools to be held successfully under the inspection of high military authorities and royal princes.' Further clauses referred to the small government grants paid in support of drill, to the need for drill to be made compulsory and to be taught by competent instructors. The concluding five clauses related specifically to the London School Board and to the contribution it could make in influencing the War Department and the Education Department 'to work together and effectively introduce drill in all schools in the country'.[16] For the Society, Major-General Eardley-Wilmot explained that it was the practice of the Society of Arts to initiate but not to continue 'beyond a certain point'. In this instance, it was hoped that the London School Board, with the continuing support of the Society, would carry on the work necessary to establish military drill firmly within the elementary school curriculum.

Impressed by the case presented to them by the deputation, the London School Board duly accepted the responsibility of preparing children attending its schools for participation in annual drill reviews, with the support and encouragement of the Society of Arts. The latter's *Journal* reported that the hand-over of responsibility had taken place, but it failed to make any acknowledgement of the contribution made by the non-Board schools which, until that time, had provided most of the participants. Having served their purpose, those schools appear to have been quietly laid down as far as the Society of Arts was concerned. Presumably the industrial and service schools had reached the 'certain point' referred to by the delegation to the London School Board and were no longer deemed to qualify for support from the Society. The teaching of drill under the London School Board merits a separate chapter, not least because of the Board's status among other local authorities.

NOTES

1. The Society had its origin in 1754, when it was set up by William Shipley to encourage innovation in commerce and manufacturing and to award prizes to promising child artists. It was one of a number of patriotic societies of that time whose supporters aimed 'to foster an orderly and industrious as well as a more prosperous Britain'. It became the Royal Society of Arts in 1908. Linda Colley, *Britons: Forging the Nation 1707–1837* (New Haven, CT, and London: Yale University Press, 1992), p. 97.
2. See note 6 below.
3. Ibid.
4. *Society of Arts, Journal* (17 February 1869).
5. Ibid. Supplement to *Society of Arts, Journal* (17 December 1869), Appendix: vii.
6. Members of the Society's Committee on Drill included the following: T. D. Acland MP, who had taken a leading part in the establishment of the Oxford local examination in 1857–58, and who contributed many speeches and pamphlets on education; Lord Henry G. Lennox MP, ex-Lord of the Treasury, who had also served as Secretary to the Admiralty and was to

be appointed the first Commissioner of Public Works from 1874–76; Sir John Pakington MP, who had twice served as First Lord of the Admiralty, and also as Secretary for War; A.J. Mundella, the Radical MP for Sheffield 1868–97, who had contributed to the framing of the Education Act 1870, and was due to serve as Vice-President of the Committee of Council on Education, 1880–85; Dr Lyon Playfair MP, who had helped organize the Great Exhibition of 1851, served as Secretary of the Department of Science and Art at South Kensington, was Chemistry Professor at Edinburgh 1859–69, and Liberal MP for the Scottish Universities 1868–85, and for South Leeds 1885–92 (he was raised to the peerage in 1892); Henry Cole, who was Secretary of the Department of Science and Art from the 1850s until 1873; Captain Donnelly RE, who served the Department of Science and Art for some 40 of its 46 years of existence and whose name often appeared in elementary school log-books as an examiner for the Department; R. R. W. Lingen, who was Permanent Secretary to the Education Department from the resignation of Kay-Shuttleworth in 1849 until 1870; E. C. Tufnell collaborated with Kay-Shuttleworth in establishing Battersea Training College for Teachers in 1840 and was Inspector of industrial schools; Edwin Chadwick was a sanitary reformer who served on the Royal Commission set up in 1833 to investigate the conditions of factory children, and was a member of the Board of Health, 1848–54; Professor T. H. Huxley FRS, Professor of Natural History at the Royal School of Mines, 1854–85, was the foremost scientific supporter of Darwin's theory of evolution and an original member of the London School Board 1870–72, who influenced the teaching of biology and science in schools; Sir Joseph Whitworth, armaments industrialist; the Archbishop of York, as representative of the Established Church; the headmasters of Eton and of Harrow, representing the major public schools.

7. *Society of Arts, Journal* (11 March 1870): 343.
8. Ibid. (18 March 1870): 397.
9. An interesting footnote might be added here: I. S. Bloch, a Polish-Jewish banker, with pacifist views, published a six-volume work, *The War of the Future in its Technical, Economic and Political Relations*, in 1897. Two years later W. T. Stead brought out an English translation under the title *Is War Impossible?*. Bloch claimed that a future war between the great industrial powers would be mutual suicide, with unparalleled levels of casualties. There would be long periods of stalemate as armies failed to get to grips in a decisive manner. 'Everyone will be entrenched in the next war … . The spade will be as indispensable to a soldier as his rifle' (cited by J. F. C. Fuller, *The Conduct of War, 1789–1961* (London: Eyre Methuen, 1972), pp. 128–30). There were few who so accurately predicted the pattern which would emerge in the First World War (1914–18), brought about by new weapons of ever-increasing potency. Bloch's ideas contrasted sharply with the conclusions drawn subsequent to the Austro-Prussian War (1866) and the Franco-Prussian War (1870–71).
10. *The Times* commented on the 'astonishing precision' of the manoeuvres as follows: 'The schools were exercised in the different movements of a battalion in the field, and the manner in which they formed lines, broke into a battalion in open column, formed close column, faced in square, "prepared" to receive cavalry, re-formed companies, and opened out into column again, was perfect, for their execution was rapid and certain, and without noise.' Less appreciatively, the *Times* correspondent drew attention to the 'old degraded workhouse character' of some of the uniforms, ignorant perhaps that, as the Society of Arts' own report observed, 'a large proportion of boys appeared in clothes and shoes made in the schools'. See report in the *Society of Arts, Journal* (24 June 1870): 693–4.
    The Prince of Teck and Princess Mary of Cambridge were the parents of Princess Mary (or May), the future consort of King George V. The Prince of Teck was accompanied at the following year's review by Prince Arthur who became the Duke of Connaught in 1874.
11. Ibid.: 693–4.
12. Ibid.: 694.
13. Ibid. (27 January 1871): 186.
14. Ibid. (2 August 1872): 753–4.
15. Newspaper reports of the 1872 review gave the ages of the boys as ranging from 6 years to 14 years. They numbered about 4,000 and attracted some 1,000 spectators. Ibid.: 753–4.

16. Clause 8 of the Society of Arts Memorial to the London School Board read:

> That the Society of Arts, Commerce, and Manufactures expresses its willingness to provide a handsome set of colours to be competed for each year, and held for the ensuing year by the school pronounced by military authorities to be the best of the year, and to give to such school a sum of £200 to be divided among the boys as a prize. (*School Board Chronicle*, 15 May 1875: 475)

4

The London School Board Drill Programme, and those of Leeds and Bradford

The sequence of events concerned with the teaching of military drill in the London Board schools merits separate consideration. The Board was targeted by the Society of Arts, and for a number of years the annual drill displays jointly staged by the Society and the School Board were a powerful advertisement for military drill instruction.

In common with other School Boards set up under the provisions of the Elementary Education Act of 1870, the London School Board found that its first task was to assess the educational needs of its area and to ascertain what existing school provision it could draw upon. Next came the decisions relating to a school building programme so that all children for whom the Board was responsible could be accommodated. Those Board schools would coexist with non-provided or voluntary schools (mostly under the aegis of the Church of England), industrial and service schools, and the like. Only then could the Board members address themselves to the related questions of the curriculum and teaching methods. The general reports for 1872 of HMIs commented that the Board had not yet opened any new schools, preferring to be thorough rather than hasty in its decision-making. Temporary accommodation was found in chapels, mission halls and similar buildings, and those often inadequate and crowded rooms had to suffice for the time being.

EARLY PROPOSALS FOR THE TEACHING OF DRILL

The issue of drill arose on a motion introduced by Mr Hepworth Dixon, a barrister and historian Board member, in February 1871. His proposal was 'That means shall be provided for physical training, exercise, and drill, in every Public Elementary School established under the authority of the Board'. Dixon drew attention to the high level of rejection of recruits to the Horse Guards as compared with similar recruits in Europe. He went on to press the Board to play its part in 'training up a

53

new generation into a higher condition for well-being and well-doing'. The ability of the masses to contribute to the defence of their homes and their liberties depended not on 'any special enthusiasm to be evoked by lyrics and leading articles', but rather on 'the rules laid down, and ... the habits acquired, by physical exercises year after year'. He asserted that it was 'by such rules [that] the natural enthusiasm was trained and organised, and by such habits [that] the bodily power lying at the root of all armed force was gradually trained and tempered to the highest mood'. Dixon anticipated that such teaching would result in 'no measurable expense' so long as the Board exercised strict control of the operation, and the willing co-operation of the children would be assured if 'a certain heroic cadence' was introduced into that part of the school curriculum.[1] The motion was carried unanimously, but not before a number of members of the Board had insisted that physical training should not be introduced into schools for military ends.

It is interesting to note that this first proposal was for a broad provision which included the teaching of 'physical training, exercise and drill'. However, Dixon made no secret of the fact that he saw the proposed programme as one which would serve the interests of the military. Members of the Board were unanimous in appreciating the need for some appropriate form of physical instruction, but there were some reservations in response to Dixon's association of the teaching with military requirements and the general question of national defence.

Some five months after this decision the writer of 'Miscellaneous Notes' in the *School Board Chronicle* predicted:

> We have little doubt that our School Boards will establish drill in every school under their control, partly because such a form of discipline tends to habits of order, regularity, steadiness, system and method; partly because it tends to strengthen the constitution and to invigorate the health; and partly because it tends to foster a patriotic and military taste amongst the masses of the people.[2]

The writer was probably correct in his identification of the three-fold nature of the current support for the teaching of drill in elementary schools. Those who provided elementary instruction had always sought to encourage orderliness, regularity and obedience in their young charges. To those traditional requirements were now added those which would provide both a robust workforce and a means by which sectional demands associated with a developing working class could be deflected into national aspirations and responsibilities. It was the third of these reasons which was to be most closely questioned, particularly by representatives of the working classes. As members of school boards, trade union committees and other *ad hoc* bodies they were in a position to monitor developments which might threaten or abuse fellow workers or their children.

When the Education Department restricted the recognition of drill under Article 24 to boys only in 1872, the London School Board called for the matter to be revised so that it could once more count as school attendance for girls as well as for boys. The Department's reply pointed out that since the provision referred to 'systematic military drill' it was unsuitable for use by girls. This did not deter the London School Board (or others) from continuing its provision of drill to either sex.[3] The quarterly return submitted in the summer of 1873 confirmed that 7,695 boys had been drilled, while that of the following November reported that nearly 5,000 girls had participated in the drill exercises.[4]

The Education Department's annual Codes were supplemented in London by the Board's own Code of Regulations for the guidance and direction of its teachers. That of 1873 included music, now a grant-earning subject, and drill among the essential subjects of instruction, with singing and physical exercises for infant schools. Where the Education Department did not categorize a subject as compulsory in its annual Code, any local authority undertaking to teach it did so at its own expense. From time to time this was the way forward, with official recognition and funding following what was already an established practice in many schools.

The London School Board's regulations with regard to drill required that

> Drill must be taught in every school during part of the time devoted to actual instruction. It has been ascertained from the Education Department that a teacher holding a certificate from the Board drill instructor, will be regarded by the Department as a 'competent instructor' of drill under Article 24 of the New Code.[5]

In order to qualify for a Board certificate, teachers were required to pass an examination in preliminary drill, turning, marching and company drill. Their instructor was Sergeant-Major Sheffield and the Board's *Regulations in Regard to Drill* were clearly taken from an Army drill manual. Those who were awarded a certificate were qualified to teach military drill.[6] Nothing in the regulations related to any other form of drill or physical exercise.

Five months after the Regulations for Drill were issued, Sergeant-Major Sheffield reported that between 50 and 60 teachers were ready to qualify as competent instructors of drill.[7] There must have been some discussion with respect to a possible drill review, as the Board's drill instructor reported in July 1873 that 'He could send about four hundred children to march past, if it were not that the teachers were generally unwilling to be drilled with the children.'[8]

MEMORIAL IN SUPPORT OF DRILL BY THE SOCIETY OF ARTS

The question of a drill review surfaced again in May 1875 with the memorial in support of drill presented by the Society of Arts. The Board's School Management Committee was asked to give the matter their consideration. At a Board meeting in July, Mr Lucraft unsuccessfully submitted an amendment to the proposal prepared by the School Management Committee which would have adjourned the matter for one month. His concern was that reviews or inspections of boys 'in military fashion' tended to create a passion for glory. The Board's drill instructor reported that over 5,300 boys could be assembled, and claimed that they would present a creditable spectacle. After due consideration the School Management Committee's recommendations in favour of a drill inspection in Regent's Park were endorsed.[9]

On the day preceding the review, Mr Lucraft returned to the fray. The chairman attempted to assure him that the Board would continue with its teaching of 'ordinary drill' and did not contemplate instruction in military drill, even though the New Code permitted it. This semantic distinction is difficult to accept. The teachers' qualifying certificate certainly called for proficiency in teaching military drill. Whilst the expense of staging the review would be met by the Board, Mr Lucraft was assured that refreshments for the bands would not be paid for out of the rates.

THE DRILL INSPECTIONS ARE STAGED

Some 6,000 children duly participated in the event which was fully reported in *The Times*. Much credit devolved upon Sergeant-Major Sheffield, while the teachers were congratulated for their work 'in drilling the small units of humanity to act on the word of command'.[10]

Not everyone was pleased at this development introduced by the London School Board. A circular from the Peace Society invited the Board's co-operation in opposing military drill, parades and inspections in connection with Board schools. The Peace Society stated that it did not believe that the London School Board had the slightest idea that it was working in the interests of the War Office. Whether the Board made any response is not apparent from the report of the Peace Society's action as reported in the *School Board Chronicle*.[11]

The London School Board's second annual drill review and inspection took place in Regent's Park in July 1876, with some 9,500 boys assembled in 238 companies. Bands were in attendance from the Caledonian Asylum, Feltham, Strand Union and Forest Gate district schools; few, if any Board schools would have been in a position to furnish a band at that time.[12] The 'Society of Arts Challenge Banner for Excellence in Military Drill' was awarded to the Kender Street School, Greenwich. This provides further evidence that there was confusion as to the kind of drill which was being taught and inspected in London. On the one hand, Mr Lucraft was assured that only 'ordinary drill' was being taught in Board schools, while on the other, the banner awarded to the winning school was for proficiency in military drill.

Similar arrangements were made in 1877, but a year later the London School Board decided by 22 votes to 5 to discontinue 'public drill'. Mr Benjamin Lucraft moved the resolution, objecting to the practice on grounds of cost[13] and because he considered that it served no good purpose. Those were his publicly stated reasons, but since he was a member of the Peace Society[14] it is reasonable to assume that he had more positive reasons for objecting to drill instruction in the Board's schools. Lucraft claimed that hundreds of parents had asked him to try to stop the military drill which they believed was leading their children 'to think more of military glory than was needful'.[15] He suggested that such teaching contributed to a spirit of jingoism: 'Thousands of children were taken to Regent's Park, with the music playing and banners flying, to go through all sorts of military evolutions before the public.'[16] Although only one of the four clergymen members of the Board supported Lucraft, on this occasion he was successful, with the result that, at least for the time being, the public drill display was out of favour. At the request of the Society of Arts their banner was returned for safe keeping.[17]

A significant step in the direction of physical instruction on the Swedish model was the Board's invitation to Miss Löfving of Sweden to become Lady Superintendent of Physical Education, a post she took up in 1878, but did not stay more than a year. Mathias Roth had persuaded Mrs Westlake, a member of the London School Board, to press for the appointment of such an instructor.

The drill lobby was by no means exhausted, however, and there was further correspondence between the Society of Arts and the Board. Subsequently, in June 1879 it was unanimously agreed by members of the London School Board that drill competitions should be reinstated, though with numbers restricted to 400. The drill instructor was to be required to select the ten schools whose drill proficiency assured them a place in the competition.[18]

In the hope of getting the resolution of 25 June rescinded, Mr Lucraft presented to the Board a memorial from the Workmens' Education Committee. The memorialists regretted the Board's volte-face and hoped:

> that there was no desire existing on the part of the Board to develop the spirit of militarism which drill in school evidently awakened and fostered; and they had hoped that at no distant day the drill-sergeant would disappear altogether from the Board schools. They called attention to the fact that the principal promoters of drill in public schools were advocates of conscription, whilst the memorialists themselves abhorred a system which was the root of the terrible evils which afflicted the continental nations. They prayed the Board to reconsider and not to sanction any further efforts to inculcate the military spirit in the rising generation.[19]

On this occasion the decision to continue with drill was only carried by 13 votes to 11, which makes the unanimity of the June decision difficult to appreciate. Possibly the matter was raised on the earlier occasion when known opponents of military drill were absent.

In October 420 boys drawn from the agreed ten schools were drilled by Sergeant-Major Sheffield in the grounds of Lambeth Palace. The Society of Arts Challenge Banner was once more raised, to be won on this occasion by Thomas Street School in Limehouse.[20]

The report of the 1880 Drill Competition which appeared in the pages of the *School Board Chronicle* demonstrated that by no stretch of the imagination could the drill be defined as other than military in character. The account read:

> The boys marched past in open column, then counter-marched, and returned in quarter-column. Then they marched past again in double quick time, and deployed to the left in fours, then advanced in line, changed front to the right, and retired by fours. They then formed in line, and were inspected in separate companies by Colonel Battersby, of Chelsea College.

After several other evolutions the boys formed in square to be addressed by the inspecting officer.[21] Non-military readers of this account of the proceedings may justifiably have been mystified by the technicalities of the various manœuvres, but they could have been in no doubt that they were reading about military drill and about no other kind of exercise.

Members of the public who enjoyed the spectacle of the annual drill competions organized by the London School Board could, as from 1880, witness adult displays of militarism. From that time annual Naval and Military Tournaments were staged in London, at which scenes and incidents illustrative of British naval and military prowess were enacted. In 1892, for example, attention was focused on the Zulu War, and in 1894 on the Sudan. These latter occasions in their turn may well have stimulated interest in and support for the displays presented by those of more tender years.

It was now the turn of the London Council for promoting International Arbitration to register its protest.[22] It did so at a meeting held on 18 September 1880, when it took note of the parents who had protested to the Council about the drill practices, and resolved:

> That this council have observed with considerable regret the extreme military character of the drill to which the children in Board schools are subjected, and consider that a simpler manual exercise, with improved gymnastic apparatus, would answer all the requirements of healthy physical development.[23]

THE SWEDISH SYSTEM

In 1881 the London School Board returned to the question of the teaching of girls' physical training. Miss Bergman (later Madame Bergman-Österberg) was appointed to superintend this teaching and to arrange classes for teachers. Two years later the Board's annual drill inspection incorporated a display by young girls, aged between 4 and 7 years, and sporting white caps and red ribbons. Under Bergman's command they counter-marched, exercised and sang. On this occasion the venue was Knighton, the country home of the Chairman of the London School Board, and the distinguished visitors included the Prince and Princess of Wales, and the Vice-President of the Committee of Council on Education.

The Swedish system of physical education continued to gain support at the relative expense of military drill, but it was still with a measure of reluctance that the London School Board agreed to adopt it for boys in 1883. Care was to be taken 'that the Military Drill required by the New Code of the Education Department in the case of boys be not interfered with'.[24] Suffice it to add that military drill qualified for attendance, and physical exercises at that time did not. However, the Board decided to appoint Captain Haarsum for a six-month engagement in 1884 to introduce Swedish gymnastics for boys.

Though the annual drill reviews continued to be held, with both Board and voluntary schools competing for honours, the Society of Arts last reported them in its *Journal* of 1887. Significantly the review held that year was seen as a means of arousing public interest in 'physical education'. The Cross Commission also received evidence from Miss Bergman, now Mme Österberg, on the teaching of Swedish gymnastic exercises – another step forward towards its acceptance.

In 1888 a Swedish drill competition for girls was held in the Royal Albert Hall, with the boys' drill competition staged in the grounds. That same year Sergeant-Major Sheffield died, having served as the London School Board's drill instructor continuously from his appointment in 1872. The Board took the opportunity to make two new appointments: a Swedish Organizing Master of Physical Exercises in Boys' Departments and Thomas Chesterton to superintend an English system of physical education. The latter drew its inspiration from the work of Archibald MacLaran who had developed a system of gymnastic exercises utilizing apparatus designed to develop the whole body. His reliance on apparatus distinguished his system from the Swedish one, but apparatus would not be appropriate for young children, and there is little mention of its use. After a two-year trial period in which both approaches were tried out, the Board abolished the former post and gave its support to the English system which included drill, and which, in the experimental period, had proved more popular with the teachers.

PHYSICAL EDUCATION DISPLAYS REPLACE DRILL REVIEWS

By 1896 the Education Department, through changes in the Elementary Code and in its guidelines to HMIs, had demonstrated its abandonment of military drill in favour of physical exercises and games. Similar developments were apparent in the London School Board's annual displays. The annual drill reviews of the previous two decades were replaced in 1896 by a physical education display presented in a crowded Royal Albert Hall. The programme, 'from which the Board have found it on the whole best to eliminate the competitive element', included a performance of military drill by three schools followed by physical exercises presented by children drawn from 11 schools. The display included: 'free exercises, a flag race, sailors' hornpipe, wand drill, skipping-rope drill, dumb-bell drill, and a new and important feature, swimming drill'.[25] It may be recalled that the drill review staged by the Society of Arts as early as 1870 had included swimming competitions, although later reports failed to make any mention of events other than the military drill. The 1896 display contained none of the militaristic flavour of earlier years, even the competitive element had been 'eliminated'. There was but a token nod in the direction of military drill, perhaps so as not to disappoint certain schools. The performance was confined to three schools – in marked contrast to the massed displays, march-pasts and reviews which the Society of Arts had set in train.

DRILL IN THE PROVINCES

The debate concerning the relative merits of military drill as compared with other forms of physical instruction engaged the critical attention of the providers of elementary education throughout the country. Decisions had to be taken by School Boards and their various committees, and by school managers, based on their interpretation of the annual Codes, the advice and opinions of visiting HMIs, and their own sensitivity to the needs and character of the local community. Certain School Boards, such as the London School Board and those which served major conurbations, tended to provide models for less powerful and less wealthy bodies to implement as best they could.

THE LEEDS SCHOOL BOARD AND DRILL

Leeds and Bradford School Boards served medium-sized cities experiencing problems peculiar to their own industrial and cultural situations. The report of the Leeds School Board's own Chief Inspector of Schools for the year ending 30 September 1892 presented an account of the physical instruction in schools under the Board's control. It stated:

> For years past the Board has employed a drill sergeant, who devotes the whole of his time to visiting the schools to teach the boys military drill. Each school is visited once a fortnight. Of the great value of the drill no one can have a doubt who has been

present on one of the annual field-days, when the schools assemble and go through their evolutions. It is pleasing to observe the firm tread, the upright carriage of the boys as they march past, and the precision with which they perform their exercises. The competition for the banners which the Board awards on such occasions is very keen, and it is no easy matter to adjudicate upon the merits of rival schools.[26]

The Chief Inspector reported that during the current year musical drill had been introduced into girls' schools, and gymnastics appeared in the curriculum of the city's central higher-grade school. From the log-book of the Cross Stamford Street Boys School it appears that the annual inspections were generally held at the Leeds Rifles' parade ground, Carlton Barracks, with the exception of 1885 when the venue was the Agricultural Gardens.

The general tenor of this report suggests that Leeds, in common with other cities and large towns, kept a watchful eye on educational developments in the metropolis, and to a considerable extent accepted as a model the practices appertaining to the London School Board. Certainly the annual field-days, when the Leeds elementary schools competed for the Board's banners, were based upon the drill displays organized by the London School Board.

Again, discussions on the physical training of children by members of the Leeds School Board in March 1895 mirror the changes which were taking place in London and elsewhere. The Revd J. Longbottom moved the acceptance by the Leeds School Board of a revised scheme of physical training in which military drill and physical exercises both had a place. He suggested that such an elaborate scheme as was now proposed would not be necessary in country districts, but, 'Where the children were crowded into the streets for their only playground, and had little opportunity for the development of their physique, such a scheme as this became imperative ...'[27] Indeed in this observation he appears to have anticipated the advice given by the Education Department to members of the Inspectorate in the Code for 1896–97.[28] Mr Parker supported the proposals advanced by the Revd J. Longbottom, adding that he hoped the new scheme of the Leeds School Board would deliver a death-blow to the annual drill competition. He was quickly satisfied on that score; the Report of the Chief Inspector of the Leeds School Board, which appeared in September 1895, stated that the new scheme of physical education had been implemented while the annual drill-day and competition had been discontinued. By way of explanation the Chief Inspector reported that those aspects of military drill which had been retained were intended to constitute 'an aid to discipline and to precision and smartness in class movements', whereas the physical exercises had been introduced the better to strengthen muscles and limbs, and to improve general physique.

It emerged from his report that the initiative for assembling the schools at a central location had originated with the local HMI, 'who preferred to see the drill collectively rather than in separate schools'. One is left to conjecture whether this decision was made on educational grounds, or because a model for corporate drilling already existed in the influential London School Board, or because it was convenient and less demanding of the HMI's time. The Board's Chief Inspector stated that since the HMI had now intimated that he no longer wished to examine the schools on a joint annual basis, the Board saw no reason to continue the 'drill-day'. In retrospect the Report commented that the competition had exerted 'a most stimulating effect in improving the general character of the drill; but, on the other hand, the competition had become so keen, that teachers were tempted to give undue time and attention to it'.[29] There, as elsewhere, the danger had been that the educational value of the drill had tended to get submerged in a drill performance and spectacle.

DRILL UNDER THE BRADFORD SCHOOL BOARD

Neighbouring Bradford had the burden of providing for more half-timers than any other town or city. Nearly 10,000 of its children in 1875 were spending half their time at school and half in 'gainful employment' in local mills and factories. Since October in that year the School Board had employed Sergeant J. Ryan as drill instructor. The local HMI, Mr Rooper, reported in 1884–85 that 'Throughout the Bradford district little or no interest appears to be taken in physical education.'[30] His criticisms may well have been instrumental in precipitating an inquiry which the Board duly conducted in its schools.

The Sixth Triennial Report of the Bradford School Board covered the period up to 30 November 1888. It reported that while Sergeant Ryan 'conscientiously discharged his duty to the best of his power', it was considered that other supplementary arrangements needed to be made. After consultation with head teachers it was decided that 'Physical exercises, and especially in the use of dumb-bells and staves should be encouraged in all schools.' Head teachers were asked to submit schemes for consideration and the Drill Superintendent was required to report on the extent to which physical training had been adopted under the Board's jurisdiction. So that teachers should be familiarized with the teaching techniques associated with physical exercises, arrangements were made for 'practical model lessons' to be given for the benefit of teachers and the general public by Mr S. Bott, Physical Exercises Superintendent under the Birmingham School Board. A predictable outcome of this snub to Sergeant Ryan was his speedy resignation, and Mr H. F. Pearman of Birmingham, who had studied and practised under Bott, was appointed Physical Exercises Superintendent. He was charged with the promotion of physical exercises in all the Bradford Board schools and was required to set up classes where head and assistant teachers could learn the new methods and techniques.[31] It is interesting to note that the Cross Commission recommended the extension of the teaching of physical exercises on the models provided by the London and Birmingham School Boards.

The scheme put into operation by the Bradford School Board in 1889 required that ten minutes should be allocated to physical exercises every day, with a weekly drill of half an hour. Mindful of the poor physical condition of its children and particularly of the physical and mental stresses to which its half-timers were subjected, teachers were instructed that exertion should never be severe or prolonged. The drill practices now recommended for weekly use had a minimum of military influence as compared with the military drill which was fast losing favour among school Boards.

Gone too from many schools were the army drill instructors, and for that alone there were many who rejoiced. It would be unwise, however, to infer from these major developments that the issue had been finally resolved and that military drill instruction in schools had been laid to rest. That was not the case. What had been achieved was that alternatives had emerged which were generally considered to be more efficient and more acceptable, that is if the concern was with the health of the nation's children and not with advance preparations for future military conflicts.

NOTES

1. *School Board Chronicle* (18 February 1871): 12.
2. Ibid. (29 July 1871): 350.
3. A report of the proceedings of the School Management Committee dated 14 March 1873 drew attention to the representation sent to the Education Department asking them 'to remove the restriction contained in the New Code of 1872, and to allow attendance at drill for girls as well as boys, to count as school attendance' (*School Board Chronicle*, 22 March 1873: 127).

4. Ibid. (8 November 1873): 438.
5. London School Board, School Management Committee Report of 14 March 1873, *School Board Chronicle* (22 March 1873): 127.
6. The Code of Regulations for the Guidance of Teachers under the School Board of London included a section 'Regulations in regard to Drill' which stated that:

    > In order to qualify themselves for a Certificate from the Board drill instructor, teachers are required to pass an examination in the following subjects:
    > (i) Preliminary drill – Teachers to take their own boys and form them into companies according to strength. To extend them in open file, and to put them through extension practices and motions.
    > Turnings – Right, left, and right and left about.
    > Marching – Slow and quick time. Balance step on the halt and on the move. To change step.
    > (ii) Company drill – The boys to be arranged into companies sized from both flanks, numbered and told off into half-companies and sections. To be put through the formations, right, left, and right and left about, as a company. To increase and diminish the front. To form company square. To form fours right, left, deep, or about. (*School Board Chronicle*, 22 March 1873: 128)

7. Ibid. (2 August 1873): 103.
8. Ibid. (26 July 1873): 79.
9. Ibid. (17 July 1875): 55.
10. *The Times* (23 July 1875): 11.
11. *School Board Chronicle* (7 August 1876): 141.
12. The Revd J. W. D. Hernaman's report on drill in West Lambeth, 1878–79, pointing to the value of school bands as an aid to discipline, has already been referred to. As an example of their effectiveness he drew attention to the marching of the older boys of South Lambert Road Board School, but the identity of the band is not clear.
13. In the previous year the cost to ratepayers amounted to £160.
14. *The Times* (23 July 1875): 11.
15. *School Board Chronicle* (6 July 1878): 7.
16. Ibid.
17. Ibid. (3 May 1879): 416.
18. Ibid. (28 July 1879): 606.
19. Ibid. (9 August 1879): 125–6.
20. Ibid. (18 October 1879): 375.
21. Ibid. (31 July 1880): 112.
22. The London Council for Promoting International Arbitration was one of many bodies encouraging the use of arbitration to settle international disputes. Some progress in that direction was made at the Peace Conference at The Hague in 1907.
23. *School Board Chronicle* (25 September 1880): 328.
24. P. C. McIntosh, *Physical Education in England since 1800*, rev. edn (London: Bell, 1968), p. 114.
25. *School Board Chronicle* (28 November 1896): 590.
26. Leeds School Board, *Report of Chief Inspector of Schools for Year ending 30 September 1892*, p. 17.
27. *School Board Chronicle* (30 March 1895): 340.
28. *Code for 1896–97, Revised Instructions to HMIs*, p. 102.
29. Leeds School Board, *Report of Chief Inspector of Schools for Year ending 30 September 1895*, pp. 17–18.
30. *Report of CCE, 1884–85* (C.-4483-I), p. 276.
31. Bradford School Board, Sixth Triennial Report, *Report of Proceedings during the Three Years ending 30 November 1888*, pp. 100–1. Birmingham School Board had developed a system of physical exercises in 1880 utilizing staves, dumb-bells, horizontal and parallel bars. The equipment was available to any of their schools desirous of adopting the system. Bradford's scheme used staves and dumb-bells, but does not mention the horizontal or

parallel bars, which in any case would only be suitable for older boys. A maximum of 60 pupils per teacher was permitted under the scheme; large numbers would severely restrict the use of equipment requiring personal supervision and assistance. For details of the agreed scheme of physical exercises in force in Bradford in 1889 see below, Appendix A.

5

The Earl of Meath's Campaign for Drill and Physical Training

Individuals who were anxious to participate in the furtherance of imperialist, nationalist or militarist ambitions found that there were many avenues open to them. For some a seat in the Lords or Commons beckoned; for others there were organizations set up with specific briefs such as the National Rifle Association (established 1860), the Primrose League (1884), the Navy League (1895), the Victoria League (1901), the League of the Empire (1901), and the National Service League (1902). Paul Kennedy has shown how such pressure groups as these tended to be 'much more consolidationist, protective and conservative' than earlier 'progressive' organizations had been.[1] Female involvement tended to be in a supportive role to essentially male-dominated organizations. A body such as the Society of Arts was encouraged to extend its brief, as we have seen in Chapter 3. Within the public and private sectors of education and in some grammar schools there was scope to develop military training through army classes and corps. Boys' uniformed and semi-uniformed organizations were staffed by men who wished to promulgate military practices among the young, predominantly working-class members of society. Many individuals expressed their support for imperialism through essays and articles in the national or local press or through more substantial publications. Needless to say, this literature was almost entirely male.

A MAN OF MANY PARTS

Reginald Brabazon, 12th Earl of Meath,[2] devoted his considerable energies across an impressive range of activities, from his seat in the House of Lords, through a number of organizations that he initiated and in which he played an active part, and in his writings and speeches. His wife both supported him and had her own concerns which she pursued enthusiastically. Meath's encouragement of good health, physical training and recreation in England was matched by his unswerving support for imperialism and its institutions. In 1908 he was a prime instigator of the Duty and Discipline Movement (see below, Appendix B).

HEALTH, RECREATION AND PHYSICAL EDUCATION

In July 1881 Meath contributed an article entitled 'Health and Physique of our City Populations' to the *Nineteenth Century* journal.[3] Posing the question as to how good health could be brought to the poorer quarters of our cities, he suggested that school meals, free where necessary, and the encouragement of physical exercises, could make significant contributions. The exercises should be conducted out-of-doors where practicable, but, failing that, the schoolroom would have to suffice, with apparatus such as ropes and a trapeze suspended from the ceiling during physical instruction lessons. He also saw the need for physical and intellectual exercises to coexist in schools and for all School Board masters to have some knowledge of gymnastics.

Meath's 'Open Spaces and Physical Education' first appeared in the *National Review* of December 1886, to be reprinted in *Some National and Board School Reforms* (1887). One of the many bodies he initiated was the Metropolitan Public Gardens Association. He used this organization as a vehicle through which to address similar memorials to the Cross Commission (then assessing the progress of elementary education since 1870) and to the School Board of London. The memorials drew attention to the need for 'increased facilities for the physical training of the young of both sexes, and further provision for their wholesome recreation', particularly with respect to the needs of larger towns and cities. Specific proposals included:

(1) recognition in the Elementary Code of physical training as an obligatory subject of instruction;

(2) support for the introduction of instruction in physical training in all training colleges;

(3) playgrounds in public elementary schools to be kept open, under supervision, for the use of children and young people between and after school hours;

(4) the granting of powers to local public bodies to purchase land for open or covered gymnasia and for recreation grounds for the general public.

At a later date he was to claim that 'these efforts afterwards resulted in the adoption by the Government of a system of physical instruction in all elementary schools'.[4] Though he was not justified in taking sole credit for that achievement, there is no doubt that he was a tireless and indefatigable champion of that and other related causes.

THE LONDON SCHOOL BOARD

Fully appreciating the power of the media of his day, Meath frequently exploited it. Subsequent to his memorializing of the Cross Commission and of the London School Board he addressed a letter to the editor of the *Daily Chronicle* on 30 December 1886. In it he publicized the fact that he had arranged for 1,142 letters to be dispatched to the various school managers in London, asking for their suggestions as to the most fruitful way of using playgrounds in the best interests of child health. Some of the replies which he received advocated systematic instruction in gymnastics and lamented the lack of governmental financial support. Mr Bousfield, chairman of the influential Works Committee of the London School Board, wrote to say that he had read the correspondence from school managers and was impressed by the importance attached to physical instruction and by the offers of help in its promotion. In his opinion the London School Board would be sympathetic to the proposal whereby physical training facilities would be provided by the Board with supervision funded and provided by the Metropolitan Public Gardens Association. He endorsed the view that physical training should be recognized in the Elementary Code and that it should be a grant-earning subject. Prophetically, he continued:

> I believe that in the first European war in which England is engaged our lamentable experience of the staying powers of many of our urban recruits will, of a certainty, oblige the nation to insist, as a simple matter of safety, on more careful attention being paid to the physical strength of the mass of the population. Why should we wait for bitter experience to force us to do what reason and public spirit show now to be necessary?[5]

Mr Bousfield's warning did not have to await British involvement in a European conflict to be borne out by events. One of the gravest defects to be exposed during the Boer War was the poor physical condition of so many of England's volunteers drawn from the working classes.

Both lack of foresight and the danger of procrastination were demonstrated in an article by Charles Bearsley in which he pointed to the absence of adequate physical training facilities, even in the newest and supposedly most efficient Board schools.[6] He claimed that playgrounds were often too restricted to cater for physical training and games, a criticism echoed by the Revd T. W. Sharpe HMI in respect of the London schools.

A National Physical Recreation Society was set up under the presidency of Herbert Gladstone MP to promote the physical education of the working classes. Meath appealed for public support in favour of this body and for positive changes in the Elementary Code. Measures such as these, he claimed, 'will bring up a generation of English men and women, physically capable of bearing the burden of the high civilisation and extended empire they have inherited from their forefathers'.[7] This statement exemplifies Meath's philosophy and attitude, which indeed was shared by many imperialist reformers at that time; in his case it was coupled with a genuine concern for the welfare of the lower classes.

ACTION IN THE LORDS

On 13 May 1889 Meath introduced a motion in the Lords which was critical of the Elementary Code's inadequate provision of physical education facilities for children attending elementary schools. His supporting speech claimed that physical education was 'almost entirely ignored in the Code', in spite of the problems arising from the enormous growth and concentration of population in our cities. He had been able to find a mere two paragraphs in the Code which contained any reference at all to physical education. Section 12, subsection F provided for military drill for boys under an instructor for two hours a week, or 40 hours during the school year. Section 89 directed that: 'The income of the school must be applied only to the purposes of the school, and the school authorities are not allowed to pay the whole or even part of the salary of a teacher of drill unless he is also the drill teacher in several schools.'[8] To support his case he quoted Sir James Crawford, Director General of the Army Medical Department, who had informed a recent meeting of the British Medical Association that 'the masses are of inferior physique to what they were twenty-five years ago'.

Replying for the Government, Viscount Cranbrook pointed to the financial difficulties which accompanied the introduction of any new subjects into the curriculum. Physical training was 'creeping in gradually', while 'large bodies of the teachers themselves are being trained in military drill'. He informed Meath that now was not the time to adopt the motion or to amend the Code, and indeed support was not forthcoming from fellow peers in respect of the motion.[9] Viscount Cranbrook's unsympathetic response did not prevent the Government from amending the Code within a year of his statement to the contrary in the Lords.

The *School Board Chronicle* in 1892 reported yet another venture in which the Earl of Meath was actively associated. Under his presidency the British College of Physical Education was opened for the purpose of providing 'both high class and elementary education in the principles, theory and practice of physical education based on present knowledge of the structure and functions of the human body and the laws of health'.[10]

THE CASE FOR MILITARY DRILL

Meath's advocacy of physical education did not mean that he had rejected military drill, as he made clear in a lengthy article, 'Compulsory Physical Education', which first appeared in the *North American Review* and was later incorporated into his book, *Social Aims* (1893). Military drill should not be neglected, he claimed; it had value in teaching 'prompt obedience and alertness of mind and body'.[11] *Social Aims*, jointly written by the Earl and Countess of Meath, comprised a collection of articles which had already been published elsewhere. These had been revised and updated in an attempt to encourage others to engage in philanthropic ventures. One of the Earl's contributions was 'The Decay of Bodily Strength in Towns'. In it he referred to the Turnverein, or National Gymnastic Association, established in Germany 80 years previously to provide a thorough training in gymnastic exercises for the whole population. Many people believed that the work of that Association had contributed to Germany's defeat of France in 1870; indeed, the French response after the war was to provide 'manly exercises' for their youth. 'Perhaps', said Meath, 'it will be necessary for us to undergo some such national humiliation' as the French had experienced. He added that there were implications 'for the arts of peace' too, and concluded:

> This question of Physical Education is one … which all classes of the community should support: the working men for their own sakes and for that of their children; military and naval men for the reputation of their country's arms; philanthropists and divines for the love of their fellow-men; employers and capitalists for the sake of improved trade; and statesmen lest they find that the Britain which they profess to govern is sinking before their eyes, borne

down by no foreign foe, but undermined through physical causes which might have been avoided but for the blindness and obstinacy with which they have fixed their gaze on distant objects and questions of '*haute politique*', to the neglect of nearer and less interesting but more indispensable reforms connected with the health and physique of the people of Great Britain and Ireland.[12]

Elsewhere in *Social Aims* he hazarded the view that: 'The future destinies of the world will probably lie, in a great measure, in the hands of the sons and daughters of Anglo-Saxon blood.'[13] Clearly it was not the products of the elementary schools who would be summoned to undertake the safeguarding of England's imperial mission. But the 'prompt obedience' and 'alertness of mind and body'[14] of more humble citizens would ensure that they too could play their part in the grand design.

There were many such stirring calls for England's imperial destiny to be accorded the support necessary for its fulfilment. Only if the nation's manhood was physically and mentally fit and alert could the challenge be met. For the future, the generation still at school had to be prepared for the role it would play. Meath and others of like mind were determined that the cause should not fail through lack of attention to the physical aspects of education.

THE PHYSICAL EDUCATION IN ELEMENTARY SCHOOLS BILL

In 1890 Meath introduced a 'Physical Education in Elementary Schools' Bill which, in effect, consisted of a single clause:

> The school authority for every elementary school in any populous town shall make fit and proper provision to the satisfaction of the inspector for the instruction and practice of all scholars of both sexes in physical education and exercises connected therewith, and no school or department of a school shall receive the higher of the two principal grants under section 101 of the new code of regulations issued by the Education Department ... unless the requisition of this section be complied with to the satisfaction of the inspector as aforesaid.

By way of explanation, he added:

> The expression 'physical education' is declared to mean any system of recognised physical exercises or drill (which may

include swimming) which shall receive the approval of the Education Department and of the school authority. 'Populous towns' include the county of London and all such boroughs and urban sanitary districts as have a population exceeding 15,000.[15]

Meath suggested that the proposals of the National Physical Education Recreation Society provided a suitable model for implementation. It envisaged a daily half-hour of bodily training after dinner or elsewhere in the afternoon session. For boys under the age of 8 years the instruction was to comprise marching with or without music; older boys were to have exercises with dumb-bell exercises, etc., in addition to marching. The programme for girls was to comprise marching, figure-marching, dumb-bell exercises, etc., either with or without music. Where practicable, children of both sexes were to be taught to swim. It was proposed that the cost should be shared equally by the Government and by the rates (local government taxation).

Meath was only able to get an 'airing' for his Bill as its introduction came too late in the session for it to be proceeded with. A second attempt in 1891 was no more successful. The democratic process of government depended, then as now, to a considerable extent on persuasion and on the creation of a climate, both in parliament and in the country at large, in which prospective measures could be considered sympathetically, particularly so in the case of social legislation. In that context it could be argued that Meath's abortive Bills of 1890 and 1891 were not fruitless exercises. They contained specific proposals drawn up from guidelines provided by a specialist body; the opportunity to associate physical instruction with music was recommended (the latter being an established grant-earning subject since 1872); the needs of children of different ages were recognized, as were the special requirements when physical education was extended to girls. There was at that time a growing realization of the importance of specific aspects of girls' education, such as physical instruction and domestic economy, if their role in the nurturing of future generations as yet unborn, was to be recognized and encouraged.

The Elementary Code, as recently amended in 1890, included 'suitable physical exercises' and military drill, the latter for boys only, among subjects which counted for attendance purposes. Meath's Bill would have made the teaching of these compulsory if schools were to qualify for the higher level of grant under Article 101. If the time was not quite ripe for that step to be taken, the delay was short-lived, as the necessary changes to the Code were made in 1895.

CONDITION OF THE POORER CLASSES IN TOWNS

The outstanding value of the contribution made by the Earl of Meath lay particularly in its broad base. In *A Thousand More Mouths Every Day*,[16] he was principally concerned with the problems associated with the rapid expansion of the urban population, which had resulted in two out of every three people in England living in towns of over 4,000 inhabitants. Of the pressing need to address that situation he wrote:

> The physical condition of the poorer classes in our large towns demands the serious attention of both the people and the Government. It is impossible to pass through the streets of a manufacturing town without being struck by the diminutive size, narrow chests, and generally unhealthy appearance of the working-class population. The thought forces itself upon one, that such were not the men who fought England's battles of yore, and raised her to her present position amongst the nations. What if another conflict with united Europe should be forced upon her?[17]

What, indeed? The question which Mr Bousfield had also raised in 1886 was not a hypothetical one; it was engaging the serious attention of an increasing number of concerned people in England. Meath was determined to ensure that sufficient public pressure was aroused as to force the Government to act. His efforts demonstrate the extent to which an individual campaigner, in his case with the advantage of a peerage and access to influential individuals and bodies, could contribute to the realization of necessary reforms.

NOTES

1. Paul Kennedy, *The Realities behind Diplomacy: Background Influences on British External Policy 1865–1980* (London: Collins/Fontana, 1985), p. 57.
2. Reginald Brabazon was born the second son of the 11th Earl of Meath, but his elder brother died in childhood and it was as Lord Brabazon that he entered Eton in 1854. His hopes of entering the army were overruled by his father, who wished him to embark upon a career in the Foreign Office. He entered the diplomatic service in 1868, the year of his marriage to Lady Mary Jane, daughter of Thomas Maitland, 11th Earl of Lauderdale. After appointments in Berlin (during the Franco-Prussian War), The Hague and Paris, he was promoted to the post of Second Secretary in Athens. This posting was considered unacceptable by both his own parents and his wife's parents. In the face of this opposition from the two families he tendered his resignation, and thereafter he and his wife courageously decided to devote themselves to 'the consideration of social problems and the relief of human suffering'. See Earl of Meath, *Memories of the Nineteenth Century* (London: John Murray, 1923), p. 201. On the death of his father in 1887 he succeeded to the title as the 12th Earl of Meath.
3. Subsequently published in Earl of Meath, *Some National and Board School Reforms* (London: Longmans Green, 1887), pp. 1–13.
4. Earl of Meath, *Memories of the Nineteenth Century*, p. 231.

5. Earl of Meath, *Some National and Board School Reforms*, p. 34.
6. Charles Bearsley, 'Physical Training in Elementary Schools', in *Some National and Board School Reforms*, pp. 27–32.
7. Earl of Meath, *Social Arrows: Essays* (London: Longmans Green, 1887), p. 77.
8. This would have tended to keep drill instruction out of the hands of the school's own teachers who might well have been less amenable to the more militaristic aspects of drill which were accepted as a matter of course by the peripatetic drill sergeants engaged by many local authorities.
9. *House of Lords Debates*, Third Series, Vol. CCCXXXV, cols. 1815–29 (13 May 1889).
10. *School Board Chronicle* (23 July 1892): 91.
11. Earl of Meath, 'Compulsory Physical Education', in Earl of Meath, *Social Aims: Essays by the Earl of Meath and the Countess of Meath* (London: Wells Gardner, Darton & Co., 1893), pp. 245–6.
12. Ibid., pp. 22–3.
13. Ibid., p. 254.
14. Joseph Chamberlain made a similar point to Meath's when he delivered an address at the Royal Colonial Institute dinner on 31 March 1897:

    it is a gigantic task that we have undertaken when we determined to wield the sceptre of empire. Great is the task, great is the responsibility, but great is the honour: and I am convinced that the conscience and the spirit of the country will rise to the height of its obligations, and that we shall have the strength to fulfil the mission which our history and our national character have imposed upon us.

    (Charles W. Boyd (ed.), *Mr Chamberlain's Speeches*, Vol. II (London: Constable, 1914), pp. 2–5, cited in G. Bennett, *The Concept of Empire: Burke to Attlee, 1774–1947* (London: A. & C. Black, 1953), pp. 319–20.)
15. *House of Lords Debates*, Third Series, Vol. CCCXLVI, cols. 1249–334 (10 July 1890).
16. In Earl of Meath, *Social Aims*, pp. 98–133.
17. Ibid., pp. 122–3.

6

The Boer War, 1899–1902

THE SITUATION IN SOUTH AFRICA: BRITISH VS BOERS

The British and the Boers had clashed periodically since Britain had acquired the Cape of Good Hope at the time of the Napoleonic Wars. By the end of the nineteenth century the situation in South Africa was that the Boers occupied the more or less independent republics of Transvaal and the Orange Free State, while the British were settled in Cape Colony, Natal and Rhodesia.

Discovery of gold in the Transvaal attracted many British adventurers. They formed the greater part of the foreign population in the republic, paid about 80 per cent of the taxes, but enjoyed no citizenship rights. In 1897 an attempt was made to infiltrate the Transvaal from Bechuanaland (now Botswana) and link up with a planned rising in Johannesburg. This conspiracy, in which Cecil Rhodes played a significant part and to which the British Colonial Secretary, Joseph Chamberlain, turned a blind eye, was an ill-conceived fiasco.[1] It was, however, the precursor of the seemingly inevitable war which broke out two years later. Halévy makes the assessment that it was not a conflict of interests where a compromise could always be sought. Rather it was 'a conflict of two nationalities, two faiths, two passions, two absolutes. Between absolutes, force is the sole arbiter.'[2] That certainly appeared to be the judgement arrived at by both parties. Ostensibly the immediate issue centred on the deprivation of citizenship rights of non-Boers in the Transvaal; however, the fundamental question to be resolved was that of primacy in South Africa.

THE OUTBREAK OF WAR

After presenting an ultimatum, which they were confident the British would not consider seriously, the Boers launched a preventive attack, taking advantage of the fact that the main British forces were not yet assembled. The three small railway towns of Ladysmith, Mafeking and Kimberley were invested before the three divisions, which the British judged to be adequate to overcome the Boers, had sailed from their home ports.

Since the Crimean War, the only European-style conflict in which Britain had been engaged was a three-month campaign in 1877, also against the Boers. On that occasion the annexation by British forces of the Transvaal had resulted in unexpected military and diplomatic defeats. Short, punitive campaigns against native forces in what were called Queen Victoria's 'little wars' were what the army had trained for, and that was the kind of warfare they intended to impose on the Boers in the campaign of 1899. Interestingly, the latter did not even have an army as such. They relied upon local 'commandos' of irregulars, farmers and their sons, mounted on horseback, but equipped with modern European weapons.

Preliminary attempts by British forces to relieve the railway towns were disastrous. A succession of defeats known collectively as 'Black Week', 10–15 December 1899, led to Lord Roberts replacing General Buller as Commander-in-Chief, and Lord Kitchener being appointed as Roberts' Chief of Staff. Fresh offensives in the New Year relieved Ladysmith, Mafeking and Kimberley, and captured Bloemfontein, Johannesburg and Pretoria. The two Boer republics were annexed and the president, Paul Kruger, fled to Europe.

Those who expected a swift end to the conflict as a reward for these victories were to be bitterly disappointed. A long drawn-out guerrilla campaign was waged by the Boers, drawing from their opponents a response directed against commandos and civilians alike. Kitchener assumed command of the British forces. A wide-ranging network of blockhouses was established to limit the freedom of action of the Boer irregulars; detention camps for women and children were set up; farms burned, and domestic animals destroyed. Exhaustion was apparent on both sides when the conflict finally ground to a halt and the Boers surrendered in May 1902.

CASUALTIES OF WAR

The war endured for two and a half years, with heavy casualties on both sides. Britain's original expeditionary force of 85,000 men had expanded to some 450,000, including volunteers from the self-governing colonies. It was the largest army that Britain had ever despatched abroad. Cholera and enteric fever accounted for two-thirds of the British casualties, which altogether totalled 22,000 deaths. Of the 24,000 Boer deaths as a result of the war, it was estimated that women and children accounted for 20,000, mostly as a result of the appalling conditions in the concentration, or detention camps.

There had been three Commanders-in-Chief and other changes among the staff as the British military establishment attempted to come to terms with an unconventional adversary. An interesting professional assessment was provided by the official German historian who described the war as not merely a contest between rifle and bayonet, but also a contest 'between the soldier drilled to machine-like movements and the man with a rifle working on his own initiative … . War had been proclaimed between rigid formulas and untrammelled healthy common sense.'[3] Smokeless powder gave the enemy a priceless advantage, that of presenting an unseen target; couple with that the use of a long-range, small-bore, high velocity magazine bullet, and the balance tilted towards defence and away from attack. The use of protective trenches was a further asset. Pakenham, in his study *The Boer War* makes these points and goes on to make the point that 'not until the bloody stalemates of the Dardanelles and Flanders' was this lesson to be learned.[4] The financial cost of the war exceeded £200 million – an indication that modern warfare was an extremely expensive undertaking.

The condition of the rank-and-file soldiery had also given cause for concern. For every 1,000 men enlisted in 1899, 330 had had to be rejected as unfit; a year later 280 in every 1,000 were rejected, but the standard of acceptance may well have become less strict as the war progressed. Further, it was estimated that only two out of every five volunteers remained as effective soldiers. The level of recruitment for lower middle-class and white-collar youths reflected to a significant degree the appeals of patriotic propaganda, but for working-class volunteers the economic situation at home was perhaps an equally potent indicator. Major deficiencies and defects required comprehensive remedies; within the decade major army reforms and programmes aimed at the improvement of the health and physique of the lower classes were to be tabled by governments of the day.[5]

BADEN-POWELL

Colonel Robert Baden-Powell was the officer in command at Mafeking during the siege. His jaunty dispatches from the beleaguered town continued to be telegraphed throughout that time and did much to lift the spirits of those who could only follow events at a considerable distance. When relief came, there was an enthusiastic outburst of relief and joy, celebrated throughout the length and breadth of Britain. As Richard Price puts it, 'Even the absurdity of Baden-Powell's position at Mafeking was turned around into a heroic touchstone of British ingenuity and virility.'[6] An example of this ingenuity was the formation of an improvised cadet corps – the model from which the Boy Scout movement was later to emerge. A new word was coined to describe the relief celebrations – *Mafficking*, defined as 'extravagant demonstrations of exultation'.

SCHOOLS AND THE WAR

Schools throughout the land were given holidays so that the children could join in the rejoicings as besieged towns were relieved. Meanwood Church of England School in Leeds, for example, coupled the event with the Queen's birthday, the school being closed for the day on 24 May 1900. They had another holiday on 27 June to celebrate the occupation of Pretoria by British troops. (And on 23 January 1901 the school log-book recorded the solemn ending of the Victorian era: 'The school bell was not rung today owing to the death of Her Majesty the Queen yesterday at 6.30 p.m.'[7])

School log-books carried surprisingly little evidence of any direct influence of the war on classroom teaching, which to a great extent continued to reflect the rigidity of elementary education. Occasionally there was reference to a particular incident which the head teacher found worthy of comment, as when the girls of Standards VI and VII of the Wolverhampton Street Girls' School, Dudley, wrote letters describing the war in the Transvaal in November 1899. It is not clear whether this was a schoolroom exercise only or whether the letters were actually posted. Possibly the latter, because 12 months later girls in the same standards joined a Correspondence Bureau and wrote letters to girls at Kilburn School in Derby.[8] In Bristol the initiative came from the Chairman of the Bristol School Board. After the relief of Mafeking he requested head teachers of schools to encourage children to compose letters congratulating the Queen on her 81st birthday and the relief of Mafeking. From the letters he received the Chairman drew up a 'comprehensive message' using a few of the children's own phrases which he telegraphed to Her Majesty. In return the Chairman received a telegram despatched the same day thanking the children for their loyal salutations. Ilford despatched a similar telegram.[9]

School readers had traditionally featured stories of national heroes; it is interesting to have evidence of the broadening of this trait to include the humble private soldier among their number. Pitman's Readers, issued in 1901, carried an introduction which stated: 'We shall read with pride of the good and valiant men, who either fought our country's battles against a foreign enemy, or strove against all attempts of tyrant rulers, to rob the people of their rights and liberties and even gave up their lives willingly in their noble efforts' (p. 6).

Inevitably, the war infiltrated the school playground. Howard Spring recalls:

> The Boer War was in full swing. In the play-ground we played Britons and Boers: a primitive pastime which consisted of chasing the Boers and lamming them with belts when they were caught. We all wore in our lapel buttons bearing the photographs of Gatacre and Buller, Roberts, White and Kitchener; and those boys were greatly admired whose mothers could afford the popular extravagance of sending them to school dressed in little replicas of a private's uniform.[10]

The wearing of miniature 'sailor-suits' was quite common among Victorian and Edwardian children; however, the extension of the practice to soldiers' uniforms is not so well documented. Nor could we it expect to be: in normal times, the sailors were the nation's darlings, not the soldiers.

A similar incident to the one narrated by Howard Spring occurred in the playground of Kenilworth National School, but on the latter occasion a boy named Willie Burton fell and broke his leg. He and his playmates must have been most surprised to receive a letter postmarked Bloemfontein and signed by the Commander-in-Chief of the British Army. It read:

> Dear Willie Burton,
>
> I am sorry to hear that in a fight which recently took place at Kenilworth National School you had the misfortune to break your leg. I hope that by the time this reaches you, you will have recovered, and that when you grow up you will be a soldier, and perhaps some day rise to command our troops in an engagement. Please tell all the other boys in the National School how glad I am to hear of the pleasant sham fights they have been having. Believe me.
>
> Yours truly,
>
> Roberts[11]

Bloemfontein having been occupied without a fight, it was time to write letters home; Roberts wrote to the Queen on 15 March 1900, and some time later to Willie Burton. Not every body of school managers, sensitive though they would have been of the honour bestowed on one of their pupils, would have wished for such whole-hearted encouragement of rough-and-tumble sham fights, with their attendant risks to limbs and tempers. But some boisterous playground activities were to be expected, if only as a brief respite from the rigours and formality of the classroom.

RENEWED INTEREST IN MILITARY DRILL

If the curriculum as a whole continued with very little change during the period of the Boer War, there was renewed interest in efforts to secure a firm place for military drill in the elementary schools. Heightened levels of patriotism in society at large encouraged the proponents of military drill to persist in or to renew their pressure on School Boards and others who were responsible for the provision of elementary education. Among that number was C. C. Perry whose article 'Our Undisciplined Brains: The War Test' appeared in the *Nineteenth Century* of December 1901. Perry strongly advocated the establishment of militarism throughout the structures of society, as was the case in Prussia: 'Universal schooling on the one hand, and universal conscription on the other, are the two pillars on which the most powerful State in Europe is raised.' He deprecated the English tendency to abuse and ignore the soldiery in peacetime, but then to praise them lavishly in times of emergency.[12] Rudyard Kipling had made the same point in his *Barrack Room Ballads*, though in more colourful fashion.

SIR LAUDER BRUNTON AND MILITARY TRAINING IN SCHOOLS

Military training in schools was considered by Sir Lauder Brunton to be an essential element in Britain's defence measures. In anticipation of a discussion arranged for 3 July 1901, he wrote to Colonel Pennington, summarizing his views on the matter. He assumed that he did not need to claim that Britain's military defences were inadequate or that her regular army must be enlarged either by volunteers, by conscription, or by enforcing the Militia Ballot Act. Conscription was not considered an acceptable alternative, rightly so, in his opinion, but he felt strongly that every male citizen should know how to act in defence of his country. That particular claim on a man's services was as vital to Britain's security and future as was the requirement that he should be able to read and write. It followed, therefore, that the military training of boys was as necessary as the teaching of the three Rs, and there seemed to be no reason why the curriculum should not accommodate such instruction. Timetable adjustments could reduce the amount of time devoted to writing and arithmetic, and old war games such as 'Prisoner's base' and 'I spy' could be updated into 'mimic games of modern warfare'. Brunton saw the military training as consisting of physical exercises, drill and marching, scouting, a knowledge of guns and shooting practice. As will be seen, even infant school children were included in his proposals.

> Small children of four or five might be trained with toy guns made entirely of wood, and which could be supplied at a penny each or even less.
>   For proficiency in drill with these they might be promoted to aim at a candle with caps[13] and as soon as they were big enough to manage it, they might learn to take a rifle to pieces, to put it up again, and to clean it. Proficiency in aiming with caps and in working with the rifle might be rewarded by taking the boys to a rifle range, which would require to be provided for every school.[14]

Those progressions were intended to take boys by the age of 14 to the level of drill-training which it might take a soldier three years to learn, so that the 14-year-olds could take an equal place at the shooting ranges with grown men.

A subsequent statement by Brunton in answer to newspaper correspondence pointed to the necessity of such a course of training being systematic and progressive, 'culminating in cadet corps armed with rifle or carbine and trained to regular military exercises'. His advocacy of skirmishing, scouting, use of cover, etc. is interesting in view of his later involvement in Baden-Powell's Boy Scout movement.[15] Colonel R. L. A. Pennington submitted his own views on *Physical and Military Training in Schools*,[16] both he and Brunton stressing the need to develop intelligent responses in addition to more formal drills.

The publication of a poem by Kipling in *The Times* elicited a response by Brunton. He referred to Kipling's observation that there was more interest in football and cricket matches than there was in an engagement in South Africa. While Brunton expressed no desire to extinguish interest in traditional team games he did suggest that more attention might be given to the encouragement of war games, to shooting and to manoeuvre. By such means the country might rid itself of Kipling's reproach, the justice of which he did not deny.[17]

ACTION BY SCHOOLS

Many local authorities and schools responded to the calls for a more overt military character in drill programmes in boys' schools and departments, and for some this implied the handling of weapons. At a full meeting of the Mitcham School Board on 5 February 1900, the Clerk reported that he had written to the Director General of Ordnance to enquire about the possible supply of carbines for drill instruction in the schools. In response to his request, he had received a sample carbine and a form of agreement by which the Board would be required to undertake to use the carbines for drill purposes only, and not to sell or otherwise dispose of them. The sample weapon was a discarded cavalry Martini-Henri carbine which had been cut across the barrel to render it unserviceable. A charge of one shilling and sixpence (1s 6d) would be made for each carbine supplied. The School Board Management Committee had recommended the purchase of 36 carbines for each of the three groups of schools under the control of the Board. By the narrow majority of two votes the School Board decided to defer any action until the Education Department required it.[18] The positive response by the office of the Director General of Ordnance in forwarding both a form of agreement and a sample carbine suggests that an established procedure was being followed.

At Rye, the School Board decided to apply for 50 such carbines for drill purposes.[19] Elsewhere, School Boards experienced varying degrees of support for proposals to teach military drill or to purchase weapons discarded by the army. Rarely were School Boards unanimous in their decisions and sometimes they were called upon to consider communications from bodies or groups objecting to any such provisions. The Evangelical Free Church Council of Sheffield, for example, protested against the proposal of the local School Board to introduce a system of military drill using dummy rifles: 'We suggest that the company training of children in this way is a violation of parental feeling and right, and an unwarrantable exercise of the power intrusted to you by the electorate.' This and another letter of protest were ignored by the School Board, whose School Management Committee recommended that dummy rifles, similar to the ones used by the Boys'

Brigades, should be obtained for use by Standard VII boys.[20] Drill practices employed by brigades elsewhere may well have suggested to other School Boards and managers the possibility of following suit.

In April 1900 the Western Quarterly Meeting of the Religious Society of Friends held at Worcester expressed concern that

> Many of the proposals [for military drill] made in councils and local committees are in the direction of using these exercises as a means of fostering the war spirit, forming cadet corps, and instilling in the hearts of scholars admiration for war, contrary to the peaceable spirit and teaching of Christ.

Sympathy was extended to individual members of committees and managers of schools who were trying to maintain their Christian principles even when finding themselves in a minority. It was recognized that many teachers attempted to instil 'the goodwill and sense of justice which exalt a nation', and that many parents objected to schools being made 'the medium for inculcating the war spirit'. Quakers were insisting that conscientious objection to war and to the preparation for war should be respected.[21]

The Rifle Club movement responded to the worrying news issuing from South Africa in the early months of 1900 by encouraging the formation of new clubs. It was hoped to extend the movement into the working classes through working men's clubs and boys' clubs, but the attempts were stubbornly resisted. The ready-made elitist structure inherent in the rifle clubs was unacceptable, and appeals for a patriotic response fell largely on deaf ears.

THE EARL OF MEATH AND THE LADS' DRILL ASSOCIATION

The Lads' Drill Association was set up following an article by the Earl of Meath in the *Fortnightly Review* at the time of the 1897 Jubilee. His concern was the perceived inadequacy of Britain's armed forces to defend the empire which was 'an object of jealousy and of hatred in the eyes of more than one great European power'.[22] The aim of the Association was to promote the provision of 'systematic physical and military training of all British lads, and their instruction in the art of the rifle'. As President and Chairman, Meath wrote to the London School Board in the summer of 1900, enclosing a copy of the Annual Report and asking the Board to consider the teaching of military drill if they had not already done so. He suggested that a deputation might perhaps be allowed to express the views of the Association. All this was familiar ground for the London School Board, who had been similarly approached by the Society of Arts, in 1875. The Board's long experience in the teaching of drill and physical training prompted a confident response to Meath. Their letter referred to their investigation of continental practices and to consultations with the medical profession. They had evolved 'a wholesome scheme of physical exercises ... which is incomparably superior to any military exercises ... Physical exercises, as taught in the schools of the London School Board, improve the bodies of the children, though they may not, except indirectly, promote the interests of the Army.' Skilfully reversing Meath's suggestion of a deputation to enlighten the Board, they offered to send tickets of admission to their next display in the Albert Hall so that the LDA officers could judge for themselves the system in operation. Failing that, visits to schools could be arranged during school hours.[23]

Lord Roberts was invited to the Albert Hall display the following year, but it was his stand-in and military secretary, General Sir Ian Hamilton, who attended. The programme included free movements, figure marching, wand and garland drill, dumb-bell exercises, organized playground games, etc., each performed by a separate school. He commented that the armies of the future would require not only brave men, but also men of 'high individual intelligence' which could only be acquired by a good education. 'Physical education', he said, 'was too noble to be ruined by fierce competition.' The Chairman of the School Management Committee asssured him that the element of competition had been eliminated from the displays.[24] That was obvious in that each participating school had the responsibility for presenting its own allocated aspect of physical exercises. It would be interesting to know what reports reached Lord Roberts, Vice-President of the LDA, and the Earl of Meath, its Chairman and President. Though rebuffed by the London School Board, neither ceased to advocate the teaching of military drill to schoolboys.

'SPURIOUS IDEALS OF PATRIOTISM'

Towards the end of 1900, Sir Joshua Fitch addressed the College of Preceptors. He accepted the importance of cherishing one's country but protested against 'the encouragement of such spurious ideals of patriotism as found vent in singing *Rule Britannia*, waving the Union Jack, and boasting of our triumphs'. Referring to proposals to establish military drill in schools, he claimed the purpose was not to assist physical development but to make soldiers. If that were so, then other agencies than schools should be employed. What were needed were lessons on the privileges enjoyed as Englishmen and an appreciation of 'the extent of the unpaid services which a country like ours demanded from the public spirit of its citizens'.[25] Fitch was one of the few inspectors of schools to have been educated at, and to have taught in, an elementary school. He certainly took a different line from many of his fellow inspectors.

HMI REPORTS ON MILITARY DRILL

Pressure in support of military drill was echoed in the Lords and the Commons, both of which rang with rhetorical pleas for the nation's youth to be trained to serve their country. School inspectors were also active. The Report of the Board of Education for 1899–1900 showed that some of HMIs demonstrated their support of military drill through accounts of general practice and of individual initiatives in their general reports. Mr Burrows, HMI responsible for the Portsmouth district, reported significant progress in physical training since he had taken charge four years earlier:

> In all boys' schools military drill, with and without arms, always accompanied by instrumental music, is the rule. In mixed, in girls' and in infants' schools some form of musical and Swedish drill, always with music, and including ball play and dancing, has been adopted. Boys on leaving the Portsmouth schools have attained to such proficiency in military drill that a large cadet corps might be formed if local funds and local energy were available.[26]

The Portsmouth schools, including two large voluntary schools, certainly displayed a surprisingly wide range of physical activities. In May 1900 a display of physical drill by both boys and girls, to the music of school bands, was held in the town hall under the auspicies of the Lads' Drill Association.[27]

In the same Board of Education report, HM Chief Inspector Mr Rankine, of the Metropolitan Division, described an experimental schoolboys' camp organized by the headmaster of Cripplegate Ward School. Boys paid twopence for a fortnight's stay at Shalford, near Guildford, during the summer vacation. Boating, swimming, fishing and rambling were programmed, and a portion of each day was devoted to military drill. Mr Davis, the headmaster, and his two colleagues all held War Office certificates, and gave instruction in drill and musketry. Martini-Henri 'rabbit rifles' sighted up to 33 yards were used for shooting at targets; after two weeks' practice 75 per cent of the boys, whose average age was 12½ years, scored bulls' eyes at a range of 60 yards. The cost of the camp, including transport, averaged 1s 5½d per head. Mr Rankine concluded: 'Does not a movement of this kind contain a germ of something greater which even the War Office might not think it beneath its dignity to encourage? And perhaps the Admiralty might follow suit...'.[28] This again raised the controversial issue, not only of young boys handling weapons, but of actually firing them. Neither the War Office nor the Admiralty showed any inclination to intrude into the Education Department's area of responsibility, and why Mr Rankine should express it as a matter of dignity on the part of the War Office is not clear beyond its obvious rhetorical appeal.

Sir William Richmond RA went even further than Mr Rankine in a letter sent in January 1900 to Mr T. Mullett Ellis, the honorary secretary of the War Emergency Committee. Mindful perhaps of the tactics employed by the Boer commandos he tendered quite specific proposals:

> All Board Schools should drill the pupils; they should be taught both to ride and use the rifle. Military drill should be a necessity of every Englishman's education. Upon leaving the Board Schools the authorities should select the strongest and most suitable lads to form a reserve force liable to be called out at any time ...[29]

Sir William could, and perhaps did, then return to his easel, leaving others to consider how boys in inner-city areas were to be given the opportunity of indulging in riding lessons. Even if physically possible there remained the question of meeting the very considerable costs which would be incurred. Unfortunately the *School Board Chronicle* did not carry a report of any response which Mr Mullett Ellis might have made. H. A. Vachell's novel *The Hill* had a Harrow boy leaving school for the Boer War and planning to take three polo ponies with him, but not even the public schools appeared to consider the inclusion of horsemanship as a component of corps activities.

DEBATES AND QUESTIONS IN THE COMMONS

In the Commons the Debate on the Army (Supplementary) Estimates provided an opportunity for the argument to be developed. Mr Louis

Sinclair (Romford, Essex) favoured the introduction into all elementary schools of a system of drill 'under the control of proper drill sergeants', the encouragement of cadet corps, and possibly of shooting galleries. Such a provision would be

> a means of developing the physique of the nation and would foster a feeling of ardour, patriotism, and enthusiasm which would be evoked whenever the country was menaced and in danger, and I feel sure would be the means of sowing seeds of a martial character which would be the best recruiting factor ever introduced.[30]

It has already been suggested that such reasoning may have been more appropriate when applied to the lower middle class than to the working class.

A week later Sinclair tabled a parliamentary question to Sir John Gorst, Vice-President of the Committee of Council on Education, as to whether drilling could be introduced in schools, and was given the stock answer that drill or suitable physical exercises were necessarily taught if schools were to qualify for the higher disciplinary grant in respect of older scholars. Pressing further, Mr Tomlinson (Preston) asked if care would be taken in the future to ensure that such drill would fit children for service in the army. Gorst's reply was that: 'In great towns it is done, but obviously, it would be impossible in a country village, where there were only perhaps thirty children taught by a school-mistress, to have military drill.'[31] Avoiding the question as to whether the drill would fit boys for army service, Gorst's reply that 'it [drill] is done' lacked the qualification 'in some schools', leaving the inference that the practice of military drill was universally applied in large towns and cities. That was manifestly not so. A similar exchange between Mr Sinclair, Mr Powell Williams, the Under-Secretary of State for War, and Sir John Gorst arose when Mr Sinclair asked whether the War Office would consider consulting with the Education Department 'with a view to introducing sergeants to teach boys drill in all elementary schools'. Mr Powell Williams' terse response was that the suggestion had already been adopted, after which Gorst gave an identical reply to that given on 26 February.[32] Was the Under-Secretary of State for War so ill informed as to claim that army sergeants were drilling boys in all elementary schools when clearly that was not true? At no time would it have been accurate to state that army personnel had been accorded access to *all* elementary schools, even where military drill was taught. Sir John Gorst's oblique reference to 'drill or suitable physical exercises', with no direct reference to military drill, went unchallenged. Certainly, when these responses to Sinclair's questions were made, the teaching of military drill was progressing slowly as compared with other forms of physical instruction. The Committee of Council on Education report for 1899 showed that of the 31,173 elementary departments under separate head teachers, 2,659 were teaching military drill while 9,115 were teaching physical exercises, and it was the latter which were gaining most ground.[33]

Mr Sinclair's campaign in the House of Commons continued with unabated vigour. When he attempted to use the debate on army estimates to press the War Office to introduce company and squad drill in elementary schools the Speaker quickly called him to order. It was, he ruled, a line of argument more relevant to the education vote than to the army estimates.[34] The distinction between the responsibilities of the Education Department and of the War Office was not to be blurred in the furtherance of the militaristic interests of Mr Sinclair and his colleagues.

A full debate on physical and military instruction in state-aided schools took place in the Commons on 30 March 1900. Sir James Fergusson (Manchester, Northeast) referred to the order paper, calling attention to the desirability of providing physical and military drill for boys in all state-aided or rate-aided schools as an obligatory part of the curriculum. He suggested that such a measure would be advantageous to the physical and mental development of the nation's youth and 'would conduce to national defence'. In his speech, he drew attention to the schools under the inspection of Mr Burrows (see above), and commented: 'Nobody desired to have the boys treated as soldiers, or to see militarism introduced into the schools, but it was desirable that there should be such physical training as was best secured by simple military methods of drill.' Mr Yoxall, MP for Nottingham, West (who served as General Secretary of the National Union of Teachers, and was the first certificated elementary teacher to become an MP), observed that a great deal of physical exercise was already provided and hoped that there would be no attempt to press for military drill. Mindful of the current war in South Africa, which had no doubt precipitated the debate, he claimed:

> The great thing in the future would not be company drill and squad drill, close order, forming fours, and marching by rank and file, but skirmishing and sharpshooting ... [and he did not see how] in public elementary school playgrounds skirmishing or sharpshooting could be practised ... Any proposal to make military drill compulsory could not be in harmony with existing conditions in thousands of schools.

These observations were relevant to the situation in South Africa, the northwest frontier of India and perhaps elsewhere in the empire, but to those who looked with concern at the possibility of a European war, traditional training would not so readily be set aside. Yoxall would also know that physical exercises of a non-military kind were favoured by the majority of School Boards and by fellow members of the teaching profession.

Sir John Gorst spoke as Vice-President of the Committee of Council on Education. He said that the Code clearly placed responsibility on local school managers, practically compelling that form of drill or other physical exercise 'as is suitable to the conditions of the school and practicable under the circumstances'. As to whether such drill should have a military character was left to the discretion of local managers. The present system was, in his opinion, satisfactory.

That position was supported by Mr John Burns (Battersea),[35] who accused Fergusson of having not gymnastics, but militarism as his goal. He seized the opportunity to state the socialist position – the fear that military drill would make the working class even more of a recruiting ground for soldiers than it was already.

> If you want to stimulate patriotism you are not going to make generals by giving men gaudy uniforms, or make patriots by teaching children barrack-yard drill … If the army wants recruits you have two great recruiting sergeants – one is poverty, which procures you 95 per cent, and the other is patriotism, which gets you 5 per cent.

Attempts to increase that 5 per cent through the teaching of military drill in the school playgrounds would be opposed by the working classes. 'They won't have it', he concluded.[36] This was a fitting response to the claims of Louis Sinclair MP during the debate on the army estimates some six weeks previously.

This debate was significant in that the socialist position was stated more firmly than hitherto in the Commons; it distanced socialists from the current wave of patriotic fervour and focused attention on the poverty which drove many working men to take the Queen's shilling on enlistment. Rudyard Kipling had referred to this practice in a song by Ortheris in a short story, 'The Courting of Dinah Shadd'.[37] Gorst showed clearly the Government's reluctance to enter into the contest between military drill and other forms of physical training. By placing responsibility on local school boards and school managers the Committee of Council on Education could, through the issue of Codes and the instructions and guidance it issued to members of the Inspectorate, influence the course of developments. That policy, displayed elsewhere, enabled it to avoid accusations of partisanship which might otherwise have been levelled at it.

THE 1901 CODE

The Code for 1901 showed the direction in which the Committee of Council on Education was going. In reviewing it, the *School Board Chronicle* noted that the term 'Physical Training' replaced the more narrow 'Physical Exercises'. The recommended physical training 'should be regarded as an integral and important part of the curriculum of every public elementary school'. A 'Model Course' was to be published, setting out a minimum programme which could be met even by small schools, and that could be supplemented by 'further and more varied Physical Training, including, where possible, systematic instruction in swimming, cricket, etc.'. Not less than one hour per week for each class, nor more than half an hour on any one day, should be timetabled for physical training and, where possible, the teaching was to be in the hands of the regular teaching staff of the school.[38] No mention here of drill, or of the use of peripatetic army sergeants to be responsible for its teaching. There is, in contrast, every indication that schools were expected to move towards physical training programmes which were varied in content and supplemented by the systematic teaching of swimming and organized games. Would the influential proponents of military drill see in this Code the end of their long-fought campaign? Certainly it offered them little hope or encouragement.

EDUCATION FOR A NEW CENTURY

In 1899 a Board of Education was set up, incorporating the existing Education Department, the Science and Art Department and the educational work of the Charity Commission. In 1900 when it appeared that the Boer War had almost run its course, the Conservative Government went to the country in the so-called Khaki or Patriotic Election. The Marquess of Salisbury's manifesto for the Conservative Party referred to 'the brilliant success of Lord Roberts and his Army', before admitting that there were 'some imperfections in our own armour of defence', which had emerged in the course of the war which otherwise might have gone unnoticed. Such defects needed to be investigated and removed 'in the light of scientific progress and the experience of other powers'.[39] This latter reasoning was perhaps more prophetic than was realized at the time, for both scientific progress and developments on the Continent were to make an indelible mark on Britain's armaments programme, particularly as it concerned the navy. The Labour Party manifesto called for the abolition of the standing army and the establishment of a citizen force, adding that the people should decide on peace or war. Bernard Shaw offered a proposal whereby the army would be replaced, 'by giving to the whole male population an effective training in the use of arms without removing them from civil life. This can be done without conscription or barrack life.' The half-time system would be extended to the age of 21, with half of that time (previously given to education) devoted to military training. Voluntary enlistment thereafter would provide the army with its necessary recruits.[40] Other schemes to train the young in military accomplishments were not lacking, though it is unlikely that any which did not depend on a full conscription programme were as radical as Shaw's proposals.

The Conservatives emerged with a comfortable majority; Salisbury was prime minister, and the Duke of Devonshire at the Board of Education, with Sir John Gorst as the Minister for Education. Gorst's determination to curtail the power of the School Boards and to ensure the future of the denominational schools was supported by the Duke of Devonshire. These aspirations found expression in a new Education Bill by which the existing School Boards would be replaced by Local Education Authorities responsible for both elementary and secondary levels of education. Some 300 County and County Borough Councils would streamline the work previously tackled by over 2,500 School Boards and nearly 800 school attendance committees. The new bodies were to be known as Part II Authorities (Part II of the Bill). Borough Councils with a population exceeding 10,000 and urban districts with more than 20,000 inhabitants were to be Part III Authorities, and as such were to be responsible for elementary education only. Board schools were to be known as Provided schools while voluntary schools were to be called Non-provided schools. As the new LEAs were to exercise control over all secular education, rate aid would be forthcoming to Non-provided schools. It was anticipated that the county councils would be 'relatively conservative in their administration of education'[41] as compared with the School Boards. The Bill became law in December 1902.

CONCERNS ARISING FROM THE BOER WAR

The heady optimism of the early days of the Boer War had given way to disappointment, disbelief and anger as the British forces experienced humiliation, and the physical condition of the common soldiers raised grave concern.

In a letter written by Sir Edward Grey, the Foreign Secretary, to the American President, Theodore Roosevelt, he said:

> Before the Boer War, we were spoiling for a fight. We were ready to fight France about Siam, Germany about the Kruger telegram, and Russia about anything. Any government here, during the last ten years of last century, could have had war by lifting a finger. The people would have shouted for it. They had a craving for excitement, and a rush of blood to the head. Now, this generation has had enough excitement, and has lost a little blood, and is sane and normal.[42]

While Grey may have made a reasonably accurate assessment of the mood of the country at that time, his reasoning as to the efficacy of a little blood-letting as a surgical device in the interests of national sanity and normality may be questioned. In much the same vein, L. S. Amery suggested that the war had been the nation's Recessional after the giddy pomp of the Jubilee year. The arrogance and contempt engendered by many years of peace and prosperity had given way to 'a truer consciousness both of our strength and of our defects, and has awakened an earnest desire to make those defects good'.[43]

Liberal contributors to *The Heart of the Empire – Discussions of Problems of Modern City Life in England*[44] attempted to shift the focus from the periphery of empire to the very heart, London, and to the condition of its inhabitants. Bentley B. Gilbert, in his introduction to the book, suggested that its authors saw the Boer War as a symbol of what was corrupt in British life. He suggested that the book not only presented the anti-imperialist standpoint, but, 'It argues, in contemporary terms, that imperialism and domestic social reform are incompatible alternatives.'[45] Masterman's contribution 'Realities at Home' sadly observed that programmes of reform, though known to statesmen, tended to emerge only as election fodder or in parliament when political points could be made. It was, he observed, 'the day of other and noisier enthusiasms'.[46]

Sidney Webb had no confidence in either of the principal parties' ability to address the situation; he proposed that a new party should be formed to implement a policy of 'national efficiency'.[47] Both Asquith[48] and Rosebery[49] spoke forcefully in favour of their versions of a national efficiency programme which would encompass the extension and updating of national education and state action to tackle deficiencies in health and physique. In 1902 the Liberal League was set up with Rosebery as president, providing a platform for the promotion of imperialism and social reforms by Asquith, Haldane, Grey and others.

Benjamin Seebohm Rowntree's inquiry into working-class York, in which he and his investigators visited all working-class households in the city was a timely exercise. His *Poverty: A Study of Town Life* (1901) and Charles Booth's *Life and Labour of the People of London* (1889–1903) provided graphic evidence of the incidence of poverty in two cities, embracing the young, the old, the sick and the unemployed.

END OF THE WAR: THE LESSONS TO BE LEARNED

Elementary school log-books recorded the end of the war without undue emotion. The headmaster of Newmill National School near Huddersfield assembled his pupils on 2 June 1902 and, after a brief address, the singing of 'Soldiers of the King' and 'God Save the King', followed by three cheers, the children were dismissed for the day.

There were certainly many lessons to be learned, both in the conduct of war and in the maintenance of a healthy population to serve the nation's needs in war and in peace. Rudyard Kipling spoke to, and for, the people of England in his poem 'The Lesson 1899–1902'. He reminded them that the lessons learnt from the Boer War would serve them well as a business people; it was, he suggested, only right that their 'most holy illusions' were exposed in order that the real issues were addressed.[50]

Sober it was, perhaps only Kipling could have dared utter it, but the warning was timely. Sooner rather than later the country would have to confront the reality of its situation or be left irrevocably behind by her imperial competitors. Britain could not continue to bask in the reflected glories of past achievements, whether military, political or economic.

The old queen had gone, so had the old century: this was clearly the time to review the situation and see what the future might hold.

NOTES

1. Known as the Jameson Raid, after its leader, Dr Jameson. He led a force of nearly 400 Rhodesian mounted police and 125 volunteers drawn from Mafeking in Cape Colony. The plan was to make a dash for Johannesburg, link up with an Uitlander rising, and take over the Transvaal. In the event, there was no rising and the Boers harried Jameson's forces into surrender. Jan Smuts was later to claim that the Jameson Raid was 'the real declaration of war in the Great Anglo-Boer conflict'.
2. E. Halévy, *History of the English People in the Nineteenth Century. Vol. V, Imperialism and the Rise of Labour* (London: Benn, 2nd rev. edn, 1951), p. 73.
3. *The War in South Africa, a German Official Account* (English edn, 1906), Vol. II, p. 336, in Major-General J. F. C. Fuller, *The Conduct of War 1789–1961* (London: Eyre Methuen, 1961), p. 39.
4. T. Pakenham, *The Boer War* (London: Weidenfeld & Nicolson, 1979), p. 574.
5. See below, Part II, in particular, Chapter 9.
6. Richard Price, *An Imperial War and the British Working Class: Working Class Attitudes and Reactions to the Boer War, 1899–1902* (London: Routledge & Kegan Paul, 1972), Introduction, p. 1. See also R. N. Price, 'Society, Status and Jingoism: The Social Roots of Lower Middle Class Patriotism, 1870–1900', in Geoffrey Crossick (ed.), *The Lower Middle Class in Britain* (London: Croom Helm, 1977).
7. Log-books of Meanwood C. E. Schools, Leeds (1900 and 1901).
8. A. Penn, 'A Historical Survey of Curricular Development in the Elementary Schools of Dudley ...' (Dissertation, Dip. Ed., Birmingham University, 1963), p. 76.
9. *School Board Chronicle* (2 June 1900): 593, 595.
10. Howard Spring, *Heaven Lies about Us* (London: Constable, 1939), pp. 18–19. He was the author of many popular novels. Cast toy soldiers produced by William Britain's company were popular toys. Kenneth D. Brown writes:

   Whenever a conflict broke out between 1893 and 1914 the appropriate model figures appeared on the nursery floor almost as soon as their real life counterparts took the field. The Boer War saw the appearance of the City Imperial Volunteers and the Imperial Yeomanry, along with Boer soldiers hastily adapted from other figures.

   From 'Models in History: A Micro Study of Late Nineteenth-Century British entrepreneurship ...', *Economic History Review*, 42 (November 1989): 528–37.
11. *School Board Chronicle* (2 June 1900): 608.
12. *Nineteenth Century* (December 1901): 897–901.
13. Brunton had written a letter to *Nature* on 17 May 1900, in which he stated that

   It was not generally known that the explosion of a percussion cap on a gun will cause a current of air sufficient to extinguish a candle at a distance of ten or fifteen feet ... [To blow out a candle at that distance the sighting had to be] nearly as accurate as that required to make a centre with a rifle at 100 yards.

   He claimed that one old muzzle-loading gun would serve to instruct many children, and 240 caps could be purchased for no more than a shilling.
14. Sir Lauder Brunton, *Collected Papers on Physical and Military Training* (published privately, 1915), 3 (2 July 1901).
15. Ibid., 'Military Training in Schools', 4 (1901).
16. Ibid., 5 (1901).
17. *The Times*, letter to the editor (7 January 1902).
18. *School Board Chronicle* (31 March 1900): 328.
19. Ibid. (25 August 1900): 178.
20. Ibid. (24 February 1900): 198–9.
21. Ibid. (5 May 1900): 487.
22. Earl of Meath, *Memories of the Nineteenth Century* (London: John Murray, 1923), pp. 328–9.
23. *School Board Chronicle* (18 August 1900): 150.

24. Ibid. (13 July 1901): 37–8.
25. Ibid. (3 November 1900): 491. Fitch was a Chief Inspector of Schools and an Inspector of Elementary Training Colleges for Women. He helped found Girton College, Cambridge, and the Girls' Public Day School Company.
26. *Report of the Board of Education, 1899–1900*, General Report for East Central Division by the Revd C. D. Du Port, pp. 272–3.
27. *School Board Chronicle* (5 May 1900): 476.
28. *Report of the Board of Education* (1899–1900), General Report for the Metropolitan Division by Mr King, p. 327.
29. *School Board Chronicle* (27 January 1900): 97. Richmond's suggestion that 'the strongest and most suitable lads' from the Board schools should be selected to form a reserve force had been earlier proposed by Lieutenant-General Havelock-Allan in 1897. Havelock-Allan envisaged a scheme whereby boys leaving school at 14 who had 'a special facility for bearing arms', and who were physically strong, should progress to further military training until the age of 21. He anticipated that some two million trained men would thus be available by the end of a period of 12 years. From that number he expected that sufficient volunteers would come forward to meet the needs of 'a popular campaign'. This scheme was advanced as an alternative to his suggestion that all able-bodied boys from age nine years should receive two hours training a week on their half-holidays. At the age of 21 they would join the Volunteers. Should his parents or guardians refuse to so bind a boy at age 9 to 'this small amount of patriotic duty' they would be required to pay for every stage of his education. Lieutenant-General Sir Henry Havelock-Allan, 'A General Voluntary Training to Arms versus Conscription', *Fortnightly Review*, LXI (1897): 85–97.

    In a letter to the editor of the *Fortnightly Review*, the Earl of Meath suggested, quite reasonably, that to withhold free education from those refusing permission was itself a measure of compulsion. Earl of Meath, letter to the editor, *Fortnightly Review*, LXI (1897): 972–4.
30. *House of Commons Debates* (Hansard), Fourth Series, Vol. LXXIX, cols. 409–10 (19 February 1900), 'Debate on Army (Supplementary) Estimates'.
31. *House of Commons Debates*, Fourth Series, Vol. LXXIX, cols. 1102–3 (26 February 1900), 'Questions'.
32. *School Board Chronicle* (10 March 1900): 249.
33. See above, Table 1, p. 36. It may be recalled that the New Code of 1875 allowed a special grant for satisfactory discipline and organization; it was not until 1890 that variable grants for discipline and organization were introduced. Both inducements encouraged the teaching of some sort of drill but much was left to the discretion of visiting inspectors and to local School Boards and managers.
34. *House of Commons Debates*, Fourth Series, Vol. LXXX, cols. 655–7 (12 March 1900), Supply (Army Estimates).
35. John Burns (1858–1943) left school at the age of 10 to become an engineering apprentice, his father being an engine fitter. He joined the Social Democratic Federation in 1884, founded the Battersea Labour League in 1889 and was an MP from 1892–1918. Between 1905–14 he served as President of the Local Government Board, the first workman to be in the Cabinet, and as President of the Board of Trade in 1914, from which post he resigned in protest against the war.
36. *House of Commons Debates*, Fourth Series, Vol. LXXXI, cols. 831–48 (30 March 1900), 'Physical and Military Instruction in State-aided Schools'.
37. Rudyard, Kipling, from 'The Courting of Dinah Shadd', *Macmillan's Magazine*, Vol. LXI (November 1889 to April 1890): 393.
38. *School Board Chronicle* (6 April 1901): 365. Circular 452 of 20 June 1901 addressed to HMIs refers them to the 'general instructions' in respect of the 'Model Course' and adds:

    But the efficiency of the instruction should be judged primarily by the effect upon the general bearing and physique of the children. Habits of willing obedience, attention, and orderliness should result from the physical training; and if the movement of classes which takes place in the usual routine of the school are smartly and quietly executed this may be taken as evidence of its success.

The Circular also sings the praises of school bands 'or even a single instrument such as a drum or fife or violin' to secure precision of movement. 'A fife-and-drum band in Boys', or a string band in Girls', Schools can be formed at a trifling expense and would be available for outdoor work. Members of such school bands should, however, receive their due share of the physical training.'

39. F. W. S. Craig (ed.), *British General Election Manifestos, 1900–1974* (London: Macmillan, 1975), p. 3.
40. Bernard, Shaw, *Fabianism and the Empire* (Manifesto by the Fabian Society, 1900).
41. Eric Eaglesham, *From School Board to Local Authority* (London: Routledge & Kegan Paul, 1956), p. 179.
42. G. M. Trevelyan, *Grey of Falloden* (1937), pp. 132–3, cited in A. J. Marder, *The Anatomy of British Sea Power: A History of British Naval Policy in the pre-Dreadnought Era 1880–1905* (London: Frank Cass, 1972), p. 20.
43. L. S. Amery (ed.), *The Times History of the War in South Africa, 1899–1900*, Vol. I (London: Sampson Low, 1900), p. 11.
44. C. F. G. Masterman (ed.), *The Heart of the Empire – Discussions of Problems of Modern City Life in England* (first published London: Fisher Unwin, 1901), ed. with intro. Bentley B. Gilbert (Sussex: Harvester Press, 1973).
45. Ibid. (Bentley B. Gilbert), Introduction, p. xv.
46. Ibid. (Masterman), p. 4.
47. Sidney Webb, *Twentieth-Century Politics: A Policy of National Efficiency*, Fabian Tract 108 (Fabian Society, November 1901).
48. Asquith's speech at a dinner in his honour, 1901. Quoted by Bentley B. Gilbert, in the Introduction to C. F. G. Masterman, *The Heart of the Empire*, pp. xx–xxi.
49. Lord Rosebery, speeches at Chesterfield (16 December 1901) and at Glasgow (10 March 1902), *Liberal League Publication Number 37*.
50. Rudyard Kipling, 'The Lesson 1899–1902' (Boer War), in *The Definitive Edition of Rudyard Kipling's Verse* (London: Hodder & Stoughton, 1940), p. 299.

PART II

Drill and the Curriculum: Developments up to the First World War

'The real issue of the first decade of the Twentieth Century was not over rate aid to the voluntary schools (now a fact) but whether the country could afford to neglect any longer the more material aspects of child welfare.'

(W. H. G. Armytage, *Four Hundred Years of English Education*, p. 201)

'... we must train the whole youth of the nation to arms, so that, while the Navy may count securely upon adequate reserves, the trained manhood of a great nation may support a voluntary professional highly-trained Army. Only thus can we maintain our position in the world. Thus, too, we can give a sense of duty, discipline, obedience, and responsibility to hundreds of thousands who are without it, and improve the deteriorating physique of our large and growing urban population.'

(Duke of Wellington, letter to the editor, *The Times* (5 April 1902): 9).

7

The Model Course of Physical Training and Interdepartmental Committee Findings, 1902–04

THE POLITICAL CLIMATE

In the aftermath of the Boer War, arguments for or against the teaching of military drill to the youth of the country reached new heights. It is not difficult to see why this should have been so. The war itself stimulated debate on military matters, and the very poor physical state of so many volunteers was a cause of national concern. But there was too a political dimension, as Britain sought to extricate itself from a position of 'splendid isolation' and to seek more positive relationships with continental rivals. In 1904 Britain agreed an *entente cordiale* with France, and a somewhat looser arrangement with Russia three years later, neither of which involved any binding military co-operation. A rival grouping, the Triple Alliance, was formed by Germany, Austria-Hungary and Italy, though the latter was to drift away later. So long as there was an approximate balance between the two alliances the likelihood of a major European conflict was contained, but the possibility of British intervention raised the stakes, certainly in the opinion of Germany. Europe was splitting into two as far as the major powers were concerned: an ominous threat to future peace. For Britain, the possibility of military involvement in Europe increased the need to address the modernization and reform of the armed forces to face different challenges from those experienced in policing the empire. Inevitably, attention was focussed on issues such as conscription and the military training of youth.

HALDANE'S SUPPORT FOR THE EDUCATION ACT OF 1902

Clearly the nation's schools were destined to play a key role in any remedial scheme to restore Britain's standing and to face with confidence the challenges of the new century. Haldane, a Liberal parliamentarian who had supported the Boer War, considered the 1902 Education Bill as a matter of great urgency: 'It is vital to our interests, essential to our position as a nation, and necessary for the preservation of our commerce, our Navy, and our Empire.'[1] Ever a staunch advocate of any moves which would raise the country's education and technical training so as to be more comparable with continental rivals, Haldane was assiduous in his reference to the Prussian system of education as a model worthy of emulation.

A MODEL COURSE OF PHYSICAL TRAINING

An advance notice of 'A Model Course of Physical Training' appeared in the *School Board Chronicle* of 6 April 1901, during the Boer War. The proposals stated that a minimum course would be compiled such as would satisfy the needs of even small schools. More varied programmes would be allowed including systematic instruction in swimming, cricket, etc. Instruction, where possible, should be given by the regular teaching staff of the school. But a Memorandum on Physical Training, issued in August 1902, and addressed chiefly to rural schools, appeared to contradict that apparently broad-based approach to physical training. With the co-operation of the War Office, non-commissioned officers from local military depots would be able to assist where necessary, although it allowed that a preferable solution lay with the ordinary teachers and heads of schools who should themselves seek qualification.[2] At a time when non-military forms of physical training were clearly the preferred option of the schools the suggestion that the army should participate in the new teaching programme must have surprised and disturbed many teachers. On the other hand, those who supported the teaching of military drill in schools would welcome the Model Course as a measure which might lift the flagging support within local authorities and individual schools for military-style drill.[3]

Following consultation with the War Office, the Board of Education issued in 1902 a 'Model Course of Physical Training for use in Upper Departments of Public Elementary Schools'. Expressing surprise at this co-operation, Mr Cremer, a radical MP, asked what authority the two departments had to act jointly in that matter. He was informed by Sir John Gorst, Vice-President of the Committee of Council on Education, that the Model Course was issued by the Board of Education only, under its general powers.[4] There was indeed considerable and mounting concern at the whole tenor of the new Model Course which relied heavily on military training models and so ran counter to recent developments which favoured more generalized forms of physical exercises. The Board of Education may well have accepted sole responsibility for issuing the new course, nevertheless the influence of the War Office was indelibly stamped upon it. A significant appointment was that of Colonel G. Malcolm Fox, formerly Inspector of Army Gymnasia, to serve as the Board of Education's Inspector of Physical Training with the task of introducing a system of drill through the use of peripatetic instructors. Further, the Model Course encouraged schools to employ instructors 'who should, if possible, have been trained in the Army Gymnastic Course at Aldershot'.[5] Taken together, Fox's appointment and the recommendation that Aldershot-trained instructors should be appointed demonstrate a determined attempt to accord military drill a significant role. If further evidence be needed, schools were advised to consult *Infantry Training, 1902* and the *War Office Handbook* in this matter.

OPPOSITION TO THE MODEL COURSE

Within a few months of the publication of the Model Course a deputation from the NUT waited upon Lord Londonderry (the Board's President since August 1902 after Balfour became prime minister) to register its protest. The NUT was particularly concerned at 'the pitiful spectre in fields near big towns of school-mistresses aged 50–60, compelled to undergo drill by sergeant instructors'.

Dr Macnamara (Camberwell, North) was most active in denouncing the Model Course in the Commons. On 23 February 1903 he questioned the Secretary to the Board of Education as to whether he would consider replacing the recently issued Model Course by one more suited to the needs of young children. Sir William Anson (who had superseded Gorst in the Cabinet reshuffle of August 1902) replied that the Board had no present intention of making any replacement, but added that it was considering the publication of an 'introduction' to the Model Course 'showing the steps by which the series of exercises in it may be progressively acquired'. The Board was, he said, prepared to consider alternative schemes having the same scope and aim as the Model Course.[6]

On the occasion of the education vote, Dr Macnamara returned to the question of the new physical training requirements which he identified as an attempt 'to introduce a purely military system of drill in all the elementary schools of England and Wales'. He compared the text of the Model Course with the *Red Book*, an instruction manual for drilling army recruits; from which only a few crude alterations had been made in the process of adaptation. For example, under the heading 'Exercises with Staves' the word *staff* was substituted for *rifle*, but the instruction still referred to the butt end of the staff.[7] Dr Macnamara pointed out that the physical training in the *Red Book* comprised about 75 per cent leg exercises and 25 per cent arm exercises, with no attention paid to the neck, side, abdomen, chest or, above all, breathing exercises. In fact, he considered that some of the exercises were 'absolutely harmful'. Colonel Onslow, the author of the drill manual, had stated that the exercises were never intended for training young children, neither were they suitable for that purpose. Dr Macnamara drew attention to a recent series of articles in *The Times* which had suggested that it was necessary to maintain an association between the school and the army. One article had stated: 'Some system of elementary military training, including the use of the rifle, should be introduced in all schools in order to lay the foundations of a military spirit in the nation.' After drawing attention to a Royal Commission Report on Physical Training in Scotland issued a few days previously, which had recommended that a skilled Committee should be appointed to draw up a model course, he urged that the Board of Education should do likewise for England and Wales.

Sir John Gorst (MP for Cambridge University and late Vice-President of the Committee of Council on Education) spoke in support of Dr Macnamara, but excused the Secretary to the Board of Education from criticism as he thought the scheme had been issued 'without his knowledge and approbation'! MPs have been known to go to considerable lengths to defend a colleague, but to suggest that the Secretary to the Board had been kept in ignorance of an important measure must have stretched the credulity of those present in the House. Gorst thought that the many teachers in elementary schools who had learned Swedish drill were better fitted to teach the military authorities than the latter were to teach them. Further support for Dr Macnamara came from John Burns who was highly critical of 'this attempt by military men to make our elementary schools a recruiting ground for the Army'.

Sir William Anson replied for the Government, claiming that the Model Course was suitable for the upper classes in the elementary schools. However, the Board of Education was aware of its inherent difficulties. He admitted that 'It was very difficult to be learned by female teachers, while certain of the requirements could not apply to children of tender age or to girls.' Having been compiled 'for use in Upper Departments' it is strange that he found it necessary to suggest that 'certain of the requirements' were not suitable for young children. He concluded, perhaps to the surprise, and certainly to the satisfaction of critics of the Model Course, by saying that if it were necessary, and he thought it would be, the Board of Education would be 'prepared to appoint a Departmental Committee to inquire into the best form of physical training for children'. This statement was welcomed by Macnamara, who thereupon withdrew his motion.[8] In answer to a further question in July, A. J. Balfour said that the Government was considering the question of appointing a Commission on Physical Training for England and Wales.[9]

The Board of Education seems to have been unable or unwilling to resist the pressure of the War Office, and of militarists generally, for the teaching of military drill in the elementary schools. The Model Course bore considerable evidence of hasty adaptation and a woeful lack of appreciation of developments which the Board had previously countenanced and indeed encouraged. Anxiety at the state of the army and of potential recruits had no doubt contributed to this hasty decision-making process.

The general reports of HMIs showed their concern at the situation, though their criticisms were somewhat hesitant and reluctant. A Mr Howard commented that there were instances where local drill instructors had been employed who were ignorant of the Model Course or who had introduced their own drills without submitting any scheme for approval. Such a report must have been read with some apprehension as to the potential consequences on the children's well-being in such instances. Mr Leaf wrote of the situation in Sheffield:

> One Board school faces the public boldly. The master says: 'For military drill we take all the general *squad* drill and develop into *company* drill, introducing *battalion* drill as far as we are able, and these are practised on the road when out *route-marching*. From play to marching in fours, about twenty seconds. Few teachers care for such publicity. We practise marching over rough ground, and the boys are keen to keep their formation intact.'

Clearly, in this instance, the drill came from the *Red Book* in completely unadulterated form. One is left to wonder what the parents thought of this procedure; it appears that few of the teachers were either impressed or indeed willing to participate! Elsewhere, a slightly shocked Mr Cornish reported:

> I visited a school the other day where a small girl pupil teacher, with her hair down her back, was calling out 'Squad! 'Shun!' to a class of little boys, in the most military fashion. It may seem a small matter, but yet it is perhaps possible that if the word 'squad' could be changed to something of less unfortunate sound, the change would be acceptable – to teachers of girls, at least.[10]

THE MACCLESFIELD PATRIOTIC ASSOCIATION

Meanwhile in 1902 *The Times* was running a series of articles on 'National Training and National Defence', beginning on 20 March with 'Military Drill in Schools', by a Correspondent. The writer called for some form of universal training for the young, suggesting that the strength of a people lay not so much in its material resources or its geographical extent, as in 'its physical vigour, martial spirit, and trained intelligence'. He suggested that 'until quite lately' physical education had, with a few exceptions, been entirely neglected. In fact there had been a dramatic improvement in the 12 years since the Code of 1890 drew attention to physical exercises and introduced variable grants for discipline and organization. The six-fold increase in the number of departments teaching physical exercises between 1891 and 1899 has already been referred to.[11] He was also apparently unaware of the hostile reception accorded to the Board of Education's Model Course, which he described as 'quite excellent of its kind', and 'likely to be of the greatest possible service'.

He went on to describe the achievements of a Patriotic Association founded in the Macclesfield area of Cheshire in the spring of 1900 'when the first lessons of the war were fresh'. The object of the Association was to encourage physical training and military drill among the 10- to 16-year-olds. Matters were simplified by virtue of the fact that all the 14 town schools and 12 country schools in the district were voluntary, or non-provided schools. That meant that individual approaches could be made by the Association to the managers and head teachers for permission to 'drill all boys of suitable age at its own cost and free of any charge to the schools'. Having received encouragement from all 26 schools, the Association engaged drill instructors, and secured the use of a central drill-hall for the use of schools which did not have covered playground areas. By the winter of 1900 every school was being drilled, and the total average attendance on parade was about 1,500. The response of the Education Department to this initiative was to request that efforts be made to drill the children at their own schools and to train the local teachers so that they could take over the instruction. However, a year later the Association was superintending the drill of over 2,000 children and also giving instruction in drill procedures to male and female teachers in its own drill-hall. A large class of non-commissioned officers was formed from the more proficient boys, and rifle-shooting classes were begun on a miniature range. It was estimated that the Association incurred a cost of between £5 and £6 per school for providing drill facilities. Having achieved success in its training of boys of school age the Association aimed to keep alive the interest of school leavers until such time as they were old enough to join the local Volunteers. This appeared to have been a particularly successful attempt to institute a locally organized and locally funded programme of military training for the young.

A number of Working Men's Rifle Clubs were set up at this time and an Association was formed to co-ordinate their work under the presidency of Lord Roberts. Those clubs would look for new members among lads who had received some form of military training at school, such as that provided under the Macclesfield scheme.

CADET BATTALIONS FOR WORKING-CLASS BOYS

In the House of Lords on 16 December 1902 the Earl of Meath asked whether the Government's attention had been drawn to the speech delivered by Field Marshal Lord Roberts at Pietmaritzberg two years earlier, in which he had pointed out that all males in Natal were required to join a corps and learn how to shoot. Roberts had expressed the hope that the mother country would learn from one of her children and insist that all boys should join the cadet corps. The evidence of Lieutenant-General Sir Ian Hamilton to the Royal Commission at Edinburgh in September 1902 was also referred to, in particular his plea that all British boys should be taught to handle rifles, to shoot, use the bayonet, march and skirmish. 'Young Boers between the ages of twelve and fifteen were little vipers, and had sent many a good man to his long account. In their native land boys of fifteen would make excellent soldiers.' Curiously, differences between the veldt and industrial Britain were not drawn by Hamilton; the 'native lands' were in fact not comparable; and if the defence of the homeland was the prime concern, then surely different criteria would need to be applied. Hamilton was perhaps alone in proposing publicly that boys should undertake bayonet practice along with other, more common, military skills.

Meath referred to the nine existing cadet battalions, catering for working lads of 14 years and upwards. Independent of Volunteer battalions, they were largely maintained by their own officers, at a cost of £2 to £5 a head.[12] An interesting example of a cadet battalion for working-class boys was that set up by the late Colonel A. S. Salmond (who died from wounds received at Stromberg in South Africa). The battalion had enjoyed the support of Octavia Hill – the well-known philanthropist – and of a number of gentlemen working with boys in south London. From an initial single company in Southwark the unit expanded until it had detachments in eight London districts with a total strength of over 600 cadets. The Hackney and Stepney companies were maintained by Eton and Haileybury public schools respectively.[13] This practice linked existing provisions for ex-elementary school youths with the cadet corps of public schools through the supply of senior NCOs provided by the latter to act as instructors.

A PROPER CONCERN FOR MILITARY REQUIREMENTS

In 1902 Sir Lauder Brunton, consulting physician to St Bartholomew's Hospital, and a strong advocate of military drill, hosted a private dinner at the Reform Club. The guests included Haldane, Buckle (editor of *The Times*), Sir Henry Craik (representing education), Sir Henry Conyngham of the Home Office and Colonel Stopford (replacing Lord Frankfort, who was then fatally ill). Brunton summarized their assessment of the current situation as follows: 'it was decided that in the present temper of the country any attempt to try and get military training in schools was quite hopeless, and it was decided that the only possible thing was to try for physical training'.[14] This is an interesting observation and one to be borne in mind when considering his strong advocacy of military training in the early years of the century.

Responding to an editorial in the *Spectator* of 10 January 1903, Brunton agreed with the writer that it was necessary for the nation as a whole to display a proper concern for its military requirements. He repeated his views with respect to the incorporation of military training into the school curriculum, but in this communication he suggested a minimum age for involvement of 7 years, so relieving the infant school children (and their teachers) of the burden of the penny guns which he had previously proposed for their use. Any suggestion that rifle training might tend towards militarism was peremptorily dismissed: 'Could any peoples be freer from this [militarism] than the American settlers … , or the Boers?' he asked, reminding his readers that the former had defeated the British, and that the latter had almost succeeded in doing so. In both cases shooting had been taught from childhood.[15] The societal differences between settlers in America or South Africa and the industrialized inhabitants of Britain were not drawn. A gun would have sat easily on the shoulder of a settler in protection of his holding or in hunting for food, with no thought of militarism in his or anyone else's mind. His children would also have been introduced to a gun and taught to use it as a matter of course. The same could not be claimed with respect to children in industrial Britain without inviting accusations that such action was militaristic in character.

THE INTERDEPARTMENTAL COMMITTEE EXAMINES THE MODEL COURSE

As forecast, an Interdepartmental Committee was set up to examine the much-criticized Model Course of Physical Exercises. It had Mr J. Struthers as its chairman, and included Colonel G. M. Fox, two medical men and a woman among its nine members. Its brief was:

> To examine the Model Course now in use, to judge how far it should be modified or supplemented, and to consider what principles should be followed, in order to render a Model Course, or Courses, adaptable for the different ages and sexes of the children in public elementary schools.

The Report was published in 1904, the Committee finding that:

> As a result of our investigation we do not consider the 'Model Course', as presented to us, to be a suitable course for use in schools, in part because certain of the exercises included in the course seem to us unsuitable as elements of a compulsory course, but chiefly because the course as a whole does not seem to be constructed on well defined general principles educed from a consideration of the function of physical exercise as a necessary element in a well ordered course of general education for children.[16]

It would have been surprising had they not come to that conclusion. The Committee asserted that physical exercise formed only a part of a much larger question, that of school and personal hygiene, which would demand of future teachers some practical knowledge and experience of 'child study'. As far as the teaching of physical exercises was concerned the view expressed was that there were obvious advantages in having them taught by the ordinary class teacher. There were reservations, however. It was unreasonable to assume that teachers 'in or beyond middle life', who were often the only teachers in rural schools, should be compelled to qualify for such teaching. To safeguard the curricular requirements, specially qualified instructors should be employed to teach in a group of schools.

> Fortunately there is at present a considerable and increasing supply of persons, chiefly women of good general education, who have undergone a systematic course of preparation (extending over two years or more), for becoming instructors in physical exercise.[17]

This clause was a significant one; the Committee did not look to the army for suitable instructors of physical exercises, and indeed their recommendations implied that there was no need to stray beyond the educational field in the search for well-qualified teachers. The Committee had also established to their satisfaction that there were already sufficient women qualified to teach physical exercises for the scheme to be implemented without undue delay. Colonel Fox must have been able to accommodate this shift in policy; having been appointed initially to implement the Model Course, he sat on the Interdepartmental Committee which demolished it, and continued to serve as a Board of Education Inspector of Physical Training until 1908.

The need for ample playground space for playing games was stressed, as was the provision of a hall or unoccupied classroom for regular and systematic physical exercise lessons, if need be on a shared basis with other schools. Appendix 1 comprised a 'Syllabus of Physical Exercises', which drew attention to the need for both physical and educational effects to be taken into account.[18] Children over the age of 12 were to have the use of light dumb-bells, staves (or barbells), and Indian clubs, with dance movements added to the balance exercises, and swimming drill. A general warning was given concerning the use of music, which, though it might help prevent fatigue, could detract from 'will training' in muscular movements. It was not recommended for older children except in marching and dance movements.

Only in considering 'Additional exercise' for pupil teachers and older scholars was there any suggestion that a Service Manual might be consulted, and then, 'along with other modern books on the subject', teachers might turn to the *Handbook of Physical Training adopted by the Admiralty*, ignoring reference to the *Red Book* of army drill which had so profoundly influenced the Model Course. *The Times* of 7 February 1901 had reported that a new Drill Book was to address 'the earlier stages of the recruit course' of military training necessitated by recent experience of war in South Africa,[19] but that manual does not appear to have been considered suitable by the Committee. Nowhere in the Syllabus nor in the Committee's Report itself is the term *military drill* employed. But it had not been considered possible to eradicate it from the 'Class Arrangements', which recommended that classes should be formed 'in two ranks, shortest on the right, tallest on the left'. And the position of *attention*, described in great detail, closely followed military norms, though it was now recognized that it was a position of strain which should not be held for more than half a minute at a time.

Circular 515 recommended that Local Education Authorities and school managers should give 'early consideration' to the new syllabus, the Board of Education stating that: 'The Syllabus should be adopted in all Public Elementary Schools as soon as is reasonably possible.' It stipulated at least an hour a week for formal lessons, divided into either two or three equal periods, and daily recreative exercises 'constantly practised'. Signed by Robert Morant, Permanent Secretary to the Board, the Circular also advised: 'Where possible, a system of taking physical measurements of the children at regular intervals should be instituted.' This comment reflected the growing interest in *child study*, and the belief that appropriate records of children's growth and development were an essential part of the monitoring process.

THE INTERDEPARTMENTAL COMMITTEE INTO PHYSICAL DETERIORATION

As we have already seen, after the Boer War, Sir Lauder Brunton became increasingly immersed in efforts to establish the causes of physical deficiency, to encourage physical education, and to promote the military training of the young. His concern at the level of physical deficiency was shared, among others, by General Sir Frederick Maurice and by Sir William Taylor, Director-General of the Army Medical Service. In a letter to *The Lancet* (14 February 1903), Brunton claimed that information was needed as to the causes of physical deficiency, the best means of remedying the defects, and the best available in the short term. He acknowledged that responsibility lay with the Government, and as there was no board of health, which would have been the appropriate body to gather information, he proposed the appointment of a small commission which could usefully look into the three points which Maurice had earlier indicated: poor dental health, flat feet and poor physique.[20] Brunton repeated his urgent call for a Royal Commission in a letter to the *Manchester Guardian* on 2 April 1903. Sir William Taylor, in his capacity of Director-General of the Army Medical Service, addressed a memorandum to the War Office which (certainly in the opinion of Brunton) precipitated the appointment of an Interdepartmental Committee. Its brief was to investigate the extent of 'Physical Degeneration'; this was criticized by Taylor as placing unnecessary emphasis on past conditions, for which no records existed which could provide necessary evidence, instead of focusing attention on the current problem of physical inefficiency. Be that as it may, the Committee sat for 11 months, took a great deal of evidence from those most closely associated with the condition of the lower classes from whom recruits were drawn, and published its findings in a three-volume Report in 1904. This Report constituted the first major official investigation into the health of the nation, though in pursuit of its brief more prominence was accorded to the question of deterioration than to inefficiency. It did, however, make the point that 'In order that the present acknowledged evils may be removed, complacent optimism and administrative indifference must be attacked and overcome.' This comment reflected the evidence tendered by General Sir Frederick Maurice, whose perceptive investigations into the physical examination of prospective recruits laid bare a number of inadequacies. He had found that in many instances the inspecting doctors passed men, not because they were fit, but because they were not so defective as many others passing before them. As he reported to the Committee: 'Their eyes had got wearied with the classes they were inspecting.' He added that the problem was more often caused by being 'improperly nurtured' from babyhood than from any hereditary deterioration. The worst conditions were not necessarily found in the hearts of large cities and industrial towns, but more probably in large villages and small towns which were expanding without proper organization. Maurice supported this claim with reference to a report by the Manchester Sanitary Association and a statement by the chairman of the Medical Health Board of Chester County Council.[21] This was a valuable corrective to any assumption that major problems of health and physique were confined to cities and large towns. Rowntree and Booth had exposed the inadequate conditions in those areas of population; Maurice had now demonstrated that the problem was a much wider one.

The Committee accepted that 'the sacrifice of infant life is enormous' (para. 277), having previously remarked that

> Except where parents are affected by syphilis or drunkenness, the child inherits at birth a good physique, and if properly cared for in infancy and childhood it may grow up strong and healthy, although its father and mother may be physically weak from bad surroundings. (para. 247)

Unfortunately, as the Committee admitted, the chances of proper care being available and forthcoming were not always good. It called for a physical census to be carried out in schools and factories, and to be subsequently extended to cover the whole population.

The Report suggested that much could be achieved by voluntary organizations, though it did demand statutory powers to compel the provision of physical training for both boys and girls. It said that the state should train teachers of physical exercises, and that local authorities should provide gymnasia and instructors. A major concern was the fate of boys who had left school at the age of 14: for them continuation classes were recommended in which drill and physical exercises were to feature prominently, with due exemptions for members of recognized and inspected clubs and cadet corps.

THE NEW CODE OF REGULATIONS FOR ELEMENTARY SCHOOLS, 1904

On 18 and 19 April 1904 copies of the *Report of the Interdepartmental Committee on the Model Course of Physical Exercises* were laid before the Commons and Lords respectively, to be followed on 21 June by the *Report of the Interdepartmental Committee on Physical Deterioration.* And in issuing a New Code of Regulations for Elementary Schools in the same year, Morant (Permanent Secretary to the Board of Education since 1903) took the opportunity to endorse their corporate philosophies. In his preface to the Code he wrote:

> The school must afford them [the children] every opportunity for the development of their bodies, not only by training them in appropriate physical exercises and in encouraging them in organised games, but also by instructing them in the working of some of the simpler laws of

health ... . The corporate life of the school, especially in the playground, should develop that instinct for fair play and for loyalty to one another which is the germ of a wider sense of honour in later life.

Perhaps these words can be accepted as a summary of some at least of the lessons of the Boer War as they affected the populace generally, and the younger and more vulnerable members of society more particularly. Within the next three years Acts of Parliament were to secure for the nation's children legislation relating to school meals and to medical inspection, both of which were projected in the Interdepartmental Reports.

A SHORT STEP FROM PHYSICAL TO MILITARY TRAINING

A conference was held at the London County Council Education Offices in November 1904 to consider the possible establishment of a national or central school for physical education on the lines of the Royal Central Institute in Sweden. Noting this event, the *Times* leader suggested that what was required was an English system rather than a Swedish one. The argument in favour of an English system had already been decided by the London School Board in the early 1890s, but that did not necessarily carry with it an implication that a national or central school of physical education similar to that existing in Sweden lacked merit. While agreeing that a start had to be made with general physical efficiency, the writer suggested that as boys grew up they needed to learn how to use their physical efficiency 'for the defence of the Empire'. In effect, he said that physical training should merge into military training, and that the reward for financing the whole operation would be reaped when the trained youths joined the Colours.[22] The universal provision of cadet battalions such as Meath described above could be seen as an ideal intermediary stage between school-based military training and local Volunteer units.

A NOTE OF CAUTION

Lest too much reliance came to be laid upon education in the future, O. Eltzbacher attempted to give a general warning, based upon his observations of the achievements or failures of Britain's military leaders in South Africa.[23] He began by claiming that 'Education, after having been more or less neglected for a long time in Great Britain, has now become an all-powerful panacea in the eyes of the British public and of the British politician ... [it] is to work wonders in every way.' He went on to make the point that few indeed of the nation's leaders in a wide field of activities had been 'trained' to leadership either in school or elsewhere, and so far as military matters were concerned, the untrained solder was often as effective as the trained:

> Many observers have been struck by the curious phenomenon that our most highly educated officers had on the whole so little success against the Boer officers, who were not only quite unlearned in the science of war, but also mostly uneducated, and sometimes grossly ignorant in elementary knowledge, peasants who had perhaps not even heard the names of Frederick the Great, Napoleon and Moltke, whose every battle our erudite officers had at their fingers' ends.

From his perusal of the Army List he had established that the most successful officers in the Boer War – Lord Roberts, Lord Kitchener, Sir John French, Sir George White, Sir Archibald Hunter, Sir Ian Hamilton, Lord Dundonald, Sir Hector Macdonald, and General Baden-Powell – had none of them passed through Staff College. On the other hand, the late General Colley, who had lost Majuba, was a Staff College professor, while General Gatacre, who was defeated at Stromberg, and Generals Kelly-Kenny, Hildyard, Hart and Barton, none of whom had served with 'conspicuous success', had all passed through Staff College. From these instances, the author suggested caution lest erudition and education stifled the exercise of common sense and practical experience. This he advanced as one of the as yet unlearned lessons of the Boer War.

And on that cautionary note we close this chapter. We have seen how the fumblings of the Board of Education and its complicity with the War Office threatened to undo much that had already been achieved in the physical education of scholars in elementary schools. The Model Course had been subjected to a thorough inquiry and found quite unsuitable for school use, the use of army drill instructors had been abandoned, and attention directed instead to the keeping of accurate records of child development. Circular 515 encouraged LEAs and school managers to waste no time in introducing the new syllabus. The Interdepartmental Committee into Physical Deterioration had reinforced those findings and added its own recommendations which aimed to focus attention on health issues. Morant usefully summarized the findings of the two Committees in his New Code of 1904 from which there would appear to be little opportunity for any radical departure.

115

NOTES

1. *House of Commons Debates*, Fourth Series, Vol. CVII, col. 704 (5 May 1902).
2. *School Board Chronicle*, 68 (16 August 1902): 155.
3. This is reinforced by a Commons' statement made by Sir James Fergusson in which he drew attention to 'the circular recently issued by the Board of Education in concert with the War Office, making such provision as was suitable for *drilling* [my emphasis] boys in the Public Elementary Schools, the great bulk of whom left school at 12 years of age' (*School Board Chronicle*, 67 (15 March 1902): 265).
4. *House of Commons Debates*, Fourth Series, Vol. CVIII, col. 376 (15 May 1902).
5. Sir George Newman, *The Building of a Nation's Health* (London: Macmillan, 1939), p. 270.
6. *House of Commons Debates*, Fourth Series, Vol. CXVIII, col. 482 (23 February 1903).
7. Dr Macnamara proffered the following extracts as examples of the near identity of the two texts:

The Infantry Drill Book
Before the squad is put in motion, the instructor will take care that the men are square individually and in correct line with each other. Each recruit must be taught to take a point straight to his front, by fixing his eyes upon some distant object and then observing some nearer point in the same straight line, such as a stone, tuft of grass, or other object.

The Model Course
Before the squad is put in motion, the *teacher* will take care that the *scholars* are square individually and in correct line with each other. Each *scholar* must be taught to take *up a straight line* to his front, by fixing his eyes upon some object *on the ground* straight to his front, and then observing some nearer point in the same straight line, such as a stone or other object.

(Note that amendments in the Model Course are in italics; the writer does not anticipate that tufts of grass will necessarily be available to view.)
8. *House of Commons Debates*, Fourth Series, Vol. CXIX, cols. 1292–332 (19 March 1903).
9. *House of Commons Debates*, Fourth Series, Vol. CXXV, cols. 693–4 (15 July 1903).
10. *Report of Board of Education, 1901–2*, HMI General Reports for 1902, p. 25.
11. See above, Table 1, p. 36.
12. *House of Lords Debates*, Fourth Series, Vol. CXVI, cols. 1295–312 (16 December 1902).
13. *The Times* (18 April 1903): 10.
14. Sir Lauder Brunton, *Collected Papers on Physical and Military Training* (privately published, undated, but letter is dated 1915), Preface.
15. *The Spectator*, letter to the editor (24 January 1903).
16. *Report of the Interdepartmental Committee on the Model Course of Physical Exercises* (1904), p. 5. For similarities between the Model Course and Australian practice see below, Appendix C.
17. *Report of Interdepartmental Committee*, pp. 7–8.
18. Ibid., 'Appendix 1, Syllabus of Physical Exercises'. The Syllabus began by stating that

(1) The primary object of any course of physical exercises in schools is to maintain, and, if possible, improve the health and physique of the children. This may be described as its *physical effect*.
(2) But the exercises which conduce to this result may, if rightly conducted, have an effect scarcely less important in developing in the scholars qualities of alertness, decision, concentration and perfect control of mind over body. This may be styled the *educational* effect.
(3) These two effects are to some extent blended in every suitable exercise and, according to circumstances, now the one aspect of the exercise, now the other, is to be regarded as important … .

19. *The Times* (7 February 1901): 11, 'Army Drill Reform'.
20. Sir J. F. Maurice (pseudonym 'Miles'), 'Where to Get Men', *The Contemporary Review* (January 1902): 78–86.

21. The statement by the Chairman of the Medical Health Board of Chester County Council was to the effect that the death-rate of infants in the first year after birth was not 200 or 300 per 1,000, but 800 per 1,000. *Report of the Interdepartmental Committee into Physical Deterioration*, Vol. 2 (1904), pp. 11–13.
22. *The Times* (17 November 1904): 7.
23. O. Eltzbacher, 'The Disadvantages of Education', *The Nineteenth Century and After* (February 1903): 315–18.

8

1905: A Significant Year

The response of the Board of Education to the two Interdepartmental Committees which had reported in 1904 appeared to have reinforced its position regarding the superiority of physical education over military drill and the desirability of keeping instruction firmly in the hands of its own qualified physical education teachers. However, supporters of the military training lobby were not prepared to allow the matter to rest there. They found a powerful advocate in Field Marshal Lord Roberts.

LORDS AND COMMONS DEBATE UNIVERSAL MILITARY TRAINING

The Lords' debate on Universal Military Training in February 1905 showed that many peers were in favour of military training being provided, particularly for boys still at school or in the years immediately following. Field Marshal Earl Roberts' article in the January issue of the *Nineteenth Century* was quoted by the Earl of Meath as a seminal statement:

> I maintain that it is the bounden duty of the State to see that every able-bodied man in this country, no matter to what grade of society he may belong, undergoes some kind of military training in his youth, sufficient to enable him to shoot straight and carry out simple orders if ever his services are required for national defence.

Meath suggested that an appropriate step would be for the Government to appoint a War Office and Board of Education Interdepartmental or other Committee, to consider and report on the best means of carrying such training into effect. He went on to quote from the speeches and correspondence of Lord Rosebery, Lord Methuen, Admiral Lord Charles Beresford, Major-General Sir Edmund Barrow and others, all of whom favoured that kind of training. During the course of the debate support came from the Earls of Stanhope, Egerton and Ranfurly, but Lord Balfour of Burleigh advised caution lest the military side of the question became confused with the educational side. He did not agree with the proposal to institute compulsory military training in all schools. The Under-Secretary of State for War, the Earl of Donoughmore, agreed that it was necessary to engender discipline and a spirit of patriotism, but he remained unconvinced that those ends could only be achieved through compulsory military training in schools. He had received protests from schools which did not want help from the War Office in case it led to the introduction of compulsory measures. Quite apart from these considerations the scheme was unacceptably expensive and he saw no practical point in appointing a committee to look into the question.[1]

Three days later during the motion for an address on the King's speech, a Mr Hunt (Ludlow) suggested in the Commons that as the country was set against conscription, it would be reasonable to make provision for two to three years of military discipline and training for boys before they left school.[2] For children at elementary schools who left at the earliest opportunity that would have required instruction to begin at the age of 9 or 10. Children in the northern textile districts where half-time was practised were already in receipt of an education which was considerably restricted, and the inclusion of military training would reduce it further.

RIFLE SHOOTING IN SCHOOLS

Sir Elliott Lees (Birkenhead) also helped to keep up pressure for military training. When the army estimates were debated in the Commons, he expressed regret that no provision had been made for the compulsory training of all boys in the use of the rifle.[3] He later (27 June) questioned the prime minister as to whether the Government would consider introducing training in rifle shooting through the medium of the Education Department. Balfour's reply offered no encouragement; he did not think that 'to the Education Department can properly be assigned the responsibility for providing the training which is contemplated under Lord Roberts' scheme'.[4] Would this rebuff be sufficient to deter any further efforts to commit the Board of Education to an involvement in the military training of youth? Certainly these and earlier attempts to involve the War Office and the Board of Education jointly in the matter had been, and were still, stubbornly resisted.

TRAINING THE YOUTH OF ENGLAND

There had certainly been a shift in General Lord Methuen's contribution to the debate in February of that year. In an article under the title

'Training the Youth of England' he referred to the Report of the Commission on the Militia and the Volunteers. He praised its members for supporting some form of compulsory military training even though they realized that their opinion would not be favourably received by the country at large. If no compulsory measures were likely to be implemented, it was clear to Methuen that a heavy responsibility rested on organizations such as the Lads' Drill Association and the Church Lads' Brigade. They would have to provide for the essential training of boys who did not come within the ambit of the cadet units attached to public and grammar schools.[5] He had voiced almost identical sentiments in September 1903 in the course of unveiling a Boer War commemmorative tablet in honour of 'the patriotic citizens of Bath and Somerset'.[6] Methuen envisaged the nation's youth reporting to the rifle range much as in Tudor times all able-bodied men were required to participate in archery practice, employing their leisure hours 'as valyant Englishmen ought to do'.[7] In much the same vein the Earl of Wemyss advocated that every youth should be trained in gymnastics, drill and sword-play. Almost as an afterthought he added shooting to his catalogue of martial activities, but his fellow peers may have begun to wonder for which war he was preparing![8]

THE EARL OF MEATH AND 'ANOTHER BRANCH OF KNOWLEDGE'

The case in favour of 'Universal Military Training for Lads' was presented at length by the Earl of Meath in an article thus titled, published in the *Nineteenth Century* (May 1905).[9] He claimed that: 'We know now, if we did not know before, that patriotism, plus five shillings a day, can with difficulty place in the field some 230,000 men on a distant shore.' However commendable that achievement in the past, Meath rightly argued that it was not commensurate with meeting Britain's current military requirements.

If the military training of boys was to be justified two questions had to be answered in the affirmative:

1. Is some form of universal military training necessary for the safety of the Empire?
2. Would such training given in youth be sufficient to meet the military requirements?

To the first question Meath gave an unqualified yes. Britain could not meet a major threat given her present forces, and there was no general support for conscription or for the militia ballot. Four objections to compulsory military service for adults were advanced: (a) it constituted an infringement of personal liberty; (b) it interfered with a man's industrial work; (c) it disorganized trade, commerce and agriculture by the withdrawal of labour; (d) there was a moral objection to housing large numbers of men in barracks. None of these objectives was seen to apply if the training was provided for boys in 'the educative period of their lives'. Schooling was compulsory and 'another branch of knowledge', associated with the use of the rifle, could be added to the curriculum without seeking their consent. The inadequacy of such a limited provision as handling and shooting a rifle would surely have quickly emerged, and pressure mounted for the introduction of other military skills, no more appropriate to the age and physique of the boys. Meath did not suggest what should be curtailed elsewhere in the curriculum to make way for rifle training.

In considering the second question Meath quoted Lord Roberts who, a few years earlier, had claimed that well-trained boys would probably become as efficient soldiers as Reserve men who had been absent from the Colours for three or four years. That response to the question assumed that the given alternative was itself satisfactory. Apparently the possibility of a well-paid professional force meeting requirements was not considered. In a climate where the continental conscript armies were not thought to provide an acceptable model, attention focused on the potential training opportunities which were identified within the schools.

LORD ROBERTS' APPEAL TO THE NATION

When Field Marshal Lord Roberts applied his considerable energies to the campaign to establish military training on a national basis, the movement received perhaps its greatest impetus. He wrote a long letter to *The Times* under the title 'Rifle Shooting as a National Pursuit', which constituted, he said, 'an appeal to the people of this country, urging them to take to heart the necessity for encouraging rifle shooting as a national pursuit, and establishing a system of obligatory physical training'.[10] Conscious of the inherently conservative nature of the British army and its reliance on tradition, he believed that it was essential that the whole nation should be concerned and involved in necessary army reforms. In support of this view he quoted the Report of the Royal Commission on the South African War which had stated succinctly that

The true lesson of the war, in our opinion is that no military system will be satisfactory which does not contain powers of expansion outside the limit of the regular Forces of the Army, whatever that limit may be. If the war teaches anything, it is this, that throughout the Empire, in the United Kingdom, its Colonies, and Dependencies, there is a reserve of military strength which for many reasons we cannot, and do not wish to, convert into a vast standing army, but to which we may be glad to turn again in our hour of need, as we did in 1899.

As Methuen had done before him, Roberts turned for inspiration and for an appropriate model to the days when skill with the longbow was achieved through compulsory practice at the butts. The twentieth-century parallel lay in rifle shooting being elevated to a national pursuit, along similar lines to those being pursued in a number of the colonies. Natal had already introduced military training into all her schools since the Boer War, and rifle clubs had proliferated in both Australia and Canada. Two existing organizations afforded the machinery necessary for furthering the popularity of rifle shooting: the National Rifle Association founded in 1860 'for the purpose of giving permanence to Volunteer corps, naval and military, and to encourage rifle shooting'; and the Society of Miniature Rifle Clubs (formed in 1901), the aim of which was to 'promote skill in rifle shooting amongst all classes of His Majesty's subjects by the establishment of short ranges for practice with miniature ammunition in every village, town and secondary school in Great Britain'.

Roberts looked to the lord-lieutenants of counties and to the mayors of important towns to give their support to his venture, and to smaller towns and villages to set up their local branches, so that every male in the country had a rifle range within reach of his home. He called for £100,000 to get the movement established.

Even were all that to be accomplished, Roberts believed that some form of conscription would still be necessary unless obligatory physical training and rifle practice were instituted in all schools and colleges 'and amongst the youth of the country generally' up to the age of 18. In addition to providing an efficient reserve of riflemen in case of need, he claimed that his scheme would 'greatly tend to increase the intelligence of the masses, develop their physique, and inculcate habits of order and discipline'.

The Times said that it would be a national disgrace if the appeal was ignored,[11] and Sir Arthur Conan Doyle (who had served in the Boer War)

122

wrote in support, calling for a law to compel every parish council to establish a rifle club and to have the power to raise the necessary money by a levy on rate-payers.[12]

Lord Raglan, President of the National Service League, echoed the complaint made by Roberts in a Lords' debate on 10 July, that the nation had already forgotten the lessons of the South African War, and that the armed forces were as unprepared as they had been in 1900.[13] The National Service League had in fact anticipated Roberts' appeal by arranging a series of five lectures in the spring of 1905 at Caxton Hall on various aspects of universal naval and military training. By the following February it had Lord Roberts, then its president, enunciating the objects of the League which, not unnaturally, bore a close resemblance to the sentiments expressed in his letter to *The Times* of 12 June 1905. Again, the absolute necessity of instilling into boys a spirit of patriotism and a sense of duty were stressed, as were the inclusion of 'universal physical training of a military character, and instruction in the use of the rifle' in the curriculum of all boys' schools. This was to be followed by further training in cadet corps, boys' brigades, etc., up to the age of 18 years, under state supervision. Roberts now made it quite clear that he required the injection of a military character into such exercises.

THE NATIONAL LEAGUE FOR PHYSICAL EDUCATION AND IMPROVEMENT

Sir Lauder Brunton's concern as to the health of the nation (see Chapter 7), finally bore fruit with the setting up of a National League for Physical Education and Improvement. The inauguration ceremony was held on 28 June 1905, at the Mansion House. It was intended that the movement should be non-political and non-denominational in character, and should seek to attain the following broad objectives:

1. To stimulate public interest in the Physical Condition of the People throughout the Kingdom.
2. To establish close Association and Centralisation of all Societies and individuals trying to combat such influences as tend to produce National Physical Deterioration.
3. To aid existing Organizations.
4. To start Organizations for Physical Health and well-being wherever none exists.

The provisional Executive Council had the Bishop of Ripon as its chairman, and included among its impressive membership the Bishops of Bristol and Hereford; Commissioner T. H. Howard of the Salvation Army; Major-General Sir Frederick Maurice; the Rt Hon. Sir J. E. Gorst; T. J. Macnamara MP; the Revd Edmond Warre, headmaster of Eton; the Lord Mayor of London; E. H. Pooley, late Secretary to the Departmental Committee on Physical Deterioration; Sir Lauder Brunton himself; and a number of eminent medical men.[14]

OFFICIAL SUPPORT FOR ORGANIZED GAMES

A significant advance in terms of regulatory codes was struck in 1905 when the 1905 Code of Regulations was accompanied by a *Handbook of Suggestions for the Consideration of Teachers and Others Concerned in the Work of Public Elementary Schools*. Its most noteworthy quality was that, for the first time, elementary school teachers were offered suggestions for their consideration rather than instructions for them to obey. However, they were reminded that the freedom they were now to enjoy carried with it an implied responsibility in its use. The *Handbook of Suggestions* encouraged the inclusion of organized games in elementary schools in the interests of '*esprit de corps*, readiness to endure fatigue, to submit to discipline, and to subordinate one's own powers and wishes to a common end'. It recommended football and cricket teams, swimming clubs and cadet corps as the means by which those qualities could be promoted, and did not envisage any imbalance in the curriculum as a consequence.[15]

Support for the acceptance of organized games has to be measured alongside the persistent encouragement of military drill by its supporters. If the latter had the more vociferous and strident advocacy among its adherents, the former enjoyed the steady, if low key, support of the Board of Education, and of progressive educationalists, including J. W. Martin, whose Fabian tract of 1894 has already been referred to. Martin had written hopefully of the time when such provisions as organized games and swimming would be commonplace for elementary schoolchildren, and other activities opened up to them. Steps were being taken towards meeting his aspirations.

Inevitably there would be those who would seize upon the opportunities for accentuating the disciplinary aspects of organized games, while others would be concerned with a more broadly based educative programme; most teachers probably fell somewhere between these two positions. If the West Riding decision to limit such teaching to half an hour per week was at all common, it would suggest that LEAs were only prepared to proceed cautiously in that area.

INFANTS AND THE NEED TO EXCLUDE MILITARY INFLUENCE

The particular needs of very young children and of girls were likely to receive scant attention so long as women were largely excluded from positions of authority and from policy-making bodies within the education service. Katharine Bathurst, one of only ten women inspectors at the Board of Education, pressed for better provision for the under-5s and for girls' education. A contribution to *The Nineteenth Century and After* in May 1905 on 'The Need for National Nurseries' deplored the drills commonly practised in infants' schools. Harassed teachers trying to cope with classes of 60 tired 'babies' adopted some sort of drill which she described as taking the following form: 'Fold arms – Sit up – eyes on ceiling (all heads are raised) – Eyes on floor (all heads are bent) – Eyes to the right – Eyes to the left – Eyes on blackboard – Eyes on me (all the sixty baby heads are wagged in unison).' She described paper-folding exercises, and needle-threading, when ten, 15 or even 20 minutes were spent in threading bodkin-sized needles. 'The discipline', she observed, 'is military rather than maternal, and can only be maintained at the expense of much healthy, valuable, and, as far as the children are concerned, necessary freedom.'[16] The philosophy of the *Handbook of Suggestions* would take time to be assimilated within the teaching profession. In the meantime there was a rigidity in practice and in discipline which often appeared closer to the military drill which had been progressively eased out in favour of physical exercises and games. The drills which Katharine Bathurst described in graphic fashion would have been welcomed by those who believed that as early a start as possible should be made if a disciplined adult population was required to answer external military threats.

A NATION IN ARMS

In July 1905 Roberts attended the annual meeting of the Lads' Drill Association, when the question of the recognition of non-uniformed brigades by the War Office was again raised. Following discussion, it was agreed to make a further approach to the War Office on the matter. Roberts was much in demand as a public speaker and as guest of honour at various rifle club meetings, but he must have been greatly disappointed at the level of response to his appeal for £100,000 to launch rifle shooting as a national pastime; in the first four months following his appeal no more than £1,000 had been contributed. Rifle clubs, however, were certainly gaining in popularity; 659 clubs had affiliated to the National Rifle Association since 1900, and membership stood at some 40,000–50,000.[17]

A *Times* correspondent (24 August 1905) suggested that those who favoured the concept of 'a nation in arms' could find a sound basis for it through the compulsory provision of military training in schools.[18] Having read that article, Major-General Sir Alec B. Tulloch subsequently wrote to say how impressed he had been by the military training of lads such as he had witnessed in the State of Victoria, Australia. On his return home to England he obtained permission to employ the local Volunteer drill sergeant for £1 a month, and set him to drill 40 local schoolboys twice a week. He bought 50 out-of-date Martini-Henry carbines at 2s each and had arms racks installed in the schoolroom. The cost of this initiative he estimated at less than twopence a boy per week.[19] Independent action of that kind appeared to be by no means uncommon, judging by the evidence reported in parliament and in the national press. To its critics it would be condemned as high handed; its success would depend on the composition of the managing body of the school, and the extent to which there were opportunities for opposing voices to be heard.

LOCAL INITIATIVES

Towards the end of 1905 *The Times* reported a number of initiatives. The Newlands Corner, Guildford Branch of the Victoria League arranged for boys attending local village schools to get weekly instruction and practice in rifle shooting on a club range;[20] the Revd T. G. Wilson announced that he had enrolled 200 lads in his 'hooligan' class at Plaistow, where they received training in drill, miniature rifle shooting and camp life; and Mr H. C. Davis set up the City of London Boys' County Camp for lads in the 14–18 age group to receive discipline, drill and shooting practice.[21] In Surrey, the Earl of Meath presented a miniature rifle, cartridges and targets to the headmaster of his local village school. He said that as a reward, the boy making the highest score was allowed to take his target home, where it was often placed on the mantelpiece by a proud mother.[22]

Ever anxious to exert pressure in high quarters, Meath sent a copy of

Field Marshal Earl Roberts' appeal to the nation, *Defence of the Empire*, to Arnold-Forster, who had replaced St John Brodrick at the War Office in October 1903. In reply he received a letter which must have given him some satisfaction: 'I am entirely in sympathy with your efforts to drill and discipline as many boys as possible; the more drill, and certainly the more discipline the people of this country get, the better.'[23]

An interesting example of collective lobbying in favour of the inclusion of military drill and the use of the rifle within the context of the school curriculum was made by the Justices of the Peace in the county of Cheshire. They memorialized the Lord President of the Council, Lord Londonderry, to that effect, suggesting that the cost should be met by the Exchequer. Lord Londonderry replied that while he supported their advocacy of rifle shooting, he considered that statutory steps would be possible only when voluntary efforts had proved to be successful.[24] His response was perhaps a predictable one, certainly there were many precedents for it.

The year ended as it had begun, on a martial note. The military training lobby had enjoyed considerable publicity, largely stimulated by the forthright statements of Lord Roberts. Support for rifle shooting and military drill had been forthcoming both in the Commons and the Lords, and among influential individuals and associations. But it was also the year of the *Handbook of Suggestions*, a noteworthy publication by the Board of Education intended to assist in encouraging teachers to adopt good educational practice rather than imposing directives through its annual codes. With the resignation of Balfour in December, the year also concluded with the prospect of a change of government, as ten years of Unionist administration, under Salisbury and subsequently under Balfour, came to an end.

NOTES

1. *House of Lords Debates*, Fourth Series, Vol. CXLI, cols 543–63 (20 February 1905).
2. *House of Commons Debates*, Fourth Series, Vol. CXLI, col. 1163 (23 February 1905).
3. Ibid., Vol. CXLIII, cols 1809–10 (30 March 1905).
4. Ibid., Vol. CXLVIII, col. 232 (27 June 1905).
5. Lord Methuen, 'Training the Youth of England', *The Nineteenth Century and After* (February 1905): 238–43.
6. *The Times* (26 September 1903): 6.
7. *The Nineteenth Century and After* (February 1905): 243.
8. *House of Lords Debates*, Fourth Series, Vol. CL, col. 740 (28 July 1905), 'Organization for War'.
9. Earl of Meath, 'Universal Military Training for Lads', *The Nineteenth Century and After* (May 1905): 734–44.
10. *The Times* (12 June 1905): 6.

11. Ibid. (12 June 1905): 7.
12. Ibid. (14 June 1905): 12. Conan Doyle served for a short time as a doctor in the Boer War.
13. Ibid. (13 July 1905): 10.
14. Sir Lauder Brunton, *Collected Papers on Physical and Military Training*, 21 (published privately, n.d., but probably 1915).
15. *Handbook of Suggestions for the Consideration of Teachers and Others Concerned in the Work of Public Elementary Schools* (1905).
16. Katharine Bathurst, 'The Need for National Nurseries', *The Nineteenth Century and After* (May 1905): 818–24.
17. *The Times* (6 November 1905): 7.
18. Ibid. (24 August 1905): 6.
19. Ibid. (8 September 1905): 10. See, below, Appendix C for similarities between the English Model Course and Australian practice.
20. *The Times* (10 October 1905): 7. The Victoria League was founded in 1901 specifically to educate the general public, including children of school age, into an acceptance of Britain's imperial role and an awareness of its significance to her survival as a leading political and economic power.
21. Ibid. (13 October 1905): 7.
22. Ibid. (1 December 1905): 3. With such a prominent local patron a school would have found it difficult not to accept his proposals.
23. *The Times* (26 October 1905): 4.
24. Ibid. (21 November 1905): 6.

9

Rifle Shooting Experiments, 1906–08

The Liberal Government formed at the end of 1905 under Campbell-Bannerman's leadership had Grey at the Foreign Office, Haldane at the War Office and Birrell at the Board of Education. The infant Labour Party had 50 seats, and John Burns became the first representative of the working classes to hold a Cabinet post, that of Minister for the Local Government Board.

THE REVD J. P. WAY ON 'MILITARY TRAINING'

Pressure for the extension of military training in schools continued. The Revd J. P. Way, headmaster of Rossall, contributed a chapter on 'Military Training' to a newly published book, *The Public Schools from Within*. He voiced the opinion of many of his colleagues when he claimed that it was a matter of vital importance to establish some universal system of military training, compulsory if possible, but at the very least, comprehensive. He wrote: 'The voluntary submission to a sound military training, as a duty, for the good of one's country and the defence of those near and dear, may indeed be said to lay a sound foundation for the finest type of Christian manliness.'[1] Clearly the Victorian concept of muscular Christianity lived on. Way looked forward to the day when the Board of Education would require military training as an essential ingredient in every boy's physical education, when the War Office would provide the necessary arms and ammunition, and the Government would use its powers to compel the provision of rifle ranges. This expectation was without foundation; the Board of Education had stated and restated its position on many occasions, and at no time in recent years had it strayed from its belief that physical training should be non-military. Neither was it likely that a Liberal President of the Board would venture to undermine the policy of his Conservative predecessors in that respect. An administration which

129

saw itself as a reforming body would not wish to divert monies from its social programmes to support or require the provision of rifle ranges. What Haldane would include in his army reform measures remained to be seen, but he would surely hesitate to intrude into the affairs of a sister department. The Revd J. P. Way's contribution to the debate was hopeful, even fanciful, given the situation.

NORTH OF ENGLAND EDUCATION CONFERENCE

The *School Government Chronicle* of 13 January 1906 reported the North of England Education Conference held in Newcastle upon Tyne which provided a platform for both physical and military drill to be debated. Captain H. Worsley-Gough, ex-army and currently an examiner in physical exercises for the local Education Committee, commended the practice of military drill on the grounds of its physical value. His view was supported by another speaker, Captain F. C. Garrett of Armstrong College, who said that he would like to see every boy familiar with the rifle. He suggested that games might be harmful through the mental strain they imposed on boys, whereas military drill provided bodily exercise while 'sparing the brain'. Other contributors to the debate followed similar lines; only one, Dr Ethel Williams, a member of the local Education Committee, took a different stance. She claimed that too much was made of military smartness in such drill as she observed, and children would be better served with simple exercise drill. The bias in favour of military training of the young by those who addressed the conference was marked.

On 27 February a deputation from the National League for Physical Education and Improvement waited upon Birrell at the Board of Education to urge the implementation of the recommendations of the Scottish Royal Commission on Physical Training, of the Physical Deterioration Committee and of other interdepartmental committees. Particular attention was drawn to physical training and to the recommendation of the Physical Deterioration Committee that compulsory evening continuation classes should provide drill and physical exercises for boys. To the various observations brought to his notice, Birrell expressed his general sympathy.[2] Such pressure indicates that Sir Lauder Brunton was determined to keep the issue of physical education at a high profile even if he did not feel it expedient to advance the arguments for military drill at that time. As we have already seen, he was conscious of the pejorative nature of the term.

PROPOSED PARLIAMENTARY GROUP TO PRESS FOR ARMY REFORMS

In February *The Times* reported that 75 MPs, drawn from the Liberal, Conservative and Labour parties, had signed an undertaking to support a new parliamentary group to press for army reforms, and had pledged themselves

> [conditionally on there being no conscription and no compulsory military service] to do all that they reasonably can to support the policy advocated by Lord Roberts, and to press especially on the consideration of the Government their conviction 'that it is the bounden duty of the State to see that every able-bodied youth should be taught to shoot straight and to obey the simple word of command'.[3]

It was expressly hoped that a system of military training in the schools would be given early and serious attention by the President of the Board of Education and by the Secretary of State for War, acting both jointly and separately. Despite previous failures to associate the two departments in furthering this concern MPs persisted in their endeavours to bring it about.

A few days later Roberts issued a statement as President of the National Service League, in which he called for teachers to instil into all boys a spirit of patriotism and duty, and for the inclusion in the curriculum of all schools a system of universal physical training of a military character and instruction in the use of the rifle.[4]

THE NATIONAL SERVICE LEAGUE AND THE LADS' DRILL
ASSOCIATION

The Lads' Drill Association met in March to consider the question of amalgamation with the National Service League along lines suggested by the Earl of Meath. Although he was not able to convince Lord Methuen, the proposal was carried by 12 votes, with two dissensions.[5] No doubt Meath considered that a stronger case for military training could be pressed by the two bodies acting in concert rather than independently. At the fourth annual general meeting of the National Service League in June it was announced that membership had nearly doubled during the year,[6] while an October meeting, which acknowledged the incorporation of the Lads' Drill Association, passed resolutions in support of rifle shooting and military exercises for boys in the context of a universal system of training.[7]

During the course of the army recruiting debate in May, Captain Kincaid Smith (Stratford-on-Avon) called for an amendment (not proceeded upon)[8] in favour of the introduction of military drill into the nation's schools. 'What harm could it do to a boy', he asked, 'to be able to walk straight and handle a rifle?' In the Lords, too, the army debates provided opportunities for pressing the case for 'the training of youth in military matters during the educative period of their lives'.[9]

APPLICATIONS TO TEACH RIFLE SHOOTING

It is pertinent at this point to show how the Board of Education responded when formal applications for permission to teach rifle shooting in schools were received. What appeared to be the first such request to be considered by Birrell came from the British School[10] at Bushey in Hertfordshire, a non-denominational school which submitted its application to the Hertfordshire County Education Committee who, in turn, forwarded it to the Board with the Committee's support in March 1906. Both Birrell and his advisers considered that the request was ill judged, both because of its unsuitability for children of elementary school age and because it did not constitute a good means of physical exercise. However, in view of the strong support from the County Education Authority and from local individuals, Birrell decided to allow rifle shooting to be taught on an experimental basis for the duration of the current school year. After that time he would give a definite decision. Three conditions were imposed: (1) it should not encroach upon the time required for proper physical exercises; (2) it should be restricted to boys who were physically fit and who had reached the age of 12; and (3) an appropriate syllabus should be submitted for approval by the Board. The cost of the experiment, estimated by the school managers to be £20 for the year, was to be met from endowment income.

This reluctantly granted permission was to cause further discomfort to the President of the Board of Education on 29 October 1906, when the Labour MP Philip Snowden asked what applications for the teaching of rifle shooting had been received and what decisions had been made. Birrell must have realized from the generalized form of the question that the questioner was not only interested in the permission granted to the Bushey school. He responded by outlining the course of action taken by him in respect of the British School at Bushey, adding that he had intended that the experiment should be confined to that school. Owing to some misunderstanding of his intentions, the Board had given similar permission to four other schools: St Wilfred's National School in Haywards Heath (East Sussex); Overbury National School (Worcestershire); Shoreham Council School (Kent); and Eynsford National School (Kent). Birrell assured the House that no further applications would be considered. The Bushey school was meeting the cost of its experiment from endowment funds, and a similar possibility may have been open to the National schools; however, Kent Education Committee made it clear that Eynsford would have to seek voluntary contributions to meet the cost. Shoreham Council School was in a different category, and one is left to wonder how it met its financial commitment. When the question of rifle shooting was first raised in Kent in July 1906 the recommendation to the Committee added that any cost should be defrayed by public subscription, and the Committee probably pursued the matter on that basis.

In answer to a question from W. R. Cremer MP, the President of the Board said:

> Rifle shooting was not regarded by the Board of Education as a necessary part of physical training, neither did the Board consider it necessary for the purpose of national defence. He was not aware of any new danger confronting the country rendering necessary increased preparations for defence in Elementary Schools, and the Board of Education was not to become a preparatory training authority and auxiliary of the Army.[11]

Cremer was Secretary of the International Arbitration League, and it was in that capacity that he had already approached Birrell. He submitted a resolution adopted by the League on 26 October, which read:

> The council of the League has seen, with deep regret, reports stating that the President of the Board of Education has sanctioned the teaching of rifle shooting in the village school of Eynsford. The council sincerely hopes that the statement is not true, and that a progressive Government does not intend to authorise or permit, for the first time, boys in State-aided schools to be instructed in the art of shooting and killing. The council is strong in the belief that the supreme object in education is to develop the moral and intellectual attributes, and, as far as possible, subdue the animal instincts, but to teach boys the art of killing under the pretext that it is necessary for purposes of defence is calculated to brutalise our youths by developing a fighting instinct and strengthening their combative natures.[12]

By associating 'the art of shooting and killing' the resolution made clear that the former could not be embraced without considering the inherent implications. Few had spelled it out so forcefully.

An indication of what was to be taught under a rifle shooting scheme appeared in the submission made on behalf of the Shoreham Council School in Kent. The instruction was to comprise:

1. construction of different parts of the rifle;
2. sight and sighting;
3. position of the body;
4. holding the rifle;
5. aim and pull off without cartridge;
6. target practice with cartridge.[13]

The Eynsford National School scheme was similar, but was prefaced by lessons in the duties of citizenship and the advantages of learning to shoot with a rifle. The Board of Education's response to the Kent Education Authority intimated that its agreement to the experimental period was reluctantly granted. It stipulated that the definite consent of parents or guardians be obtained prior to any boy participating in the rifle shooting class. The introductory lessons in citizenship, etc., contained in the Eynsford proposal, were also deleted as being *extraneous* to the course; citizenship belonging elsewhere in the school curriculum. This latter decision effectively isolated the rifle shooting classes from the remainder of the curriculum, rendering the Board's eventual decision a straightforward one on a clear issue.

On 25 October J. Ward MP tabled a parliamentary question as to whether the President of the Board of Education could comment on the statement by the Chairman of the Birmingham Small Arms Company (BSA) to the effect that the Government had adopted a miniature rifle for use in schools and that deliveries of these would shortly begin. Mr Birrell denied knowledge of the statement, assuring his questioner that as far as elementary schools were concerned the claim was without foundation, although he could not answer for what was being done by public secondary school authorities. Dr McNamara MP expressed his concern at the safety factor in respect of the use of rifles by schoolboys, referring to 'at least one fatal accident'. Birrell was sorry to learn of a fatality but suggested that accidents also arose from chemistry experiments. No further light was thrown on the alleged death.[14]

Further questioning on 30 October sought to establish whether any petitions with respect to rifle shooting had been submitted to the previous administration and refused. Birrell's reply suggested that none had been made, but his enquiries had shown that two applications had been received by the Board in 1901: one from Manningtree National School in Essex and the other from Kimblesworth Colliery School in Durham. Both applications had been refused.[15] He reminded his fellow MPs that those applications had been made before the setting up of Local Authorities to represent the views of rate-payers.

USE OF SCHOOL PREMISES

The use of school premises was, at times, an embarrassing matter for the Board of Education. During school hours responsibility lay with the Board, but at other times with the Local Authority. Thus it was all too easy for it to appear that the Board of Education favoured certain initiatives undertaken on school premises when the reality was that it was neither involved nor responsible. This was indeed so in respect of the London Schools' Recreation Guild and also in the activities of the rifle corps or club at Galley's Field Upper Standard School in Hartlepool. Sir Harry Vincent, a persistent advocate of military training in schools, asked Birrell on 14 November if his attention had been drawn to the work of the shooting club of the London Schools' Recreation Guild.[16] After drawing on the examples afforded by the cadet movement in the dominions, he asked if the President would 'enable the British boys to keep pace with their comrades in the colonies' by authorizing such clubs in state-aided schools, subject to parental approval and proper supervision of shooting ranges. Birrell replied that the School Guild's shooting clubs operated wholly outside school hours and were not part of the public elementary schools as such at all.[17] He was not prepared to be drawn into any further discussion.

CRITICISM OF RIFLE SHOOTING AT GALLEY'S FIELD UPPER STANDARD SCHOOL

Reginald McKenna succeeded Birrell on 23 January 1907, and he was the target for Mr Summerbell MP in April of that year when attention was drawn to the situation at Galley's Field Upper Standard School in Hartlepool. McKenna was asked whether the Board was in favour of rifle corps attached to elementary schools and whether inspectors had been instructed to suggest to headmasters that they should use their

135

influence to persuade boys to join such corps. In particular, he wondered whether the Board of Education was aware of the situation in the Hartlepool school where, he claimed, targets were openly displayed within the building. It was also asserted that boys were taken out of school for sighting and shooting practice on the range before the official end of the session, and that some boys had been reprimanded for absence from that instruction.

McKenna replied that no such instructions had been given to the inspectorate and that he would investigate the other allegations.[18] A week later he assured T. Summerbell that while enquiries showed that targets had been displayed in corridors but not in classrooms, no instruction had been given in school hours, and no boys had been reprimanded for absence from rifle shooting practice. Summerbell's response to this statement showed that he was not satisfied with the answers to his questions, but there the matter was allowed to rest.[19]

SCHOOL RIFLE ASSOCIATION IN LEWISHAM

Similar concerns to those raised by Summerbell formed the basis of a question in the Commons on 6 May, when W. P. Byles asked whether the position regarding rifle shooting and military drill in public elementary schools remained as stated by Birrell the previous October. On being informed that there was no change, Byles asked whether the President of the Board of Education was aware of the formation of a School Rifle Association in the Metropolitan Borough of Lewisham. He claimed that 40 of the 43 elementary schools, with a total population of some 2,600 boys, had joined, and that all those boys over the age of 12 were required to shoot with miniature rifles. Specifically he asked: 'Will he [McKenna] say whether these pupils are instructed in the art and inculcated with the duty of killing their fellow men; and whether the cost of such instruction, or any part of it, falls upon the public.' McKenna admitted that he knew of the formation of the Association but had no details of its membership. All he could say was that none of the instruction was given during school hours or at public expense.[20]

THE BOARD OF EDUCATION'S DECISION ON RIFLE SHOOTING EXPERIMENT

At the conclusion of the school year in July 1907 the Board of Education made known its decision on the experimental period of rifle shooting in

136

a limited number of schools. Letters were sent to the local authorities concerned informing them that in the opinion of the Board rifle shooting was inappropriate for elementary schools and that when the experimental period came to an end such instruction should cease.[21]

The managers of the St Wilfred's National School at Haywards Heath, East Sussex, refused to be diverted from their support of rifle shooting by the Board's termination of the agreement by which shooting was permitted. A *Times* correspondent in October 1908 reported that arrangements had been made whereby boys were taken to the firing range by assistant masters after school hours on one day a week. While regretting the withdrawal of official sanction, the managers saw some advantage in the revised organization which no longer had to be accommodated to the school timetable. The boys were also able to spend more time on rifle practice.[22]

OPPOSITION TO MILITARY TRAINING OF THE YOUNG

The Board of Education had been assailed from both sides over the highly controversial issue of military training and, in particular, of rifle shooting in public elementary schools. By the summer of 1907 it had emerged from the fray clearly on the side of those who did not wish to see any overt militarism practised in the nation's elementary schools. Opponents of military training in schools had included members of education committees, MPs, parents, trade unionists and pacifists. At its annual meeting in September 1906, the TUC made an emphatic protest against increases in armaments, and the 'insidious attempts' to introduce conscription or some other form of military service, which it saw as threats both to the interests of the working classes and to world peace.[23] A more direct attack appeared in *The Worker*, issued by the Huddersfield Socialist Party in July 1906. It deplored the speech by Lord Roberts, in which he had pressed for the compulsory military training of children:

> It is not because there is any immediate danger of a European conflagration. Indeed, if there was, the little children, whom it is intended to train in the use of arms, would not be of much value to us as a fighting force. The real reason for these alarmist speeches lies in the desire to cultivate a martial spirit amongst the populace. A peace-loving nation is not desired by the class that needs the 'minions of the law' to repress any attempt to undermine its privileges. ... Militarism never has brought, and never will bring,

permanent advantage to any people. It is a poisonous weed having its roots in a pool of lust and evil desire. It develops the worst part of men's natures ... It encourages brutality ...[24]

With hindsight it could be argued that if a war might be anticipated as having a likely duration of four or five years then the preliminary training of older school children might have some military potential. However, that was not the view of Europe's military leaders; they were preparing for a short, if brutal, engagement of mass armies. The possible need to make good manpower losses of frightening proportions was probably not prominent in their calculations. The writer's claim that the underlying intention of the militarist lobby was to inculcate a martial spirit in the young appears to be a more accurate assessment of the situation.

A WOMAN'S PROPOSAL

A contrary point of view to the above was advanced in 'An Appeal to the Women of England', a letter to *The Times* a week later. Mrs Gertrude Silver called on women to play their part in England's effort to attain national military efficiency. First of their chosen tasks was

> To encourage and induce the boys of every family and of every class to learn to drill and to shoot; by this means cultivating a better understanding of their military duties towards their country, and at the same time improving their physical condition and giving them early lessons in discipline that will later in life help them to govern themselves and others ...[25]

She elaborated a scheme whereby the country would be divided into districts, each of which would be watched over by a woman. However, subsequent issues of *The Times* failed to suggest that there was any response to her proposals, either by women or men. In general women displayed little inclination to write in support of military training of boys, and it was only when occupying some position in school management or training, or in the field of health that they were prompted to participate in the debate, and then it was usually to oppose such instruction.

Katharine Bathurst turned her attention to girls' physical education in May 1905 through an article in *The Nineteenth Century and After* with the title 'The Physique of Girls'. She began with an expression of thankfulness that a more sensible drill handbook had recently been issued which no longer required teachers, 'including old men and maidens, married women and spinsters', to be taught to form squares and 'to perform other feats drawn from a military source' by drill sergeants from local barracks. But, she complained, 'Even nuns and sisters of mercy were not excepted from the general pressure.' Within the previous three years she reported having witnessed more than one infant class where 3- to 5-year-old children were practising exercises considered appropriate for army recruits. 'Three ounce dumb-bells were provided for three year olds and six ounce ones for six year olds – a manifestly mad practice.' At a mixed school in Oxfordshire she had been greeted with a military salute by all the little girls. All too often the age and sex of pupils were ignored when the drill enthusiasts were allowed their head. She reminded her readers that two-thirds of the children in elementary schools were girls or infants, and that the number of women teachers far exceeded that of their male colleagues. Women teachers, she maintained firmly, should be trained by women specialists, and little girls should not be drilled by men. In 1904 Katharine Bathurst had submitted a report to the Board of Education with respect to the drilling by a sergeant instructor of a class of girls at a pupil teachers' centre. The exercises were being performed at a very fast pace and the Inspector was alarmed to discover from subsequent discussion with the girls that most of them were wearing stays (probably not of pliable whalebone but of material which could easily splinter) under their gym dresses. She claimed that the practice might have led to 'terrible accidents' had any stays broken while the girls were vigorously lunging forwards or backwards.[26] Her warnings with respect to both infants and girls were certainly necessary in a male-dominated society, where insufficient attention was paid to the knowledge and expertise of women.

THE MEDICAL DEPARTMENT OF THE BOARD OF EDUCATION

Two acts in 1906 and 1907 were to pave the way for further progress. A TUC-sponsored Bill 'to promote the Improvement of Education and the Physique of Children attending Elementary Schools' in 1906 foundered, but co-operation between the Liberal Government and the 29 Labour MPs ensured that a subsequent measure to make provision for *Meals for Children attending Public Elementary Schools in England, Wales and Scotland* was enacted. In 1907 the Education (Administrative

Provisions) Act empowered LEAs 'to make such arrangements as may be sanctioned by the Board of Education for attending to the health and physical condition of children in Public Elementary Schools'. Under the powers conferred by the Act, Dr (later Sir) George Newman was appointed as the Board of Education's first Chief Medical Officer. The Medical Department of the Board of Education set up that year under Dr Newman gave him general oversight of physical training in addition to his medical responsibilities. Perhaps Newman's outstanding contribution to the general improvement of the physical condition of children of school age was his insistence that regular physical examinations should be conducted and accurate records kept of children's condition and progress. His annual reports were to draw attention consistently to child health as a major factor contributing to the general well-being of the whole nation.[27]

A PHYSICAL TRAINING INSPECTORATE

Miss L. M. Rendell was appointed in 1908 as the first woman inspector to supervise physical exercises. Lieutenant-Commander F. H. Grenfell RN succeeded Colonel Malcolm Fox, and Mr Veysey and Miss Koetter were also appointed. These four specialists formed a physical training inspectorate, touring the country and organizing demonstrations of physical training for the benefit of teachers.

LORD ROBERTS' CAMPAIGN AND THE LADIES

When Lord Roberts presided over the annual meeting of the Society of Miniature Rifle Clubs at the end of July 1906 he commented favourably on the presence of women among the competitors. He was, he claimed, 'a great believer in ladies taking an interest in rifle-shooting, for they could do a great deal towards inducing men to take an interest in rifle-shooting also'.[28] It was left for the Duke of Argyll to suggest that the boys' sisters might shame them into learning how to shoot! That he did when he accompanied Princess Louise as she formally opened the Girls' High School in Leeds in October 1906. Responding on her behalf to a vote of thanks for her presence on that occasion, the Duke commented on the school premises and equipment, adding that one thing he had not seen was a shooting gallery. If the country failed to take up Lord Roberts' proposals for universal military training of the young it would fall upon the girls to make the boys ashamed of themselves by insisting on having a shooting gallery and becoming better shots than the boys. If the girls only did that they would be of great assistance to Lord Roberts, who was seeking to make the boys fit to use the rifle on proper occasions.[29]

His gallantry to the young ladies was greeted with laughter, but the 'seed-sowing' exercise was almost certainly more than just a spontaneous and amusing pleasantry.

A BOYS' BISLEY

To provide opportunities for schoolboys in non-uniformed corps to compete in rifle shooting at a national level Major-General Lord Cheylesmore suggested that a 'Boys' Bisley' might be organized to follow the annual Bisley meeting of the National Rifle Association. What *The Times* described as 'a modest beginning' was made in July 1906, when 29 masters accompanied 339 boys from public and grammar schools for a week's camp at Bisley. An average of over 50 rounds of ammunition was fired by each boy on the ranges.[30] On an adjacent site was located the camp of the London Schools Recreation Guild, comprising about 170 boys. This number included a small group sent by the Earl of Meath and about 30 Jewish boys, for whom special catering provision was necessary. Lord Roberts visited both camps, pausing to remind the boys of the Recreation Guild that it was their duty to prepare to defend their country or any part of the empire.[31] A year later the Schoolboys' Bisley attracted nearly 600 boys accompanied by 47 masters. Some 150 young marksmen of the London Schools Recreation Guild also attended, having previously attended a special service in the crypt of St Paul's Cathedral before leaving the city for Bisley.[32]

ARMY REFORMS

When R. B. Haldane presented his first army estimates in March 1906, he hinted that he wished to introduce reforms which would effect reductions in both men and money, but which would provide also a more homogeneous structure. It was his intention to incorporate the uniformed youth movements into recognized cadet units affiliated to, and feeding, local volunteer Territorial forces. During the report stage of the Territorial and Reserve Forces Bill in June 1907 the question was debated as to the lowest age at which a person might qualify for parliamentary funds payable to a Territorial Association. An attempt to remove the age limit of 16 years was narrowly lost (104 votes to 114). In his defence of the Bill as it stood, Haldane held firmly to his view that as War Minister his concern was with the reorganization of the British army and not with training in elementary schools. Boys in units attached to the latter were not of an age to contribute to the officer reserve he wished to establish, nor to the training programmes within the Territorial Forces. An exception was made in respect of the cadet corps of public (independent) schools, which he continued to draw on for his officer reserve. So far as juveniles were concerned: 'The duty of developing military training in Elementary Schools was one which he declined to assume. It came wholly within the region of education, and to that region he left it.'[33] Anyone looking to Haldane for encouragement of military training in the elementary school sector was thus likely to be disappointed. Since the Board of Education was not prepared to support it, his comments confirmed that any attempts to develop such training in the elementary schools would have to be on a spare-time, financially self-supporting basis, with no official encouragement. The use of school premises for these out-of-school activities led to some misunderstandings regarding the possible assumption that the Board of Education or the school authorities had done more than permit the use of the premises by other organizations. Haldane himself was not averse to attending an activity of this voluntary kind, as when he began 1908 by scoring a bull's-eye on the new miniature rifle-range he opened at the Jews' Free School in London. The range was intended to cater for the 1,500 London members of the Jewish Lads' Brigade, then numbering some 4,000 cadets in all.[34]

'THE SOBER JUDGMENT OF BRITISH WORKING MEN'

The attention of members attending the Incorporated Association of Assistant Masters in Secondary Schools in September 1907 was drawn to the TUC meeting at Bath earlier that month when a Mr Appleton, in moving a resolution against conscription and compulsory military training, said that trade unionists did not want to get the parson out of the schools in order to get the soldier in. The resolution was passed with only one dissension. The IAAM hoped that such remarks did not represent the 'sober judgment of British working men'.[35] Ostensibly, delegates to the Congress were concerned at the injurious effects of military training policies through 'the removal of young men from their trades and occupations at that time of life when excellence in craftsmanship is most easily obtainable';[36] however, the IAAM would have found the TUC and its membership equally resolute in a stand against such training beginning while boys were still at school.

SURREY, DERBY AND LIVERPOOL CONSIDER THEIR POSITIONS

Authorities around the country were being called upon to consider the matter of military training and rifle shooting provision for boys of school age. In Surrey a Joint Committee was appointed by the Quarter Sessions and the County Council to consider these questions with respect to schools in receipt of grants from public funds, and to consider what encouragement, if any, should be accorded to rifle clubs and rifle shooting generally in the county. Nearly 41,000 in the county's elementary schools were affected at that time or in the near future; of that number 8,607 boys between the ages of 12 and 15, and 17 over the latter age were affected immediately. There were also 2,447 boys and young men in the evening continuation schools of the county, of whom about half were affected; the remainder, who were over the age of 17, were eligible for the Volunteer corps. Three of the authority's elementary schools provided instruction in rifle shooting for older pupils with the cost met by private subscriptions. The Joint Committee decided against the recognition of military drill and rifle shooting as part of the elementary school curriculum, being satisfied that the existing physical training was 'well adapted to cultivate a proper tone of discipline and alertness'. It saw no objection to military drill and rifle shooting being included in the curricula of evening continuation schools and in rate-aided secondary schools, and recommended that financial support should be available to such schools as set up cadet corps. Strong support was given to the establishment of rifle clubs, and it was recommended that a county committee be formed under the leadership of the Lord Lieutenant and the High Sheriff of the County.[37] This review of the situation in the county is interesting in that there is a comprehensive approach to the issue covering the elementary schools, the evening continuation schools and the secondary schools. The elementary schools apart, the county was set to give every encouragement to drill and rifle shooting. A resolution couched in strong terms was moved by a councillor at a meeting of Derby Education Committee in September 1907. It informed the headmasters of its elementary schools that the

Committee 'forbade discussion or encouragement of rifle shooting on school premises'. This was opposed by an alderman who thought the proposal narrow-minded, toned down by the Mayor who suggested the matter be left to the discretion of individual headmasters, and eventually carried with the substitution of the word 'disapproved' for 'forbade'. On a previous occasion the Committee had 'declined to recognize officially' the Derby School Boys' Rifle Association, which had a complement of over 800 boys under the age of 14. The reason given was that the Association fostered a spirit of militarism.[38] From the strength of the movement in terms of the numbers of boys enlisted it would appear that it was well established on an independent basis, though probably welcoming the possibility of official recognition. In Liverpool the Director of Education, Mr J. G. Legge, expressed support for experiments in the practice of rifle shooting in elementary schools. He claimed that even if it achieved nothing else, it gave a training to the eye of the finest kind, 'and precisely the very kind of which modern civilization tends to deprive a man'.[39] It is not easy to appreciate what general advantage could result from training boys to squint through a gun-sight whilst aiming at a target. Mr Legge's observation may suggest, however, that the supporters of rifle shooting were straining to find any sort of justification for the practice to which the term 'militarist' could not be attached.

NOTES

1. Revd J. P. Way,'Military Training', in *The Public Schools from Within* (London: Sampson Low, 1906), p. 210.
2. Sir Lauder Brunton, *Collected Papers on Physical and Military Training*, 25 (published privately, n.d., but probably 1915).
3. *The Times* (13 February 1906): 9–10.
4. Ibid. (17 February 1906): 12.
5. Ibid. (15 March 1906): 8.
6. Ibid. (13 June 1906): 5.
7. Ibid. (20 October 1906): 6.
8. *House of Commons Debates*, Fourth Series, Vol. CLVI, col. 657–68 (2 May 1906).
9. *House of Lords Debates*, Fourth Series, Vol. CLXI, cols. 952–3 (24 July 1906), 'The New Army Scheme', observations by the Earl of Meath. The War Office issued a Special Army Order in January 1907 setting out Haldane's scheme of reorganization. The Yeomanry and the Volunteers combined in a Territorial Army on 1 April 1908, on which date an Officer Training Corps was also established. The Militia was formed into a Special Reserve.
10. British Schools were a product of the non-conformist British and Foreign School Society, formed in the early years of the nineteenth century to parallel the Church of England's National Schools. Few survived into the twentieth century.
11. *School Government Chronicle* (3 November 1906): 379.
12. *The Times* (27 October 1906): 14.
13. *School Government Chronicle*, 76 (22 September 1906): 239.

14. *House of Commons Debates*, Fourth Series, Vol. CLXIII, cols. 425–7 (25 October 1906).
15. Ibid., Vol. CLXIII, col. 888 (30 October 1906).
16. The London Schools Recreation Guild founded by Dr R. J. E. Hanson, a hygiene enthusiast, provided disciplined holidays for boys of City schools, with drill, shooting and play facilities, in addition to its local shooting clubs.
17. *House of Commons Debates*, Fourth Series, Vol. CLXIV, cols. 1495–6 (14 November 1906).
18. Ibid., Vol. CLXXII, col. 1569 (23 April 1907).
19. Ibid., Vol. CLXXIII, col. 702 (30 April 1907).
20. Ibid., Vol. CLXXIII, col. 1309 (6 May 1907).
21. *School Government Chronicle*, 78 (27 July 1907): 80.
22. *The Times* (2 October 1908): 6.
23. Ibid. (7 September 1906): 10.
24. *The Worker*, Huddersfield Socialist Party (20 July 1906): 2.
25. *The Times* (28 July 1906): 4.
26. Katharine Bathurst, 'The Physique of Girls', *The Nineteenth Century and After* (May 1906): 818–24.
27. Dr (later Sir) George Newman acknowledged the relationship between patriotism and the development of physical training when he wrote: 'The gymnastic movement in Europe derived its impulse from patriotism, often represented in military form, and only in later years did it draw much inspiration from the Greeks. Speaking generally, it sprang in Europe from love of country, from a sense of freedom, from a rising democratic faith in the physical improvement of the human body.' Sir George Newman, *The Building of a Nation's Health* (London: Macmillan, 1939), pp. 259–60.
28. *The Times* (30 July 1906): 7.
29. *School Government Chronicle*, 76 (6 October 1906): 277.
30. *The Times* (2 August 1906): 15; and (25 August 1906): 4.
31. Ibid. (4 August 1906): 9.
32. Ibid. (30 July 1907): 12.
33. *School Government Chronicle*, 77 (22 June 1907): 569.
34. *The Times* (27 January 1908): 10. The Jewish Lads' Brigade was set up in 1895 at the Jews' Free School in Spitalfields, 'to instil into a rising generation, from its earliest youth, habits of orderliness, cleanliness, and honour, so that in learning to respect themselves, they would do credit to their community and country'.

    The Jewish community, swollen by immigrants from pogroms in Poland and Russia, had its own particular problems. The Jewish Lads' Brigade was considered by its founders to have a part to play in helping Jewish youth to adjust to, and to play an acceptable part in, English society. In this, it differed somewhat from the aims of the Boys' Brigade, the Church Lads' Brigade, etc.
35. *The Times* (16 September 1907): 14.
36. Ibid. (6 September 1907): 5.
37. *School Government Chronicle*, 77 (5 January 1907): 8.
38. Ibid., 78 (28 September 1907): 256.
39. Ibid., 82 (9 October 1909): 289.

10

The Board of Education Stands Firm

THE ARMY ESTIMATES, 1909

Presenting his army estimates in 1909 Haldane again expressed his objection to compulsory military service. Having previously refrained from intruding into the province of the Board of Education, on the present occasion he bowed to temptation. He felt obliged to comment on the low levels of attainment of recruits to the army, three-quarters of whom entered the service with a level of education below that of a 10-year-old child (13 per cent were below even Standard 1, the level of a 7-year-old). To tackle this deficiency he advocated the need for compulsory continuation schools in which ex-elementary school children would continue their education on a part-time basis beyond the statutory school-leaving age.[1] By pressing for this educational provision he was incidentally giving encouragement to institutions in which a place might more readily be found for military training within the curriculum, though the idea may not necessarily have been uppermost in his mind.

CAPTAIN KINCAID SMITH'S LAST STAND

In 1908 Captain Kincaid Smith, MP for Stratford on Avon attempted to gain support for universal military training under the Ten-Minute Rule through a Bill to amend the Territorial and Reserve Forces Act of 1907. He was unsuccessful,[2] but a year later demonstrated the strength of his concern for this issue by resigning his seat as Liberal MP and thereafter appealing to his former constituents as an independent candidate supporting the concept of compulsory military training. At the poll in May 1909 his Unionist opponent won easily, the official Liberal candidate came second and Kincaid Smith a poor third. The Stratford-on-Avon electorate clearly did not share his concerns, and the result could be seen as a deterrent to any other MP who might contemplate taking similar action.[3]

NATIONAL SERVICE LEAGUE BILL

A National Service (Training and Home Defence) Bill, promoted by the National Service League, was introduced in the Lords on 19 May 1909 by Lord Newton, in the absence of Lord Roberts. The Bill provided for compulsory service in the Territorial Force of all male residents in the UK between the ages of 18 and 30. The Bill was not expected to go forward, but its introduction was intended to present a case for such a measure and to test public opinion.[4] The National Service League, having doubled its membership, was not downhearted; at its annual meeting in July a resolution was passed seeking to obtain from parliamentary candidates an undertaking to support the principle of national service.[5]

THE ANTI-MILITARISTS SPEAK OUT

At the other end of the political spectrum the TUC again condemned compulsory military service,[6] and both the Religious Society of Friends at a Quarterly Meeting representing Quakers in Northumberland, Durham and North Yorkshire,[7] and the Peace Society, at its annual meeting,[8] expressed their concern at growing militancy and increased expenditure on armaments. Addressing the Seventeenth Annual Conference of the Independent Labour Party in Edinburgh in 1909, Keir Hardie moved a resolution deploring the efforts of 'irresponsible statesmen, politicians and newspaper editors' in both Britain and Germany, to promote strife between the two nations, and called for a workers' crusade to counter the threat through the advocacy of cuts in arms expenditure, tribunals to settle international disputes, and the eventual abolition of war. To this resolution was grafted a second which declared the Conference's 'unabated opposition to all attempts to foster military customs in our schools or to impose compulsory military service upon the people'. The combined resolution, which was carried unanimously, further demonstrated the strength of the opposition to the drift towards war, and the mounting concern lest attempts to encourage militaristic practices in schools should succeed.[9]

ABORTIVE PHYSICAL TRAINING BILLS

In 1909 the Board of Education issued a new physical training syllabus which gave more attention to recreative exercises, though evidence of the drill tradition persisted. A new Education (Physical Training) Bill was introduced in the House of Lords by Viscount Hill, on behalf of the Hygienic League, in September 1909. A memorandum explained that the object of the Bill was 'to secure continuous physical training for the youth of both sexes up to the age of sixteen years', in order to arrest the physical deterioration which had been exposed by the Interdepartmental Committee in 1904. Paragraph 4 of the Bill allowed for the use of drill halls where local school premises were inadequate, with the proviso that the pupils were not to be allowed to use or to be taught to use 'any war weapon of any kind whatever'.[10] Children attending physical training lessons in drill halls would possibly be exposed to visual displays illustrative of rifle and drill exercises. While some adults would accept or even welcome such exposure, it would not be favoured by all parents. However temporary such arrangements, it was a proposed expediency which was not likely to receive universal acceptance. The age for total or partial exemption from school had been raised to 12 in 1899, although it remained at 11 in agricultural districts. A year later School Boards were granted powers to compel part- or full-time attendance at school up to the age of 14 instead of 13. Any attempts to enforce 'continuance physical training' to the age of 16 would be fraught with difficulties, not least those which would be voiced by employers in industrial communities and farmers in rural areas. However, with the demise of the Bill such issues were not put to the test.

In the summer of 1910 another attempt was made by Viscount Hill to introduce an Education (Physical Training) Bill to apply to elementary, secondary and continuation schools. The Earl of Meath supported the general tenor of the Bill but regretted that the use of any war weapons was to be prohibited despite the trend of public opinion which he claimed was 'in the direction of training children in military drill'. He had obviously not tested the opinions of the working classes and the trade unions on this issue. Among his own circle he could more confidently claim support for the military training of children. Lord Ampthill thought that physical training in schools needed a mental stimulus and suggested that no higher motive could be introduced than that of patriotism. The Marquess of Londonderry was sympathetic to the Bill but was not in favour of physical training being compulsory whilst other subjects lay at the disposition of the Board of Education through the Code. Other peers recommended the postponement of the Bill and that course was accepted by Viscount Hill who thereupon withdrew it.[11]

A Government Bill was launched in May 1911 which, if successful, would have abolished the half-time system and raised the leaving age to

13. After that age children would have been required to remain at school to 14 (or to 15 if the by-laws of the local authority so decreed), or attend continuation classes to the age of 16 years. The Government had earlier commissioned two investigations, by an Interdepartmental Committee on Partial Exemption from School Attendance, and by the Consultative Committee on Continuation Schools, both of which reported in 1909. 'Owing to pressure of time' this Bill was withdrawn without any discussion. Had it succeeded, the curriculum would have attracted much discussion, not least the part that physical education or military drill should play in continuation classes and schools. It would have gone a considerable way towards meeting the stated object of Viscount Hill's proposals of 1909 and 1910 as set out above.

Lord Charles Beresford attempted to secure in the Commons what Viscount Hill had failed to achieve in the Lords, but with no more success.[12] Twice in 1912 Mr Munro-Ferguson enthused on the positive effect on recruitment which would result from the introduction of a system of compulsory continuation classes in physical training, particularly if some military training was provided for the boys.[13] However, that claim had been answered by John Burns MP in March 1900 when he pointed out that 'the great recruiting sergeant' was poverty, with patriotism playing only a very minor role.

These various attempts to introduce Bills for the extension of physical training provided opportunities for views to be aired in both the Lords and the Commons on the importance of physical instruction within the school curriculum. So far as the sensitive question of a military drill element in the provisions was concerned, the lack of support from the Government suggested that the Board of Education was satisfied with its policies and with the progress being made by the local authorities. Further, it demonstrated that the Liberal Government was not prepared to allow agitation on the question of Britain's military preparedness to influence or intrude into its educational policies.

POLITICAL OPPOSITION TO MILITARISM

Both the Labour Party and the Independent Labour Party (ILP) continued to mount anti-militarist campaigns. At the annual Labour Party Conference in 1911, Keir Hardie (ILP) moved that the resolution expressing opposition to militarism should have added to it the findings of the recently held Socialist International Congress at Copenhagen. The suggested additional clause demanded 'that the principles of peace and international fraternity be taught in the public schools', (public here referring to the nation's schools, not those in the private sector). With the exception of a clause which called for possible strike action as a means of preventing war, the resolution and amendment were carried unanimously.[14] The Nineteenth Independent Labour Party Conference was held in Birmingham on 17–18 April 1911, when it was reported that some 250 meetings in favour of internationalism and peace had been organized in the previous October alone, at which appropriate resolutions had been carried. There too the findings of the Socialist International Congress were endorsed, but without exclusion of the clause relating to possible strike action.[15] For either party the teaching of military drill was incompatible with their philosophies in favour of peace and international fraternity.

THE GREAT ILLUSION AND *WHAT IS AND WHAT MIGHT BE*

The third edition of Norman Angell's *The Great Illusion: A Study of the Relation of Military Power in Nations to their Economic and Social Advantage* appeared at this time. Written two years earlier, it aroused considerable interest.[16] Angell contended that military and political power gave no commercial advantage and that it was economically impossible for one nation to seize another's wealth, or to enrich itself by overwhelming another. The book became an international bestseller but the author's stark message that not even the victors could profit in an economic sense from war appeared at a time when an inexorable march towards a major international conflict was already in train.

There was a greater measure of apprehension and reticence within the elementary education sector than was experienced elsewhere in education, not only in political terms as measured by the political parties of the left. Elementary education was, of course, subject to much closer public scrutiny at local and national levels than were the public and private schools, not least because of the official financial support it received and the consequent controls to which it was subjected. When Edmond Holmes, former Chief Inspector to the Board of Education, published his *What Is and What Might Be* in 1911, the book showed clearly the disaffection of an administrator and inspector who had come to regard the department he had served for so many years as having sold the nation's children short in terms of real education. He commented sadly that the children 'had no initiative, no spontaneous activity … they could do nothing but sit still and wait for the word of command'.[17] In similar vein, the *Report of the Consultative Committee on Attendance, Compulsory or Otherwise, at Continuation Schools*, published in 1909, warned that 'A not unnatural desire for orderly quiet ... leads imperceptibly to a military precision and a rapid simultaneity of movement and expression which if long continued must prove fatal to the better forms of education.'[18] In spite of the advances made in elementary education it is quite clear that the dullness associated with the Revised Code had not been extinguished. It is little wonder that the Board of Education preferred to look to new approaches in physical training based on the Swedish system rather than to the formal drills which had their inspiration in army manuals. Shooting practice, too, came into this latter category – it may have provided eye-training, but the stern discipline required on safety grounds alone drastically diminished its general educative value. There were too the moral aspects to be taken into consideration.

A NATIONAL CADET FORCE

All this time between 1909 and 1911 R. B. Haldane was engaged in the establishment of a national cadet force administered by the Territorial forces. The scheme was intended to embrace all uniformed youth movements, but cadet regulations, issued by the Army Council in 1910, stated that only officially recognized cadets would in future receive military and financial support. The newly formed Officer Training Corps was not to include such movements as the Boys' Brigade, which decided to retain its autonomy and religious aims. A number of questions relating to the loss of privileges previously enjoyed by the Boys' Brigade were put to Haldane in the Commons, but he remained firm. Those organizations which did not feel able to accept the War Office requirements would no longer be able to hire camping equipment, purchase disused carbines, or 'ask for Generals in full uniform to inspect them'. They would, he said, 'have to be content with a gentleman in a black frock coat'.[19] Haldane was moving inexorably towards a more professional cadet force and one which would distance itself from units whose roots lay firmly within the working class.

A chapter in *The Higher Education of Boys in England* by Cyril Norwood and Anthony Hope carried a chapter on 'The Officer Training Corps' which stressed the authors' belief that there was no inherent danger of militarism being encouraged through corps activities. Schoolmasters were not introducing 'a subtle and insidious poison into the life of the State', but 'reverting to old, simple, and proved forms of education, the inculcation of patriotism and service'.[20] Such claims lacked credibility as far as they suggested a long tradition rather than a late Victorian character. The dissociation of militarism, 'that strange something of which so many are afraid, and which so few define', from such training was questioned by those who feared an extension of similar practices for all youths up to the age of 18.

LORD HERSCHELL'S ILL-ADVISED ADVANCE AND CONFUSED RETREAT

In February 1913 the House of Lords debated the Territorial Force, in the course of which Lord Herschell spoke on behalf of the Secretary of State for War. (Since 12 June 1912, J. Seely had taken over this post from Haldane, who had aspired to the Lord Chancellorship.) Having referred to the teaching of physical training in continuation schools, which he saw as comprising gymnastics, physique and discipline, he went on to suggest that 'It might be well that the use of arms and simple military formations would add to the self-respect of the people and would lay a foundation on which a great scheme of national defence might be based...'. For the Opposition, the Marquess of Lansdowne hoped that Herschell's statement suggested that the War Office was 'seriously considering some plan', but Herschell beat a hasty retreat from his exposed position, having gone a great deal further than Haldane had done previously in his Commons statements. The noble Lord stated somewhat lamely by way of correction that he was only indicating that 'If it was desired to train the youth of the nation from the point of view of physique, that might be achieved by some scheme in connection with secondary education.' Lansdowne took advantage of the opportunity which Herschell had unwittingly presented to him, suggesting that the wearisome content of much teaching might usefully be replaced by 'some ... physical, gymnastic education involving the handling of arms and occasional military movements'. It was left to the Marquess of Crewe to restore the situation for the Government by reminding peers that Herschell had only suggested a possible development when he referred to arms training. He informed the House that the War Office did not contemplate any such system at the present time.[21] Herschell himself had revised his original statement by suggesting that he was referring to *secondary* schools, whereas his original comments were made in respect of *continuation* schools, which were intended to cater for elementary schoolchildren. Herschell seemed to have forgotten that the 1911 Bill by which the continuation schools and classes were to be set up had failed; it was not until 1918 that the issue was to be addressed in the context of a major educational Bill.

A month later in the Commons J.A. Pease was asked by J. F. P. Rawlinson whether his attention had been drawn to Lord Herschell's statement (without, of course, acknowledging the later qualifications made by Herschell and Crewe). In answer to the specific question as to whether the Board of Education would sanction 'steps by LEAs to add to the self-esteem of the people by those means', Pease emphatically stated that he would not sanction the use of arms or the practice of military formations in elementary schools, and he had not received any proposals of that kind from LEAs.[22]

THE TERRITORIAL FORCES BALLOT BILL

When the Lords gave a second reading to the Territorial Forces Ballot Bill in June, Haldane supported the teaching of physical training 'to prepare the way for subsequent military service' if boys decided to take it up. He also agreed that it was not possible to deal with physical training from which reference to organization and discipline had been excluded. But, he said, it would not be practicable to bring it under the aegis of the War Office, and the Bill was not conceived on lines which would permit it. This did not, however, preclude the inclusion of 'some of the admirable features which we witness in connection with the Boy Scouts and the Cadet Corps'. Unlike Herschell, he left few chinks for the Opposition to penetrate.[23]

General Sir Ian Hamilton's presidential address to members of the Birmingham and Midland Institute in September 1912 was concerned with the training of boys. He suggested that if one were to ask a boy what he thought of 'a competitive superboy' he would say he was a swot; the boy with the best academic record would be considered a sneak; but mention the boy sergeant or corporal and, 'here his tone became hushed, his expression solemn', such a person was 'one of the greatest men who ever lived'. He assured his audience that members of the School Cadet Corps, Boys' Brigades, Church Lads' Brigades and the Boy Scouts were not playing a silly game, but were engaged in something 'quite intensely real, more real, perhaps, than the things the fathers and mothers of those Cadets and Scouts were doing'.[24] Present-day readers may well consider his address more appropriate for a schoolboy audience than for the ears of a learned society, but it does indicate the emotional aura which permeated public appeals to patriotism and nationalism at that time.

THE DUTY AND DISCIPLINE MOVEMENT

The redoubtable Earl of Meath had yet another venture to launch, the Duty and Discipline Movement, founded on 16 June 1913, with Lady Barrington and himself as joint presidents.[25] Its objects were self-evident, and it joined the Empire Day Movement[26] and other initiatives as evidence of Meath's patriotic involvement in public life and in voluntary organizations. (See Appendix B.)

If the Duty and Discipline Movement was intended to strengthen discipline both in the home and in school and to 'counteract the many influences tending to weaken authority in the State',[27] the speeches of Lord Roberts were becoming ever more shrill in their advocacy of military preparedness against an identified potential enemy. Aged, but ever-vigorous, Roberts addressed a mass meeting organized by the National Service League in the Free Trade Hall, Manchester, in October 1912. He told his 3,000-strong audience that the time-honoured policy of the German Foreign Office was 'Germany strikes when Germany's hour has struck', and suggested that 'this excellent policy' was, or should be 'the policy of every nation prepared to play a great part in history'. The gist of his message was: 'Arm and prepare yourselves as men, for the time of your ordeal is at hand.'[28] A resolution demanding national service was carried 'with enthusiasm'. He continued his militarist campaign the following spring, visiting Bristol, Wolverhampton, Leeds and Glasgow, everywhere attracting huge audiences. In Leeds, 3,000 were admitted into the Town Hall, while his speech 'was thrown, line by line, on to a screen in Victoria-square', and in music halls and picture palaces in the city.[29]

ANTI-CONSCRIPTION CAMPAIGN

Late in 1913 an anti-conscription campaign was launched by the Independent Labour Party, with Keir Hardy, Philip Snowden and other leaders addressing meetings in London and in the provinces. In Huddersfield a public debate was held on the question 'Should the Working Class support the National Service League?'. *The Worker* reported the speeches of Mr G. W. Roberts for the National Service

League and of Mr F. Shaw for the British Socialist Party, but failed to record any vote at the conclusion of the proceedings.[30] A demonstration against compulsory military service and arms expenditure was organized by the Huddersfield Committee against Compulsory Military Service and held in the local Town Hall in February 1914. Councillor J. W. Robson, presiding, claimed that 'the highest and truest form of patriotism [was] not in working to make either the army or the navy stronger and greater, but in working for the removal of the causes that made for war'. Since he was a prominent member of the Religious Society of Friends in Huddersfield it was not surprising that his comments bore a close resemblance to the Quaker Peace Testimony. He was followed by C. P. Trevelyan, MP for neighbouring Elland and Parliamentary Secretary of the Board of Education, who successfully moved a resolution against compulsory military service. That was succeeded by a second resolution in favour of a limitation to arms expenditure, also carried.[31]

A CONTRARY VIEW

A few months later the *Colne Valley Guardian Weekly* reported an event in a rural community some distance from Huddersfield which provides a contrary view to those expressed above. When the Golcar and District Rifle Club celebrated the opening of its new pavilion in May 1914, its president, Dr Webster, claimed that such organizations merited encouragement because they tended to improve the character of the people: '[A man] who was anxious to be a good shot could not be either a bad citizen or a "loose" man. The very fact that he was trying to be a good shot steadied the man and made it incumbent upon him to be of steady character.'[32] Dr Webster, presumably a medical man, relied upon faculty psychology to substantiate his statement. The transfer of the physical steadiness required to shoot with a rifle to a general steadiness of character might be supported by the prevailing psychology,[33] but we may now consider it to be a very dubious claim. It is, however, not surprising when taking into account the perceived need to stress the civic and moral values which were attached to such activities. Comparable arguments were advanced in support of rifle shooting for boys, as we have seen.

MILITARISM: FOR AND AGAINST

In meetings convened throughout the country, either in favour of militarism or deploring it, large audiences gathered to participate in lively discussions and the passing of countless resolutions. It was inevitable that the fate of youths and boys still at school was drawn into the debate, for they constituted a potential source of recruits to the armed forces of the Crown. Debates in both the Lords and Commons wrestled with the pros and cons of army reform, compulsory military service and the contribution to be made by cadet units. The question of the form of drill to be taught in schools was also often raised. Haldane, responsible for implementing crucial reforms for the army and its cadet units, realized the importance of youth training and of appropriate physical exercises in schools. Unlike many of his fellow MPs he appreciated the different roles of the departments responsible for education and for war respectively, and did not attempt to confuse them. The political, patriotic, moral and educational aspects of these issues were fiercely argued right up to the outbreak of war in August 1914, and, indeed, did not cease when hostilities actually broke out.

ACHIEVEMENT OF THE BOARD OF EDUCATION

The final comment on this issue, as far as state schools were concerned, should perhaps rest with the Board of Education. The *Annual Report* of the Board for the year 1913–14 acknowledged that pressure had been exerted in favour of military drill and rifle training having a recognized place in a course of physical exercises, but the Board itself dissented from this, stating: 'Experience shows that physical training in elementary schools should not be less and cannot well be more, than a preparation for the more specialised forms of physical training which may properly be undertaken at a later age.' The inculcation of habits of discipline and obedience, and the promotion of 'all-round physical development' were the desired objects, and to attain them the Board was satisfied that the official syllabus of physical exercises, supplemented where possible by organized games and swimming, provided all that was necessary or desirable.

The report also commented on the remarkable progress made in terms of 'corporate spirit' in recent years. It credited this to the relaxation of control by the central authority, and offered, as an illustration, the practice of allowing children 'to walk in groups to Centres and Baths without being marched under military discipline'.[34] There had been less direct control of the schools and their teachers since the early years of the century, and more attention was being paid to the all-round education of children than had been the case formerly.

Curricular developments and changes in teaching methods extended across the whole range of subjects taught. Since the introduction of its *Handbook of Suggestions* in 1905, pamphlets had been circulated to cover many specific subjects of the curriculum and to advise on teaching methods. All the many principles advocated were to be found in some school or other. Failure to achieve success lay with those head teachers who 'have never fully realized the change in aim' or who were incapable of carrying it out. Overall, the Board suggested that 'All schools, more or less consciously, are moving away from older ideas and methods – all Education Authorities acquiesce whether or not they encourage teachers to advance with the times.'[35] The inference here is that the Board of Education considered that its policies were at least receiving the tacit support of local authorities, although encouragement and guidance would continue to be necessary at both administrative and school levels if further progress was to be made.

Those parts of the curriculum which attracted most interest from educationalists and from classroom teachers were to be found in programmes of courses arranged by local authorities. The West Riding Education Authority, for example, organized programmes at Bingley Training College which included general, specific and physical training courses. The general course in 1913 included lectures in teaching history as a preparation for citizenship, organized games, rhythmic movements and dances, arithmetic, English, handwork, reading and story-telling, infant school teaching, domestic subjects and physiology.

The *Consultative Committee Report on Attendance, Compulsory or Otherwise at Continuation Schools* (1909) had also pointed to the shift in emphasis from a rigidly imposed discipline to a recognition that there were other qualities which should underpin the process of education: 'Well-disciplined children may acquire a habit of exactness and obedience. But they will not learn self-reliance; their intelligence will not be quick to meet emergencies; their individuality and powers of initiative will not be developed.'[36] Through its annual reports and supported by the findings of consultative and other committees the Board of Education had championed a curriculum and teaching methods which were subject to educational criteria. It had withstood long and continuous pressure for the inclusion of military training and rifle shooting. At times it had wavered, it had allowed questionable experiments to be tried, it had even sanctioned a Model Course based on military rather than educational criteria, but overall its stand had been in the perceived interests of the children, and its report for 1913–14 presented a confident statement of its achievements.

NOTES

1. *The Times* (5 March 1909): 7, 8, 9.
2. Ibid. (7 July 1909): 9; (8 July 1908): 8.
3. Ibid. (6 April 1909): 11; (6 May 1909): 9.
4. Ibid. (20 May 1909): 12; (7 July 1909): 4; (13 July 1909): 11; (14 July 1909): 6–7.
5. Ibid. (1 July 1909): 11.
6. Ibid. (8 September 1909): 4.
7. Ibid. (24 April 1909): 12.
8. Ibid. (20 May 1909): 9.
9. Independent Labour Party, *Report of Seventeenth Annual Conference* (Edinburgh, 1909), pp. 83–5.
10. *House of Lords Debates*, Fifth Series, Vol. II, col. 1073 (13 September 1909).
11. Ibid., Vol. VI, cols. 166–89 (14 July 1910).
12. *House of Commons Debates*, Fifth Series, Vol. XXXIX, cols. 1500–1 (18 June 1912).
13. Ibid., Vol. XXXV, col. 981 (12 March 1912), and Vol. XLI, col. 284 (16 July 1912).
14. Report of the Labour Party Conference, 1911, pp. 113, 116, 118, in F. Bealey (ed.), *The Social and Political Thought of the British Labour Party* (London: Weidenfeld & Nicolson, 1970), pp. 75–7.
15. Independent Labour Party, *Report of Nineteenth Annual Conference* (Birmingham, 1911), p. 93.
16. Norman Angell, *The Great Illusion: A Study of the Relation of Military Power in Nations to their Economic and Social Advantage* (London: Heinemann, 1st edn 1909; 3rd edn 1911). Angell was awarded the Nobel Prize for Peace in 1933, knighted, and served as a Labour MP.
17. E. G. A. Holmes, *What Is and What Might Be: A Study of Education in General and Elementary Education in Particular* (London: Constable, 1911), p. 119.
18. *Report of the Consultative Committee on Attendance, Compulsory or Otherwise, at Continuation Schools* (1909), p. xvii.
19. *House of Commons Debates*, Fifth Series, Vol. XXII, col. 2101 (14 March 1911).
20. C. Norwood, and A. Hope (eds), *The Higher Education of Boys in England* (London: Murray, 1909), p. 446.
21. *House of Lords Debates*, Fifth Series, Vol. XIII, col. 906 (10 February 1913).
22. *House of Commons Debates*, Fifth Series, Vol. L, col. 252 (12 March 1913).
23. Ibid., Vol. XIV, col. 484 (2 June 1913). Haldane, though he had relinquished the War Office to Seely, had retained responsibility for implementing the measures which he had initiated.
24. *School Government Chronicle* (28 September 1912): 260–1.
25. See below, Appendix B for the contents of a letter from the Earl of Meath, published in *The Standard* on 15 June 1908, which he claimed led to the formation of the Duty and Discipline Movement.
26. The Empire Day Movement, with the motto 'One King, One Flag, One Fleet, One Empire' was conceived by the Earl of Meath in 1896. In a letter to *The Times* he proposed that the anniversary of the Queen's accession to the throne should be made a universal school holiday, preceded by the singing of the National Anthem and the saluting of the flag. Following extensive correspondence in *The Times*, the venture attracted support both in Britain and in the colonies.
27. See below, Appendix B.
28. *The Times* (23 October 1912): 5.
29. Ibid. (19 April 1913): 8.
30. *The Worker* (25 October 1913): 6.
31. Ibid. (14 February 1914): 5.
32. *Colne Valley Guardian Weekly* (22 May 1914).
33. Faculty psychology – the prevailing psychology which was based upon the belief that the mind operated through certain powers, or faculties, such as memory, imagination, reasoning and perception. Since these faculties needed to be exercised, it followed that the marriage of certain subject areas with one or more desired faculties was a profitable educational exercise.

An associated concept was that of the transfer of training, which held that once the faculties had been developed they would be available for exploitation elsewhere.

34. *Board of Education Annual Report 1913–14*, p. 64.
35. Ibid., p. 223.
36. Board of Education, *Consultative Committee Report on Attendance, Compulsory or Otherwise at Continuation Schools*, Vol. 1 (Cd. 4757), p. 52.

Conclusion

Throughout the period 1870–1914 there was, as we have seen, an active lobby in favour of securing an honoured place for the teaching of military drill within the elementary school curriculum. At times successes were dramatic, as when the powerful and influential London School Board was persuaded to adopt the programme proposed by the Society of Arts in 1875. Influential and patriotic individuals such as Lord Roberts raised the expectations and hopes of militarists; at other times local initiatives advanced the cause significantly. Always, however, military drill was judged alongside 'ordinary' drill or physical exercises, which did not rely upon military models, or kept them to a minimum.

As long as military drill qualified for attendance purposes, and hence for a grant, it enjoyed a distinct advantage over ordinary drill, which was not so privileged. The introduction of discipline and organization grants encouraged schools to include drill, which was perceived as an activity contributing directly to good order and discipline, and from 1890 variable grants favoured those schools whose discipline and organization sufficiently impressed HMIs to merit a higher level of grant. In that year, too, the New Code drew attention to physical exercises. The natural desire of schools to attract the higher level of grant, coinciding with favourable reference to physical exercises, must have stimulated interest in the latter at the expense of military drill. It did not, however, deter the supporters of military drill, who continued to seek opportunities to establish it in the schools.

Inevitably, the military shortcomings during the Boer War impinged upon schools, which were viewed by some as appropriate venues for teaching basic military skills. Haldane's army reforms were to stimulate further debate; however, with the exception of the ill-conceived and speedily rejected Model Course of 1902, successive governments had moved away from the encouragement of military drill towards support for physical exercises and corporate games, and Haldane himself showed little inclination to intrude into the field of elementary education in his consideration of the future of cadet units. Children's physical needs were given priority over other, external factors, particularly after the appointment of a Chief Medical Officer to the Board of Education in 1907. These developments effectively meant that any military drill provided for children of school age would have to be accommodated elsewhere than in the curriculum of the nation's elementary schools.

Throughout this study the emphasis has been on the elementary education of boys, with only passing observations on the provisions made for infants and girls. In the social climate of the time women were not expected to know of military matters, and if military drill was to be taught there would be little inducement to seek female guidance. However, as Britain's position as a world power was increasingly threatened, the role of its women as the mothers of an imperial race came to be recognized, with more attention directed to the education of girls and to their physical well-being and preparation for a supporting domestic role in society. Madame Bergman-Österberg, pioneer of physical education for girls, stated that position clearly when she claimed that her aims were 'trying to train my girls to help raise their own sex, and to accelerate the progress of the race; for unless the women are strong, healthy, pure and true, how can the race progress?'[1] There were, however, those who expressed alarm lest physical health and strength were made the principal aim of national well-being. Dr Jane Walker, at the National Union of Women Workers' Conference in 1906, was one of that number. She saw 'a danger of making a fetish of exercise', particularly as it concerned her own sex; more important for the nation, in her opinion, was intellectual supremacy, and 'immeasurably more important is our moral and spiritual prowess'.

IMAGES OF MASCULINITY

Male control extended across the whole of society. Masculinity recognized the male warrior as an ideal form, and it was in bravery, honour and glory that manhood was measured. Schumpeter (1919) claimed that: 'Aggressive nationalism ... the instincts of dominance and war derived from the distant past and alive down to the present – such things do not die overnight. From time to time they seek to come into their own.'[2] He suggested that appeals to national sentiment never failed and were unique in arousing 'the dark powers of the subconscious ... [calling] into play instincts that carry over from the life habits of the dim past'.[3] Interestingly, he differs from most writers on imperialism in his identification of deep-seated psychological promptings and instincts of an aggressive nature.

By the early 1960s social learning theory was laying emphasis on the influence of conditioning and reinforcement, of imitation and indoctrination, all of which could be identified in military drill practices. Edley and Wetherell (1995) claim that masculinity is 'historically variable and is socially, rather than biologically or naturally, produced'.[4] This is illustrated in the strength of today's youth culture and modes of dress, hair-style, and so on. In late Victorian times manly attributes encouraged within the closed communities of the public schools were imitated elsewhere; boys of all social classes read school stories which mirrored life in public schools and exalted prowess on the playing field. Activities on the games field took precedence over school corps, but the latter remained a significant feature within the public schools; with semi-uniformed brigades and the Boy Scout movement appealing to boys from working-class backgrounds. Values which were encouraged in more privileged environments were imitated elsewhere, often transmitted by individuals who were challenged to set up youth organizations in which conditioning and reinforcement, imitation and indoctrination, were all practised. 'Invented' traditions were widely practised and celebrated, as in annual Empire Day observances and massed drill parades of schoolchildren. Social learning components were similarly present in the teaching of military drill, with a sense of order, discipline and obedience to instructions paramount. Running through the entire garment of society was the bright thread of patriotism, to which sentiment appeals were constantly made. Even the youngest child could clutch a Union Jack in its fist, or sport a sailor's costume or a nurse's outfit. A knapsack and staff, a leather belt and a smart hat, with companions similarly equipped, was sufficient demonstration of one's readiness to serve Queen, or King, and country. Patriotism, that 'cohesive force of states' was spiritual, even religious in character, in the view of E. C. Wingfield-Stratford in 1913.[5] In 1939 he returned to a consideration of the phenomenon as it had found expression in 'the empire-conscious days' towards the end of the nineteenth century when patriotism meant 'an honest-to-God – or Satan – love for your country, right or wrong, – not that she ever was wrong to signify – and loving your country meant shouting, and going all out, and, at need, dying, for that empire on which, as we were constantly reminded, the sun never set'.[6]

BRITAIN AS THE CENTRE OF THE WORLD

The writing of history, as Arthur Brittan has noted, has been a privileged male activity since Thucydides, and 'until the nineteenth century was a

162

chronicle of the decisions of "great male leaders"',[7] among whom would be military and naval commanders. Those models found their way into the schools through the selective teaching of geography and history, and the pages of class readers. The style of textbooks and readers was often arrogant and nationalistic, with children constantly reminded of Britain's status as a leader of nations, with model laws and an empire-building mission which it could neither ignore nor lay down. The author of *Blackwood's Educational Series*, Vol. III, of 1883 wrote:

> We have seen England and Great Britain growing larger and larger, stronger and stronger, more and more free, more and more intelligent, until our empire has risen to be the greatest, most powerful and most respected on the face of the globe … We must learn to love our country for what she has been in the past, and what she is now, and what she is destined to become in the future.[8]

The effect of empire-building on native peoples was rarely portrayed in negative terms, although an astute child reader of Louise Creighton's *First History of England* (1889) might have suffered some misgivings on reading that 'Englishmen have gone and lived and shown themselves so strong that they have either driven out the people who lived there before or have made them do as they bid them.'[9] The notes accompanying an *Atlas of the British Empire throughout the World* (*c*. 1874) reminded scholars: 'It will be seen that the British Isles occupy the central position among the great land masses of the globe',[10] and a geography reader of 1882 stated bluntly: 'London is the centre of the land surface of the Earth.'[11] It is highly unlikely that any child in a British elementary school was ever confronted by a world map which did not depict the British Isles as occupying a central, and therefore, dominant position.[12] From this firm base Englishmen could set out confidently to strengthen and extend the empire:

> Where is the Briton's home?
> Where the brave heart can come,
> Where labour wins a soil,
> Where a stout heart can toil –
> Any fair seed is sown –
> Where gold or fame is won,
> Where never sets the sun,
> Where a brave heart can come,
> There is the Briton's home![13]

163

Here, Edward Bulwer Lytton stereotyped the positive attributes of a Britisher against which the perceived inferior qualities of other races might be judged. Anthologies of songs for use in schools also drew on the wealth of patriotic and national songs which were popular at the time. *National Songs for the School and the Home* had sections devoted to the home, the open air, the navy, the army and to patriotism respectively. Section IV 'Soldiers' Songs', related to 'valour and heroism in camp and field, self-reliance, duty and courage under the flag, touching the inner springs of feeling and sentiment, and inculcating the noblest characteristics of British nature as pourtrayed [*sic*] in History and Biography'.[14]

Male assertiveness and aggression also found ready expression in the formal drill practices and even more so in the rifle handling and shooting which were introduced in some schools. However, as we have seen, the Board of Education (which replaced the Education Department in 1899), remained firm through successive ministers in the view that rifle shooting had no place in the elementary schools. The Board did not consider it necessary for such training to be rehearsed in preparation for future military service, neither did a boy's masculine development depend upon it. But it is interesting and significant that it was necessary for the Board's position to be defended vigorously in the face of persistent questioning in both the Lords and the Commons.

EMPIRE AND MILITARISM

The war which many had feared and some had considered inevitable erupted in August 1914. Somewhat surprisingly, the monthly *Times Educational Supplement* of 4 August – the day Britain declared war on Germany – did not even hint of impending conflict. Leading articles discussed 'Religion in our Schools', 'The Wider Citizenship' and 'Physical Efficiency'. The author of the second article suggested that 'There is a persistent and unwarrantable confusion of the idea of the Empire with the idea of militarism.'[15]

The 'idea of the Empire' was a concept which teachers had addressed without fear of criticism, assisted by the extension of the curriculum to embrace geography and history, the support of HMIs, the availability of appropriate textbooks, and English readers which carried stories of the bravery of explorers, missionaries and military and naval heroes. 'Militarism', however, was ostensibly frowned upon. John Gooch claims that 'Almost all nineteenth-century writers on the army and the

State, prior to the Boer War at least, agreed that Britain was not a military nation.'[16] There was a similar reluctance to admit to imperialism. A. P. Thornton points out that the word 'imperialism' always appeared in quotation marks during Disraeli's premiership (1874–80), a practice which extended to Conservative newspapers and quarterlies.[17] He also claims:

> Nothing is filed under the heading 'Imperialism' in the archives of a nation-state that owned an empire. Foreign affairs, or external relations, are catalogued there, and a place is found for imperial administration and colonial trade; but 'imperialism' is always a listing in someone else's index, never one's own.[18]

In British eyes, 'militarism' was particularly associated with Germany: had not Prince von Bülow clearly stated that it was Germany's greatest strength?[19] Simply defined as 'the spirit or tendencies of a professional soldier; undue prevalence of the military spirit or ideals', militarism could be seen to be a quality commonly shared by nation-states which pursued the path of imperialism. On the Continent, where nation-states faced one another across common boundaries, large conscript armies were the norm. Britain, however, enjoyed island status, and looked to its army to police the empire, under the protection of a powerful navy. Only grudgingly were steps taken, under Haldane, to address the issue of a possible European war. Conscription, though deemed by some to be necessary, was seen as contrary to Liberal principle, and was not to be embraced until Lord Derby's 'shot-gun wedding between the fair maid of Liberal idealism and the ogre of Tory militarism'[20] in 1915–16. Michael Howard has pointed out that despite the well-established practice of conscription on the Continent and Britain's reluctance to follow that example, there was no difference in the response to serve one's country when the call came.[21]

THE IMPACT OF THE MILITARY ON CIVILIAN LIFE

The intrusion of the military spirit into civilian life had long been the subject matter of novels: for instance, Jane Austen's *Pride and Prejudice* and Thackeray's *Vanity Fair* both feature the effect of the military on young women! The colourful uniforms, particularly those of the officers, were splendid and eye-catching, and even when in the 1880s drab khaki uniforms were introduced, regimental bands (potent agents in encouraging enlistment) still retained their dress uniforms. Robert Giddings allies the military with the Church, law, government and royalty as establishments whose qualities are 'frozen in time', the full dress uniforms worn by the Brigade of Guards and regimental military bands preserving for all time the regimentals of High Victorian Imperialism.[22] Bands and military music enlivened many a local fête or national celebration, contributing further to the 'invented traditions' whose origins can be located in that period.

The military spirit also extended into religion: the Salvation Army (1881) had its own military-style uniforms for men and women, and offered hymns and other religious music for 'the deliverance of mankind from sin and the power of the devil'. In its early years, the Boys' Brigade (founded in 1883) drew many of its officers from the Volunteers. Weekly drill parades and Bible classes were held with the aim of furthering the cause of Christian manliness. Other bodies of a similar nature emerged, including the Church Lads' Brigade, the Jewish Lads' Brigade, and their sister organizations. The concept of Christian manliness had been championed in the mid-nineteenth century by Thomas Hughes and Charles Kingsley. The aggressive spirituality of both muscular Christianity and Christian militarism exercised powerful influences on provisions made for the young in the years leading to the First World War. A third school, that of Social Darwinism, also highlighted masculine attributes, correlating them with racist perceptions of non-Europeans. Sir Francis Younghusband wrote in 1896: 'No European can mix with non-Christian races without feeling his moral superiority over them … [which] is not due to mere sharpness of intellect, but to that higher moral nature to which we have attained in the development of the human race.'[23]

Herbert Spencer had referred to 'a military type of society' in 1886, where the process of regimentation, although most prominent in the army, affected the whole of society.[24] The military mentality as well as its modes of action and decision-making intruded into the civilian sector of such a society. In England military sentiments were widespread, symbolized by the army bands, the emergence of uniformed and semi-uniformed brigades and youth organizations, and the drill displays in which squads of schoolchildren paraded behind their bands in towns throughout the land.

Empire Day celebrations, which flourished in the post Boer War years, and indeed persisted into more recent times, were a further indication of the intrusion of militarism into imperial celebrations. In 1908 the London County Council agreed to support the venture, adding

800,000 children to the numbers participating in its observance. The following year the *School Government Chronicle* reported the arrangements which had been put in train for the metropolis.

> The day's programme begins at 9 a.m. at Cutler-street, Aldgate, with the 'Empire Day Rifle Match for Boy Marksmen' for HRH the Princess of Wales's championship gold medal and the firing by the English team for the Earl of Meath's Imperial Trophy.
>
> At 3 p.m. an Empire Day Concert will be held in the Queen's Hall. Here the presentation will be made of HRH the Princess of Wales's gold medal and other trophies and prizes. The band of HM Grenadier Guards will perform.
>
> The First Commissioner of the Board of Works has granted the use of Hyde Park for the final demonstration of the trooping of the whole of the 56 colours of the Empire.
>
> At 3 o'clock also a procession of the boys and girls will be formed in Trafalgar-square, whence they will march with their flags and their bands to Hyde Park, where the flags of the Empire will be trooped, for the first time in England, with suitable ceremonies.[25]

The whole procedure drew on military practices; with rifle shooting competitions, trooping of the colours to the music of the band of the Grenadier Guards, and a vast procession of 5,000 flag-waving children, accompanied by their bands, marching along streets crowded with spectators to Hyde Park for the triumphal climax to the day. Lord Meath impressed upon teachers that boys and girls taking part must, for safety's sake, be properly trained to obey the word of command. Here can be seen a prime example of the close integration of the civil and military components of Edwardian English society. Public celebration was insufficient, as Meath recognized; there was need also for teachers to ensure that the school curriculum reflected and encouraged the qualities which were widely considered vital to the future of Britain as an imperial power.

Many individuals and organizations whose members encouraged and perhaps practised activities of a militaristic nature were not necessarily restricted to those concerns and were often involved in other matters which were not of a military character. The Society of Arts, for example, whose encouragement of military drill has been discussed at some length, had in 1870 petitioned the Commons regretting that the Education Bill then before the House did not require a minister solely responsible for education, and calling for instruction to be provided in geography, drawing, singing, drill and moral training in all elementary schools.[26] Members of the Society's Committee on Drill comprised men with wide educational, scientific and political experience. The Society's efforts to establish military drill in elementary schools needs to be considered in this wider context, and the breadth of interest and integrity of individual members acknowledged. The societies and organizations which were set up with specific aims came into a different category, as, for example, the Navy League, the National Service League, the National Rifle Association, and the Lads' Drill Association, whose titles indicated clearly their more limited perspectives.

Sir Lauder Brunton's call for better physical training and the teaching of gymnastics attracted the ire of the writer of the third leader in the *Times Educational Supplement* of 4 August 1914, who stated tartly: 'The suggestion that this undesirable athleticism should be further encouraged by the appointment of "sports masters" is one on which no educationist would be prepared to look with favour.'[27] The athleticism of which the writer was so critical had maintained a strong lead over corps activities in public and private schools, and has been well documented by J. A. Mangan.[28] If 'athleticism, imperialism and militarism became enmeshed at the public schools'[29] this was true to a far lesser degree in the elementary schools. The public schools prepared their boys for service in the army, the civil service and other positions of authority. The elementary schools were required to teach their pupils to be obedient to their future master's needs;[30] the imperial mission for them was less clear, less defined. But those who enlisted for foreign service in India experienced a sense of superiority over the native population which had to be unlearnt when they returned to Britain. In the elementary sector team games were a late arrival, their entry eased after physical exercises replaced military drill in popularity and in educational respectability. Charles Kingsley had pointed to the association between competitive sports and moral education in his *Health and Education* (1874); by the century's end elementary schoolboys could also 'play the game'. Indeed, John Richards claims: '"Fair play" became the motto of a nation whose ideology and religious faith were subsumed under Imperialism, with its belief in the British as the elect who had a God-given duty to govern and civilise the world.'[31] However, 'Football quickly threw off the mantle of Christian sportsmanship and became a livelier and more purely plebian game.'[32] The first Schools Football Association was set up in South London in 1885, followed by others in Sheffield, Manchester and Leeds. Games were seen to have moral values as well as physical ones in the Report of the Board of Education for 1905–06:

Victory or defeat, their individual success or failure, will be far less important than 'playing the game', and from their pride in 'the school' and its good name will spring a stronger love of fair play, the power to give and take which counts for so much in the rough and tumble of life.[33]

These sentiments written in respect of elementary school children show how far the Board had moved from the earlier championing of military drill in the interests of discipline, control and obedience to instructions. Possibly with some qualification of the final reference to 'give and take', the statement might have been extracted from a book devoted to public school boys, and to qualities expected of them.

Individuals whose aim was single-minded in the pursuit of military interests were likely to be members of the armed services. Prime examples of these were General Lord Wolseley and Lord Roberts. Roberts campaigned vigorously for compulsory military training, and for that to have a firm foundation in drill and weapon-training programmes in all the nation's schools. Some headmasters and governors supported his views but the majority were largely indifferent. Roberts drew a clear line between compulsory service in the army overseas and compulsory training for defence of the homeland. Addressing the Oxford Union at the end of 1905 he claimed:

There is no 'militarism' and no 'Jingoism' in a man's being prepared to defend his country. There is no infringement of the rights of a free man in asking him to fit himself for that defence, and there is not a man, whatever his position in life may be, who would not be the gainer physically and morally for a training in arms.[34]

Although membership of rifle corps increased, his campaign to establish local rifle clubs throughout the country met with a disappointing response. His views were widely applauded at well-attended public meetings, but socialists remained suspicious that hard-won freedoms were being threatened. Interestingly, Roberts recognized the need for social reform; it was, he claimed, 'a preliminary to any thorough system of National Defence'.[35]

As we have seen, the Labour movement and the trade unions maintained a steady rejection of all demands for the military instruction of boys of school age and of any form of military conscription. They guarded what were perceived to be the interests of the working classes, and those were seen to be better expressed in terms of international fraternity than in conscript armies and the build-up of armaments. Their respective positions as representing members of the working classes focused attention on the exploitative aspect of military training; it fell to peace and international arbitration organisations to address more closely the ethical aspects.

MILITARISM AS A MEANS OF SOCIAL CONTROL

Britain in the years immediately preceding the outbreak of a European war in 1914 experienced much social unrest and many strikes by workers seeking higher wages and better conditions in their places of employment. Less than 7 per cent of the population was called upon to pay income tax; 2½ per cent of the population held two-thirds of the country's wealth. In 1914 many teachers and, indeed, some of their pupils went on strike, though for different reasons. In Paul Johnson's opinion:

> Liberal England in 1914 was a society in process of decomposition; its values and attitudes were already being pulverized under the impact of new social, political and economic forces. England on the eve of war, was in a state approaching revolution – only our submersion in a general European catastrophe averted a crisis of our national fortunes.[36]

Those who felt their privileged position threatened by unruly mobs may well have been drawn to support initiatives which focused on the inculcation of obedience, discipline and good order to the adolescent generation, and to favour other measures which might ensure that strikes and similar threats to the established order were strongly resisted. C. E. Fayle, writing in 1914, pointed to the dangers of militarism, which brought in its wake 'tyranny and reaction in domestic affairs, wars of fruitless conquest, and the cultivation of an exclusive, dominant military caste'.[37] The situation in Germany was even more tense; Karl Liebknecht claiming that militarism was 'not only a means of defence and a weapon against the external enemy', but 'it has the task of protecting the prevailing social order, of supporting capitalism and all reaction against the struggle of the working class for freedom'.[38]

As early as 1897 I. S. Bloch[39] warned that a future war would not take the form of a swift campaign, but would be a long, drawn-out contest marked by frequent stalemate and 'unparalleled casualties'. The soldiers who fought in the war came from both public (independent) and state schools. The latter were to furnish most of the infantry 'other ranks', who would be subjected to the harsh conditions of trench warfare and to the rigours of army discipline. In due course there would be inquiries and investigations into this war as there had been into the Boer War. Indeed the First World War had scarcely begun before demands for educational reform were being voiced in the *Times Educational Supplement* and elsewhere. The first leader in the *Times Educational Supplement* of 4 May 1915 recognized that now was not the time to attempt any reorganization, but it was suggested that the way ahead could be prepared if, in the course of a mental stock-taking, it was realized that there would be no return to the conditions of early 1914.[40] Meanwhile, it continued to be necessary for the Board or its spokesmen to issue reminders that 'for children up to 14 or 15 it was most desirable that military drill should not be introduced in elementary schools'.[41]

That was not the final word on an issue which had persisted for almost half a century. Indeed, the matter has surfaced again as recently as 1997 with the Conservative Government's plan for cadet units to be set up in state schools and inner-city areas. Opponents of the scheme expressed dismay that children under the age of 18 would be receiving firearms training, fears which Michael Portillo, then Defence Minister, dismissed with the answer that in such units: 'You learn guns are dangerous, you learn responsible use of guns and the harm they can do',[42] from which he argued that boys would be tempted away from the use of guns. (Sir Ian Hamilton argued in similar fashion in 1911 when he suggested that compulsory military service was a lesser danger to world peace than was voluntary service. The former 'by its very nature is a weapon that cannot be lightly used', whereas a voluntary system calls for taxes, not individual service, so that war was viewed 'with a less tragic regard'.[43]) Many critics saw Portillo's 1997 scheme as one aimed at instilling order and discipline at a time when crime and unsocial behaviour by teenagers were at an unacceptable level, reminding us of the reasons for the introduction of military drill in elementary schools over 120 years ago. In a companion article Mark Steel wrote that: 'Over the last 20 years the map showing recruitment into the Army fits almost exactly over the map showing areas of high unemployment.' He suggested that it would also coincide with the map of cadet centres promised by the Minister for Defence. And that too reminds us of John Burns' claim in the Debate on Physical and Military Instruction in 1900 that poverty was the great recruiting sergeant.

The second leader in the *School Government Chronicle* of 25 October 1906 suggested that the dispute over rifle practice was in danger of both confusing and prejudicing 'the wholesome, necessary movement towards physical care and the development of school sports'. The writer accepted that it was the plain duty of the Minister of Education to prevent the spread of militarism in the school system, but questioned whether rifle practice should be singled out for banning. It was seen to be 'as good as many games and better than some' in terms of what it did for 'physique and temperament', though the writer accepted that better sports could be provided for most boys. Absent from the editorial, however, is any reference to the ethical question as to the acceptability of encouraging boys of school age to handle rifles and shoot at targets, though the writer did agree that parental permission was necessary and that local public opinion was not able under current legislation to sufficiently influence decision-making.[44] Cremer's insistence on establishing a link between the art of shooting and of killing did emphasize the moral aspect which the International Arbitration League and other similar organizations were anxious to establish.

For some participants and for some critics, the issue of military drill was a straightforward if not a simple one. Depending on one's standpoint, it was either superior to, or inferior to, 'ordinary' drill or physical exercises. In the early days of elementary education for all it was necessary to justify a place for any form of physical exercise in the curriculum, at a time when instruction in the three Rs was so sorely needed, and so many children were attending school for the first time. Good order and discipline were qualities most in demand by teachers facing large classes, and by managers anxious to draw government grants to sustain their schools. Some form of regimented drill appeared to be most conducive to the realization of those aims, and consequently drill, drawn to a greater or lesser degree from army manuals, was introduced. Local School Boards drew up their own programmes which were implemented in the schools and subjected to the scrutiny of HMIs. A clear distinction came to be drawn between military drill and ordinary drill. Adherents of the former pointed to external advantages associated with the need to train children for the rigours of life in the armed services or in mill or factory. On the other hand, 'child studies' focused attention on the physical development of children *per se*, irrespective of any future demands which society might make. However, it was argued that, in any case, those demands would be better met if the health and physique of children were prioritized in early years. Advocates of military drill pointed out that such criteria were also met through their system, but it was difficult to apply this argument realistically in respect of infants and girls. Moral justifications were also sought. Advocates of

172

Christian militarism and of Christian manliness could find much in the military drill programmes worthy of their support, while many socialists and pacifists remained critical and apprehensive, finding 'ordinary' drill and later, physical exercises and physical education, more to their liking. It would be difficult to establish children's views on the respective merits of these two main approaches. But provisions for children out of the confines of the school, through brigades, the Boy Scout movement, and schoolboys' shooting clubs,[45] appeared to experience little difficulty in recruiting members for activities which drew on military practices and procedures. The Boy Scout movement avoided weapon training, but was ready, when war came in 1914, to respond to the call for volunteers. Within 24 hours, 2,500 Boy Scouts had been requisitioned for duties, over 100 being attached to the War Office as messengers and office boys, and others helping the police and troops to guard the East Coast and to keep watch over telegraph and telephone lines. They constituted a 'public service non-military body'.[46] John Springhall observes:

> The Boy Scouts could only have emerged against the real and imagined dangers of pre-1914 England. Scouting is one expression of a general cultural movement at the turn of the century among the European middle classes, reflecting the fears, aspirations and self-doubts of an Edwardian military caste anxious to preserve its prestige in a world disturbed by class conflict, international crisis and the threat of national decline.[47]

Those real and imagined dangers had also impinged upon the long-running debate concerning the merits of the teaching of military drill in the nation's elementary schools.

'THE METAPHORS OF WAR'

Although Britons in the nineteenth and early twentieth centuries were reluctant to admit that their country was a militaristic nation, the evidence for it being so is strong. Correlli Barnett writes: 'War, symbolized in the metaphors of war used so widely and so frequently, is deeply embedded in our institutions, thinking, recreations',[48] a view echoed by John Mackenzie, who argues that 'positive attitudes to warfare were deeply embedded in the intellectual, philosophical and cultural trends of the age'.[49] The schoolboys and young men of the early years of the twentieth century, 'saturated in the literature and imagery of militarism',[50] were ready, when war came, to volunteer for army service.

173

It was a matter of relief to the Government that the existing pressures of constitutional reform and social unrest were not compounded by the issue of conscription. Prime Minister Asquith was able to act in somewhat leisurely fashion by setting up a Joint Parliamentary Recruiting Committee in late August 1914 to encourage enlistment.[51] Not until 1916 did it become imperative to meet the appalling losses in the trenches by partial, and subsequently universal, conscription.

NOTES

1. Jonathan May, *Madame Bergman-Österberg, Pioneer of Physical Education for Girls and Women* (London: Harrap, 1969), p. 52.
2. J. A. Schumpeter, *Imperialism and Social Classes* (1st German edn 1919), P.M. Sweezy (ed.) (New York: A. M. Kelly, 1951), p. 29.
3. Ibid., p. 14.
4. Nigel Edley and Margaret Wetherell, *Men in Perspective: Practice, Power, and Identity* (Hemel Hempstead: Prentice-Hall, 1995), p. 97.
5. E. C. Wingfield-Stratford, *The History of English Patriotism*, Vol. I (London: John Lane, 1913), p. xxxiv.
6. E. C. Wingfield-Stratford, *The Foundations of British Patriotism* (London: Routledge, 1939), p. x.
7. Arthur Brittan, *Masculinity and Power* (Oxford: Basil Blackwell, 1989), p. 80.
8. Meiklejohn (ed.), *Blackwood's Educational Series*, Vol. III (1883), pp. 249–50, cited in Valerie E. Chancellor, *History for their Masters: Opinion in the English History Textbook, 1900–1914* (Bath: Adams & Dart, 1970), p. 47.
9. Louise Creighton, *A First History of England* (publisher unknown, 1889), pp. 2–3.
10. John Bartholomew, *Atlas of the British Empire throughout the World, with Explanatory and Statistical Notes*, noted in *School Board Chronicle*, 11 (February 1874): 145.
11. *The World at Home*, Standard IV Geography Reader, Nelson's Royal School series (London and Edinburgh: Nelson, 1882), p. 15.
12. It is perhaps of interest to note that delegates from 25 countries met in Washington, DC, in 1884, to decide on a common system of time and longitude. There was some international rivalry on the issue but Britain had two special claims for the site of the prime meridian and, associated with it, the base for universal time. Firstly, the Royal Observatory at Greenwich had produced the British Nautical Almanac for over a century, and that had almost universal application for navigational purposes. Secondly, the Greenwich Meridian had already been adopted in the United States and in Canada as the basis on which standard time-zone divisions for their transcontinental railway systems had been agreed.
13. Edward Bulwer Lytton, in *The World at Home*, see note 11 above.
14. R. S. Wood (ed.), *National Songs for the School and the Home* (The Penny Poets, LXV, n.d.), pp. 24, 36, 41.
15. *Times Educational Supplement* (4 August 1914): 131.
16. John Gooch, 'Attitudes to War in Late Victorian and Edwardian England', in Brian Bond, and Ian Roy (eds), *War and Society: A Year Book of Military History* (London: Croom Helm, 1975), p. 87, cited in J. A. Mangan, 'Duty unto Death: English Masculinity and Militarism in the Age of the New Imperialism', in J. A. Mangan (ed.), *Tribal Identities: Nationalism, Europe, Sport* (London: Frank Cass, 1996), pp. 12–13.
17. A. P. Thornton, *The Imperial Idea and its Enemies: A Study in British Power* (London: Macmillan, 1959), p. 30.
18. A. P. Thornton, *Imperialism in the Twentieth Century* (London: Macmillan, 1978), p. 3.
19. Prince von Bülow, *Imperial Germany* (1913), cited in R. A. Falconer, *Idealism in National Character* (London: Hodder & Stoughton, 1920), pp. 43–4.

174

20. Arthur Marwick, *The Deluge: British Society and the First World War* (Harmondsworth: Penguin, 1967), p. 80.

21. Michael Howard, 'Europe on the Eve of the First World War', in R. J. W. Evans and H. P. von Strandmann, *The Coming of the First World War*, lectures by members of the Faculty of Modern History at Oxford University (Oxford: Oxford University Press, 1988), p. 2.

22. R. Giddings, 'Delusive Seduction: Pride, Pomp, Circumstance and Military Music', in John M. Mackenzie, *Popular Imperialism and the Military, 1850–1950* (Manchester: Manchester University Press, 1992), p. 26.

23. Sir Francis Younghusband, *The Heart of a Continent* (publisher unknown, 1896), p. 109, cited in R. A. Huttenback, 'The British Empire as a "White Man's Country" – Racial Attitudes and Immigration Legislation in the Colonies of White Settlement', *Journal of British Studies*, 13, 1 (November 1973): 108–37.

24. Herbert Spencer, *The Principles of Sociology*, Vol. III/2 (1886), pp. 568–602, cited in Volker R. Berghahn, *Militarism: The History of an International Debate, 1861–1979* (Leamington Spa: Berg, 1981), p. 11.

25. *School Government Chronicle*, 81 (15 May 1909): 443.

26. *Society of Arts, Journal* (11 March 1870): 344–5.

27. *Times Educational Supplement* (4 August 1914): 131.

28. J. A. Mangan, *Athleticism in the Victorian and Edwardian Public School* (Cambridge: Cambridge University Press, 1988); J. A. Mangan, *The Games Ethic and Imperialism: Aspects of the Diffusion of an Ideal* (Harmondsworth: Viking, 1986).

29. Jeffrey Richards, *Imperialism and Juvenile Literature* (Manchester: Manchester University Press, 1989), p. 10.

30. A *Report by the Consultative Committee upon Questions Affecting Higher Elementary Schools* (1906) defined a higher elementary school as one which catered for brighter children drawn from elementary schools, who would 'as a class, complete their day school education at the age of fifteen, and thereupon go out into the world to earn a living in the lower ranks of commerce and industry. For such children there must naturally be a kind of education that is likely to make them efficient members of the class to which they will belong'.

31. Jeffrey Richards, 'Passing the Love of Women', in J. A. Mangan, and J. Walvin (eds), *Manliness and Morality: Middle-Class Masculinity in Britain and America 1800–1940* (Manchester: Manchester University Press, 1987), p. 104.

32. Alastair J. Reid, *Social Classes and Social Relations in Britain, 1850–1914* (Cambridge: Cambridge University Press, 1995), p. 39.

33. *Report of the Board of Education, 1905–6*, Vol. XXVII, pp. 24–5.

34. David James, *Lord Roberts* (London: Hollis & Carter, 1954), p. 422.

35. Ibid., p. 446.

36. Paul Johnson, in his Preface to George Dangerfield, *The Strange Death of Liberal England* (London: MacGibbon & Kee, 1966), p. 10.

37. C. E. Fayle, *The New Patriotism: A Study in Social Obligations* (London: Harrison & Sons, 1914), p. 39.

38. Karl Liebknecht, *Militarism and Anti-Militarism, with Special Regard to the Internationalist Young Socialist Movement* (first published 1907, trans. and intro. by Grahame Lock) (New York: Garland, 1973), p. 22.

39. I.S. Bloch, see above, Chapter 3, note 9.

40. *Times Educational Supplement* (4 May 1915): 63.

41. Ibid. (2 March 1915): 42.

42. *Guardian* (24 January 1997): 4.

43. *House of Lords Debates*, Fifth Series, Vol. VII, col. 294 (6 March 1911), 'Territorial Army and Home Defence'. The Earl of Portsmouth, in reference to Hamilton's contribution to a publication with the title *Compulsory Service*, in which he answered the charge that a nation in arms encouraged a spirit of Jingoism and militarism.

44. *School Government Chronicle* (25 October 1906): 345.

45. *The Times* (20 December 1906): 2. The article referred to the City Schoolboys' Shooting Club, President, Lord Roberts. The club mustered some 500 boys drawn from nine elementary schools in the City. There was no dependence on the school authorities and all

activities were conducted out of school hours. Two hundred members attended the Miniature Bisley Meeting and the team was placed second in competition with schools drawn from the whole of England.

46. Captain W. Cecil Price, 'The Practical Utility of the Boy Scouts during the War', *The Nineteenth Century and After* (September 1914): 686–701.
47. John Springhall, *Youth, Empire and Society: British Youth Movements, 1883–1940* (London: Croom Helm, 1977), p. 64.
48. Correlli Barnett, 'The Education of Male Elites', *Journal of Contemporary History*, 2, 3 (1967): 15, cited in J. A. Mangan, *Tribal Identities: Nationalism, Europe, Sport* (London: Frank Cass, 1996), p. 12.
49. Mackenzie, *Popular Imperialism and the Military*, p. 2.
50. Jeffrey Richards, 'Popular Imperialism and Image of Army in Juvenile Literature', ibid., p. 81.
51. John Gordon Little, 'H. H. Asquith and Britain's Manpower Problem, 1914–1915', *History*, 82, 267 (July 1997): 397–409.

Appendices

APPENDIX A
SCHEME OF PHYSICAL EXERCISES IN OPERATION BY SCHOOLS
UNDER THE BRADFORD SCHOOL BOARD, 1889

Ten minutes daily were to be devoted to Physical Exercises, which, with a once-weekly drill of 30 minutes, would comprise one hour ten minutes in all.
  Not more than 60 scholars per teacher to be allowed.

Exercises
(a) formation;
(b) combination movements, consisting chiefly of exercises for chest and arm;
(c) free bodily exercises – so arranged as to bring into action all the important muscles of the body;
(d) dumb-bells – (1) wrist exercises; (2) simple exercises for arms, shoulders and chest; (3) complex movements, exercising all muscles of the body;
(e) staves – as a change exercise from dumb-bells;
(f) turnings – half-right, half-left, right, left, and right-about;
(g) marching;
(h) running – an invigorating exercise, especially for the winter months – in file, pairs, fours, eights, and concluding with a simple maze.

N.B. All exercises to be taken in the playground, and b, c, d (1 and 2), f and g in the school...
  Exertion should never be severe or prolonged.

General Drill in the School Playground
Before the exercise –

Fall in	Fours right or left-wheel
Attention	Double arms' distance – extend
Eyes – Right or Left	one arm's distance – extend –
Dress	half right turn
Eyes – front	Cover
From 1 – 4 number	Front prove – distance
	Side prove – distance

(H.F. Pearman, Superintendent of Physical Exercises, *Scheme of Physical Exercises* (Bradford School Board, 1889), pp. 5–8.)

APPENDIX B
LETTER FROM THE EARL OF MEATH TO *THE STANDARD*, 15 JUNE
1908, WHICH HE CLAIMED LED TO THE FORMATION OF THE
DUTY AND DISCIPLINE MOVEMENT

A Society is sadly needed to encourage a more lively sense than at present exists amongst the rising generation of the responsibilities and duties connected with life, and to strengthen the bonds of discipline, which in recent years have been unduly relaxed, to the detriment of the community and to the danger of the State. Various efforts have of late been made to arouse the patriotism of a sleepy nation, and many warnings have been given by eminent men that, unless the British race rise to the height of their almost overwhelming responsibilities, as owners of one-fifth of the earth's surface, their Empire must assuredly fall; but few have pointed out that one of the primary causes of the universally lamented decay of a sense of duty amongst our people is the growth of indiscipline in the home, in the school, and in the State. It must be apparent to the most unobservant that there are influences at work subversive of authority. A few noisy zealots, eager to advertise themselves, and to get credit for an easy humanitarianism, are ever ready, both in and out of Parliament, to render the administration of justice and of authority difficult, and at times almost impossible. Some societies, started for very laudable objects, have permitted their zeal for humanitarianism to push them into action, which, intentionally or unintentionally, encourages such men, and is responsible for no inconsiderable weakening of legitimate authority in the home, in the school, and in the State. To counteract such pernicious influences, concerted action and unity is needed by those who believe that authority requires strengthening, and who desire to support discipline, and a more Spartan-like training of the youth, upon whose shoulders will shortly be placed the burdens of Empire. A Duty and Discipline League should be formed to correct these evil tendencies, and to encourage and support parents and teachers in the maintenance of a reasonable discipline in the home and in the school, and to form a strong public opinion which shall counteract the many influences tending to weaken authority in the State. The writer is far too busy, nor is he the right man to start such a League, but where there is a demand for a leader, a leader will be found. There are many who are firmly impressed with the need of such an organisation, and who would gladly follow an energetic and wise leader, who is willing to organise them and to place himself at their head, in an effort to attack and overthrow the forces which are slowly sapping the virile character of the British people. Let us remember that history has yet to tell us the story of a successful State or Empire founded on the quicksands of indiscipline.

(Reginald, 12th Earl of Meath, *Memories of the Twentieth Century* (London: John Murray, 1924), pp. 43–4.)

APPENDIX C
SIMILARITIES BETWEEN THE ENGLISH MODEL COURSE OF PHYSICAL EDUCATION AND AUSTRALIAN PRACTICE

There was much similarity between England's Model Course of Physical Education and Australian practice in the first decade of the twentieth century. Both countries had introduced military drill in response to pressures to provide for national defence; Britain with her eyes on her European rivals, Australia fearful of Japan, her 'Yellow Peril'. Both looked to the military to provide models of instruction and instructors, but found difficulty in relating the conflicting interests of the education and the military authorities. Both were to abandon military drill as a component of the physical training programmes adopted for general use in the schools.

Following the Australian Defence Act of 1903 a compulsory junior cadet training scheme was established for boys of twelve to fourteen years. Five years after England's Model Course, Melbourne hosted a conference of delegates from most of the Australian states, at which it was recommended that a system of physical training for all schools should be adopted, that staff should be appointed to instruct teachers and that a manual of instruction should be prepared. The Defence Department was to be directly involved, and was to meet the costs of the scheme. A second Melbourne Conference was called the following year to consider the implications of the Defence Act of 1909 on the training of boys within the junior cadet training scheme. However, the Conference widened its brief by recommending that all pupils of both sexes should follow an agreed syllabus of physical training, and proposed that such a syllabus should be based on the revised Syllabus of Physical Exercises for Schools issued in England in 1909. The Junior Cadet Training manual finally appeared in 1916 with the English syllabus in its entirety, and additional sections which included military training.

(See David Kirk and Karen Twigg, 'The Militarization of School Physical Training in Australia: The Rise and Demise of the Junior Cadet Training Scheme, 1911–31', *History of Education*, 22, 44 (1993): 391–414.)

Bibliography

Unless otherwise stated, the place of publication is London.

CONTEMPORARY (TO 1920)

Books

Alexander, A. and Alexander, Mrs, *British Physical Education for Girls* (London and Edinburgh: McDougall's Educational Co., n.d., but frontispiece photograph dated 1907).

Amery, L. S. (ed.), *The Times History of the War in South Africa, 1899–1900* (Sampson Low, 1900), Vol. 1.

Angell, Norman, *The Great Illusion: A Study of the Relation of Military Power in Nations to their Economic and Social Advantage* (Heinemann, 1st edn 1909; 3rd edn 1911).

Bartholomew, John, *Atlas of the British Empire throughout the World, with Explanatory and Statistical Notes*, noted in *School Board Chronicle* (February 1874).

Boyd, Charles W. (ed.), *Mr Chamberlain's Speeches* (Constable, 1914), Vol. II.

Brunton, Sir Lauder, *Collected Papers on Physical and Military Training* (published privately, n.d., but probably *c.* 1915).

Bülow, Prince von, *Deutsche Politik* (1913), trans. Marie A. Lewenz, *Imperial Germany* (Cassell, 1914).

Chamberlain, Joseph, *Patriotism: An Address to the Students of the University of Glasgow, November 1897* (Constable, 1897).

Chesterton, Thomas, *Organised Playground Games, Suitable for Elementary and Secondary Schools* (Educational Supply Association, 1901).

Creighton, Louise, *A First History of England* (publisher unknown, 1889).

Falconer, Sir R. A., *Idealism in National Character: Essays and Addresses* (Hodder & Stoughton, 1920).

Fayle, C. E., *The New Patriotism: A Study in Social Obligations* (Harrison & Sons, 1914).

Gorst, Sir John, *The Children of the Nation: How their Health and Vigour Should Be Promoted by the State*, ed. C. W. Saleeby, The New Library of Medicine (Methuen, 1906).

Greenwood, Arthur, *The Health and Physique of School Children* (P. S. King & Son, 1913).

Haldane, R. B., *Education and Empire: Addresses on Certain Topics of the Day* (John Murray, 1902).

——, *Army Reform and other Addresses* (Fisher Unwin, 1907).

Hayward, F. H., *Day and Evening Schools: Their Management and Organisation* (Ralph Holland, 1910).

Holmes, E. G. A., *What Is and What Might Be: A Study of Education in General and Elementary Education in Particular* (Constable, 1911).

Hughes, Emrys, *Keir Hardie's Speeches and Writings (1888–1915)* (Glasgow: Forward Printing & Publishing Co., n.d.).

Kekewich, G. W., *The Education Department and After* (Constable, 1920).

King-Harman, M. J., *British Boys: Their Training and Prospects* (G. Bell, 1913).

Macdonald, J. Ramsay, *Labour and the Empire* (Allen, 1907).

——, *Socialism and Government* (Independent Labour Party, 1910),Vol. I.

——, *National Defence: A Study in Militarism* (G. Allen & Unwin, 1917).

Maclaren, Archibald, *A System of Physical Education, Theoretical and Practical* (Oxford: Clarendon Press, 1907).

Magnus, Sir Philip, *Educational Aims and Efforts, 1880–1910* (Longmans Green, 1910).

Meath, Earl of (ed.), *Some National and Board School Reforms* (Longmans Green, 1887).

——, *Social Arrows* (Longmans Green, 2nd edn 1887).

——, *Social Aims: Essays by the Earl of Meath and the Countess of Meath* (Wells Gardner, Darton & Co., 1893).

Meath, Earl of, Legh, Cornwall and Jackson, Edith, *Our Empire, Past and Present*, 2 vols, 2nd edn (Harrison, 1906).

Mill, John Stuart, *Representative Government* (1861) in his *Utilitarianism, Liberty and Representative Government* (J. M. Dent, Everyman, 1910).

——, *Essays on Politics and Society* (Toronto: University of Toronto Press, 1977). Vol. XIX of the Collected Works of John Stuart Mill.

Nelson (publisher), *The World at Home*, Standard IV Geography Reader, Royal School series (London and Edinburgh: Nelson, 1882).

Norwood, Sir Cyril and Hope, A. H. (eds), *The Higher Education of Boys in England* (Murray, 1909).

Oakesmith, J., *Race and Nationality: An Inquiry into the Origins and Growth of Patriotism* (Heinemann, 1919).

Oncken, H., 'The German Empire', in *Cambridge Modern History*, XII (Cambridge: Cambridge University Press, 1910).

Seeley, J. R., *The Expansion of England* (1st publ. 1883; Macmillan, 1901).

Vachell, H. A., *The Hill: A Romance of Friendship* (J. Murray, 1905, 4th impress., 1950).

Waldstein, Sir Charles, *Patriotism, National and International: An Essay* (Longmans, 1917).

Way, Revd J. P., *et al.*, 'Military Training', in *The Public Schools from Within* (Sampson Low, 1906).

Wingfield-Stratford, E. C., *The History of English Patriotism*, 2 vols (John Lane, 1913).

Wood, R. S. (ed.), *National Songs for the School and the Home* (The Penny Poets, n.d.), Vol. LXV.

Journals, Newspapers, etc.

Andrews, Frederick, 'Paper in Opposition to the Introduction of Military Drill into Schools', paper read at Liverpool Health Congress, 1903, *Ling Association Leaflet*, 1, 4 (April 1904): 5–6.

Bathurst, Katherine, 'The Need for National Nurseries', *The Nineteenth Century and After* (May 1905): 818–24.

——, 'The Physique of Girls', *The Nineteenth Century and After* (May 1906): 825–33.

Birchenough, Henry, 'Compulsory Education and Compulsory Military Training', *The Nineteenth Century and After* (July 1904): 20–7.

Colne Valley Guardian Weekly (1913–14).

Daily Chronicle (30 December 1886).

Eltzbacher, O., 'The Disadvantages of Education', *The Nineteenth Century and After* (February 1903): 315–18.

Gladstone, W. E., 'England's Mission', *The Nineteenth Century* (September 1878): 569–73.

Havelock-Allan, Lt-Gen. Sir Henry, 'A General Voluntary Training to Arms versus Conscription', *Fortnightly Review*, 61 (1897): 85–97.

Huddersfield Daily Chronicle (12 January 1912–end of 1914).

Impey, E. Adair, 'Military Training Considered as Part of General Education', *Journal of Scientific Physical Training*, 5 (1913): 16.

Kipling, Rudyard, 'The Courting of Dinah Shadd', *Macmillan's Magazine*, 61 (November 1889–April 1890): 381–94.

Knollys, Lt- Col. W. W., 'Boy Soldiers', *The Nineteenth Century* (July 1879): 1–9.

Long, Constance, 'Physical Degeneration', *Ling Association Leaflet*, 2, 4 (May 1905): 1–4.

Lyttelton, Edward, 'Athletics in Public Schools', *The Nineteenth Century* (January 1880): 43–57.

Martin, J. W., 'State Education at Home and Abroad', Fabian Tract, 52 (1894).

Maurice, Sir J. F. (pseud. 'Miles'), 'Where to Get Men', *The Contemporary Review* (January 1902): 78–86.

——, 'National Health, a Soldier's Study', *Contemporary Review* (January 1903): 41–56.

Meath, Earl of, 'Health and Physique of our City Populations', *The Nineteenth Century* (July 1881): 1–13, subsequently published in *Some National and School Board Reforms* (Longmans Green, 1887).

——, Letter to the Editor, *Fortnightly Review*, 61 (1897): 972–4.

——, 'Universal Military Training for Lads', *The Nineteenth Century and After* (May 1905): 734–44.

Methuen, General Lord, 'Training the Youth of England', *The Nineteenth Century and After* (February 1905): 238–43.

Perry, C. C., 'Our Undisciplined Brains: The War Test', *The Nineteenth Century and After* (December 1901): 897–901.

Price, Captain W. Cecil, 'The Practical Utility of the Boy Scouts during the War', *The Nineteenth Century and After* (September 1914): 686–701.

Robertson, Captain J. C., 'The Introduction of Military Drill into Schools', paper read at Liverpool Health Congress, 1903, *Ling Association Leaflet*, 1, 4 (April 1904): 2–5.

School Board Chronicle.

School Government Chronicle.

Seebohm, Frederic, 'Imperialism and Socialism', *The Nineteenth Century* (April 1880): 726–8.

Shaw, Bernard, *Fabianism and the Empire*, Manifesto by the Fabian Society (1900).

Society of Arts, Journal (1869–1920).

Spectator (7 January 1902; 24 January 1903).

The Times (1870–14).

Times Educational Supplement (1912–15).

Vogel, Julius, 'Greater or Lesser Britain', *The Nineteenth Century* (July 1877): 809–31.

Webb, Sidney, 'The Workers' School Board Programme', Fabian Tract 55 (1894).

——, 'Lord Rosebery's Escape from Hounsditch', *The Nineteenth Century and After* (September 1901): 375–85.

——, 'Twentieth-Century Politics: A Policy for National Efficiency', Fabian Tract 108 (November 1901).

Wolseley, General Lord, *United Services Magazine* (1897).

Worker (The), The Organ of the Huddersfield Socialist Party (1905–15).

Official Records (State)

(i)   *House of Commons Debates* (Hansard) (throughout the period). *House of Lords Debates* (Hansard) (throughout the period).

(ii) *Reports of the Committee of Council on Education* (for the years 1870–99). The general reports of HMIs were printed as appendices.

(iii) *Reports of the Board of Education* (for years 1900–14). The general reports of HMIs were printed as appendices.

(iv) *Royal Commissions and Similar Inquiries*
Report of the Royal Commission on the Working of the Elementary Education Acts (England and Wales) (Cross) (1886–88).
Report of the Royal Commission on Physical Training (Scotland) (1903).
Report of the Interdepartmental Committee on Physical Deterioration (1904).
Report of the Interdepartmental Committee on the Model Course of Physical Education (1904).
Report of the Interdepartmental Committee on Medical Inspection and Feeding of Children attending Public Elementary Schools (1905).
Report of the Consultative Committee upon Questions affecting Higher Elementary Schools (1906).
Report of the Consultative Committee on Attendance, Compulsory or Otherwise at Continuation Schools (1909).

(v)   *Codes*
Code of Regulations for Public Elementary Schools (throughout the period).

(vi) *The Inspectorate*
Circular of General Instructions to Her Majesty's Inspectors (January 1878).
Code for 1896–97. *Revised Instructions to Her Majesty's Inspectors.*
The New Code 1897 – Circular to Inspectors, No. 153P.

(vii) *Board of Education Circulars*
452 Circular to HMIs
     Physical Training and *Model Course of Physical Training for use in the Upper Departments of Public Elementary Schools* (20 June 1901).
484 Circular to HMIs
     Physical Training (provisional arrangements) (May 1903).
515 *Circular with Report of the Interdepartmental Committee on the Model Course on Physical Exercises* (22 August 1904).
552 *Education (Provision of Meals) Act* (1 January 1907).

185

576 *Memorandum on Medical Inspection of Children in Public Elementary Schools, under section 13 of the Education (Administrative Provisions) Act, 1907* (22 November 1907).

577 *The Education (Administrative Provisions) Act, 1907* (5 December 1907).

582 Circular to LEAs. *Schedule of Medical Inspection. Education (Administrative Provisions) Act, 1907, section 13* (with *Schedule of Medical Inspection*) (23 January 1908).

727 *Revised Syllabus of Physical Exercises for Public Elementary Schools* (September 1909).

(viii) *Miscellaneous*

Handbook of Suggestions for the Consideration of Teachers and Others concerned in the work of Public Elementary Schools (1905 and 1927). *Annual Report of Dr George Newman, Chief Medical Officer to the Board of Education* (1911).

Official Records (Local)

(i) *Bradford*

School Board Triennial Reports, 1–11 (1877–1903).

Scheme of Physical Exercises in operation by schools under the Bradford School Board, 1889.

Education Committee Annual Reports (1904–14).

(ii) *Halifax*

Education Committee, Minutes (1912–14).

(iii) *Huddersfield*

Education Committee, Annual Reports (from year ending 9 November 1910–end of 1914).

Education Committee, Minutes of Education Committee and Sub-committees (10 October 1912–end of 1914).

(iv) *Leeds*

School Board, *Souvenir of Leeds School Board, 1870–1903.*

School Board, Report of Chief Inspector of Schools (1892–1902).

Education Committee, Proceedings (1904–11).

Education Committee, Annual Reports (1904–14).

Leeds Hebrew School, First Annual Report (1889).

School Log-Books

Cross Stamford Street Board School, Boys (1872–1914).

Meanwood Church of England School (1900–01).

(v) *London*

School Board, *Final Report of the School Board for London, 1870–1904* (P. S. King & Son, 1904), 2nd rev. edn.

(vi) *West Riding of Yorkshire*

Education Committee, Annual Reports (1904–14).

New Mill National School Centenary Brochure, 1838–1938.

Other Records

(i)   *Fabian Society tracts* (see also under author, where given, in Journals section above).

No. 52, J. W. Martin, *State Education at Home and Abroad* (1894).

No. 55, *The Workers' School Board Programme* (1894).

No. 108, Sidney Webb, *Twentieth-Century Politics: A Policy of National Efficiency* (1901).

(ii) *Huddersfield and District Rifle Club*

Annual Reports (1906–09).

(iii) *Independent Labour Party*

Report of the 17th Annual Conference, Edinburgh (1909).

Report of the 19th Annual Conference, Birmingham (1911).

Katharine Bruce, *Socialism and the Home*, ILP pamphlet (n.d., but advertisement dated 1909).

(iv) *Jewish Lads' Brigade*

Annual Reports (1907–20).

(v)   *Labour Party*

Annual Conference Report (1911).

(vi) *National Union of Teachers*

30th Annual Conference Report (1899).

Annual Report (1902).

(vii) *Trades Union Congress*

Annual Conference Report (1904).

Miscellaneous

Blatchford, R., *Germany and England*, pamphlet reprinted from the *Daily Mirror* (Associated Newspapers, 1911).

Glasier, J. Bruce, *Militarism*, Labour and War Pamphlet, 2 (Independent Labour Party [ILP], 1915).

——, *The Peril of Conscription*, Labour and War Pamphlet, 3 (ILP, 1915).

Glasier, Katharine Bruce, *Socialism and the Home* (Independent Labour Party pamphlet, n.d., but advertisement dated 1909).

Norman, C. H., *British Militarism – A Reply to Robert Blatchford* (ILP pamphlet, 1915), new series, 1.

——, *Nationality and Patriotism*, pamphlet (National Labour Press, 1915).

Rosebery, Lord, Speech delivered at Chesterfield, 16 December 1901 (Liberal League Publication 37).

What Her Majesty's Inspectors Say: Being their Reports (Newcastle-upon-Tyne: North of England School Furnishing Company, 1879–86).

LATER SOURCES (POST-1920)

Books

Alter, P., *Nationalism* (first published Germany, 1985), trans. S. McKinnon-Evans (Edward Arnold, 1989).

Armytage, W. H. G., *Four Hundred Years of English Education* (Cambridge: Cambridge University Press, 1969).

Ashby, Eric and Anderson, Mary, *Portrait of Haldane at Work in Education* (Macmillan, 1974).

Barker, Ernest, *National Character and the Factors in its Formation* (Methuen, 1927).

Barker, R. S., *Education and Politics, 1900–51: A Study of the Labour Party* (Oxford: Clarendon Press, 1972).

Baumgart, Winfried, *Imperialism: The Idea and Reality of British and French Colonial Expansion, 1880–1914* (New York: Oxford University Press, 1982).

Beales, A. C. F., *The History of Peace: A Short Account of the Organised Movements for International Peace* (Bell, 1931).

Bealey, F. (ed.), *The Social and Political Thought of the British Labour Party* (Weidenfeld & Nicolson, 1970).

Beloff, Max, *Imperial Sunset. Vol. I, Britain's Liberal Empire, 1897–1921* (Methuen, 1969).

Bennett, G. (ed.), *The Concept of Empire: Burke to Attlee, 1774–1947* (A. & C. Black, 1953).

Berghahn, Volker R., *Germany and the Approach of War in 1914* (Macmillan, 1973).

——, *Militarism: The History of an International Debate, 1861–1979* (Leamington Spa: Berg, 1981).

Best, Geoffrey, 'Militarism and the Victorian Public School', in B. Simon and I. Bradley (eds), *The Victorian Public School* (Dublin: Gill & Macmillan, 1975).

Bond, Brian and Roy, Ian (eds), *War and Society: A Year-book of Military History* (Croom Helm,1975).

Bowle, John, *The Imperial Achievement: The Rise and Transformation of the British Empire* (Harmondsworth: Penguin, 1977).

Brittan, Arthur, *Masculinity and Power* (Oxford: Basil Blackwell, 1989).

Brockway, Fenner, *The Colonial Revolution* (Hart-Davis/MacGibbon, 1973).

Carrington, C. E., *The British Overseas: Exploits of a Nation of Shopkeepers* (Cambridge: Cambridge University Press, 1950).

Carrington, Charles. (ed.), *The Complete Barrack-Room Ballads of Rudyard Kipling* (Methuen, 1974).

Chadwick, H. Munro, *The Nationalities of Europe and the Growth of National Ideologies* (Cambridge: Cambridge University Press, 1945).

Chancellor, Valerie E., *History for their Masters: Opinion in the English History Textbook, 1900–1914* (Bath: Adams & Dart, 1970).

Clark, G. Kitson, *An Expanding Society: Britain 1830–1900* (Cambridge: Cambridge University Press, 1967).

Colley, Linda, *Britons: Forging the Nation 1707–1837* (New Haven, CT, and London: Yale University Press, 1992).

Craig, F. W. S. (ed.), *British General Election Manifestos, 1900–1974* (Macmillan, 1975).

Crossick, Geoffrey (ed.), *The Lower Middle Class in Britain* (Croom Helm, 1977).

Cunningham, Hugh, *The Volunteer Force – A Social and Political History, 1859–1908* (Croom Helm, 1975).

Dangerfield, George, *The Strange Death of Liberal England* (MacGibbon & Kee, 1966).

Delamont, Sara and Duffin, Lorna (eds), *The Nineteenth-Century Woman: Her Cultural and Physical World* (Croom Helm, 1978).

Dixon, J. G., McIntosh, P. C., Munrow, A.D. and Willetts, R. F., *Landmarks in the History of Physical Education* (Routledge & Kegan Paul, 1957).

Eaglesham, Eric, *From School Board to Local Authority* (Routledge & Kegan Paul, 1956).

Edley, Nigel and Wetherell, Margaret, *Men in Perspective: Practice, Power, and Identity* (Hemel Hempstead: Prentice-Hall, 1995).

Eldridge, C. C., *Victorian Imperialism* (Hodder & Stoughton, 1978).

Ensor, R. C. K., *England, 1870–1914* (Oxford: Clarendon Press, 1936).

Evans, R. J. W. and von Strandmann, H. P. (eds), *The Coming of the First World War*, lectures by members of the Faculty of Modern History at Oxford University, 1984 (Oxford: Clarendon Press, 1988).

Faber, R., *The Vision and the Need: Late Victorian Imperialist Aims* (Faber & Faber, 1966).

Foot, M. R. D. (ed.), *War and Society* (Elek, 1973).

Fuller, Major-General J. F. C., *The Conduct of War, 1789–1961* (Eyre Methuen, 1972).

Giddings, R., 'Delusive Seduction: Pride, Pomp, Circumstance and Military Music', in John M. Mackenzie, *Popular Imperialism and the Military, 1850–1950* (Manchester: Manchester University Press, 1992).

Gollwitzer, Heinz, *Europe in the Age of Imperialism, 1880–1914* (Thames & Hudson, 1969).

Gooch, John, 'Attitudes to War in Late Victorian and Edwardian England', in Brian Bond and Ian Roy (eds), *War and Society: A Year Book of Military History* (Croom Helm, 1975).

Grierson, Edward, *The Imperial Dream: The British Commonwealth and Empire, 1775–1969* (Collins, 1972).

Haldane, R. B., *An Autobiography* (Hodder & Stoughton, 1929).

Halévy, E., *History of the English People in the Nineteenth Century. Vol. V, Imperialism and the Rise of Labour, 1895–1905* (Benn, 2nd rev. edn, 1951).

Hall, Donald E. (ed.), *Muscular Christianity: Embodying the Victorian Age* (Cambridge: Cambridge University Press, 1994).

Himmelfarb, G., *Victorian Minds* (Weidenfeld & Nicolson, 1968).

Hobsbawm, E. J., *The Age of Empire, 1875–1914* (Weidenfeld & Nicolson, 1987).

——, *Nations and Nationalism since 1780: Programme, Myth, Reality* (Cambridge: Cambridge University Press, 1992).

Hobsbawm, E. J. and Ranger, T. (eds), *The Invention of Tradition* (Cambridge: Cambridge University Press, 1983).

Howard, Michael, 'Europe on the Eve of the First World War', in R. J. W. Evans and H. P. von Strandmann (eds), *The Coming of the First World War*, lectures by members of the Faculty of Modern History at Oxford University, 1984 (Oxford: Clarendon Press, 1988).

Howarth, Patrick, *Play up and Play the Game: The Heroes of Popular Fiction* (Eyre Methuen, 1973).

Hyam, Ronald, *Britain's Imperial Century, 1815–1914: A Study of Empire and Expansion* (Batsford, 1976).

James, David, *Lord Roberts* (Hollis & Carter, 1954).

James, Robert R., *Rosebery – A Biography of Archibald Philip, Fifth Earl of Rosebery* (Weidenfeld & Nicolson, 1963).

Janssen, K. H., 'A Patriotic Historian's Justification', in H. W. Koch, *Origins of the First World War: Great Power Rivalry and German War Aims* (Macmillan, 1972), p. 261.

Jenkins, Gwyn Harries, *The Army in Victorian Society* (Routledge & Kegan Paul, 1977).

Kamenka, Eugene (ed.), *Nationalism: The Nature and Evolution of an Idea* (Edward Arnold, 1976).

Kedourie, E., *Nationalism* (Hutchinson, 1960).

Kennedy, Paul, *The Realities Behind Diplomacy: Background Influences on British External Policy 1865–1980* (Collins/Fontana, 1985).

——, *The Rise and Fall of the Great Powers: Economic Change and Military Conflict from 1500 to 2000* (Collins/Fontana, 1989).

——, *Strategy and Diplomacy, 1870–1945* (Collins/Fontana, 1989).

Kennedy, Paul and Nicholls, Anthony, *Nationalist and Racialist Movements in Britain and Germany before 1914* (Macmillan, 1981).

Kiernan, V. G., *From Conquest to Collapse: European Empires from 1815–1960* (New York: Pantheon, 1982).

Kipling, Rudyard, *Rudyard Kipling's Verse: Inclusive Edition, 1885–1918* (London: Hodder & Stoughton, n.d., probably 1921).

Koch, H. W., *Origins of the First World War: Great Power Rivalry and German War Aims* (Macmillan, 1972).

Lichtheim, G., *Imperialism* (Harmondsworth, Penguin, 1974).

Liebnecht, Karl, *Militarism and Antimilitarism, with Special Regard to the Internationalist Young Socialist Movement*, trans. with intro. Grahame Lock (New York: Garland Publications, 1973). (Reprint of 1917 edn.)

Lipson, E., *Europe in the Nineteenth Century, 1815–1914*, 8th edn (A. & C. Black, 1948).

Macdonald, N. P. (ed.), *What is Patriotism? Answered by Lord Allen of Hurtwood and Others* (Thornton Butterworth, 1935).

McIntosh, P. C., *Physical Education in England since 1800* (Bell, rev. edn, 1968).

Mack, E. C., *Public Schools and British Opinion since 1860: The Relationship between Contemporary Ideas and the Evolution of an English Institution* (New York: Columbia University Press, 1941).

Mackenzie, John M., *Propaganda and Empire: The Manipulation of British Public Opinion, 1880–1960* (Manchester: Manchester University Press, 1984).

——, *Imperialism and Popular Culture* (Manchester: Manchester University Press, 1986).

——, *Popular Imperialism and the Military, 1850–1950* (Manchester: Manchester University Press, 1992).

——, *Fair Play: Ethics in Sport and Education* (Heinemann, 1979).

Maclure, S., *One Hundred Years of London Education, 1870–1970* (Harmondsworth: Penguin, 1970).

Mangan, J. A., *Athleticism in the Victorian and Edwardian Public School*

(Cambridge: Cambridge University Press, 1981).

——, '"The Grit of our Forefathers": Invented Traditions, Propaganda and Imperialism', in J. M. Mackenzie (ed.), *Imperialism and Popular Culture* (Manchester: Manchester University Press, 1986).

——, *The Games Ethic and Imperialism: Aspects of the Diffusion of an Ideal* (Harmondsworth: Viking, 1986).

—— (ed.), *Tribal Identities: Nationalism, Europe and Sport* (Frank Cass, 1996).

Mangan, J. A. and Walvin, J. (eds), *Manliness and Morality: Middle-Class Masculinity in Britain and America, 1800–1940* (Manchester: Manchester University Press, 1987).

Marder, A. J., *The Anatomy of British Sea Power – A History of British Naval Policy in the pre-Dreadnought Era, 1880–1905* (Frank Cass, 1972).

Marwick, Arthur, *The Deluge: British Society and the First World War* (Harmondsworth: Penguin, 1967).

——, *Britain in the Century of Total War: War, Peace and Social Change, 1900–1967* (Harmondsworth: Penguin, 1970).

Masterman, C. F. G. (ed.), *The Heart of the Empire: Discussions of Problems of Modern City Life in England* (first published London: Fisher Unwin, 1901), ed. with intro. Bentley B. Gilbert (Brighton: Harvester Press, 1973).

May, Jonathan, *Madame Bergman-Österberg: Pioneer of Physical Education and Games for Girls and Women* (Harrap, 1969).

Meacham, Standish, *A Life Apart: The English Working Class, 1890–1914* (Thames & Hudson, 1977).

Meath, Earl of, *Memories of The Nineteenth Century* (John Murray, 1923).

——, *Memories of the Twentieth Century* (John Murray, 1924).

Minogue, K. R., *Nationalism* (Batsford, 1967).

Mommsen, W. J., *Theories of Imperialism* (Weidenfeld & Nicolson, 1981).

Morgan, Kenneth O., *The Age of Lloyd George: The Liberal Party and British Politics, 1890–1929* (Unwin University Books, Allen & Unwin, 1971).

Morris, A. J. A., *Radicalism Against War, 1906–1914* (Longman, 1972).

——, *Edwardian Radicalism, 1900–1914* (Routledge, 1974).

——, *C. P. Trevelyan, 1870–1958: Portrait of a Radical* (Belfast: Blackstaff Press, 1977).

Morris, James, *Heaven's Command: An Imperial Progress* (Harmondsworth: Penguin Books, 1979).

——, *Pax Britannica: The Climax of an Empire* (Harmondsworth: Penguin, 1979).

——, *Farewell the Trumpets: An Imperial Retreat* (Harmondsworth: Penguin, 1979).

Muir, Ramsay, *A Short History of the British Commonwealth. Vol. II, The*

Modern Commonwealth (George Philip & Son, 4th edn 1927).

Newman, Sir George, *The Building of a Nation's Health* (Macmillan, 1939).

Owen, Roger and Sutcliffe, Bob (eds), *Studies in the Theory of Imperialism* (Longman, 1972).

Pakenham, Thomas, *The Boer War* (Weidenfeld & Nicolson, 1979).

Pease, E. R., *History of the Fabian Society* (1st edn 1918; 3rd edn Frank Cass, 1963).

Perlmutter, Amos, *The Military and Politics in Modern Times* (New Haven, CT: Yale University Press, 1977).

Porter, Andrew, *European Imperialism, 1860–1914* (Macmillan, 1994).

Porter, B., *Critics of Empire* (Macmillan, 1968).

——, *The Lion's Share: A Short History of British Imperialism, 1850–1970* (Longman, 1975).

——, *Britain, Europe and the World, 1850–1982* (Allen & Unwin, 1983).

Price, Richard N., *An Imperial War and the British Working Class: Working-Class Attitudes and Reactions to the Boer War, 1899–1902* (Routledge & Kegan Paul, 1972).

——, 'Society, Status and Jingoism: The Social Roots of Lower-Middle-Class Patriotism, 1870–1900', in Geoffrey Crossick (ed.), *The Lower Middle Class in Britain* (Croom Helm, 1977).

Reader, W. J., *At Duty's Call: A Study in Obsolete Patriotism* (Manchester: Manchester University Press, 1988).

Reeder, D. A. (ed.), *Educating Our Masters* (Leicester: Leicester University Press, 1980).

Reid, Alastair, *Social Classes and Social Relations in Britain, 1850–1914*, New Studies in Economic and Social History (Cambridge: Cambridge University Press, 1995).

Rich, E. E., *The Education Act, 1870* (Harlow: Longman, 1970).

Richards, Jeffrey, 'Passing the Love of Women', in J. A. Mangan, and J. Walvin (eds), *Manliness and Morality: Middle-Class Masculinity in Britain and America 1800–1940* (Manchester: Manchester University Press, 1987).

——, *Happiest Days: The Public Schools in English Fiction* (Manchester: Manchester University Press, 1988).

——, *Imperialism and Juvenile Literature* (Manchester: Manchester University Press, 1989).

——, 'Popular Imperialism and the Image of the Army in Juvenile Literature', in John M. Mackenzie, *Popular Imperialism and the Military, 1850–1950* (Manchester: Manchester University Press, 1992).

Roberts, Robert, *The Classic Slum: Salford Life in the First Quarter of the Century* (Manchester: Manchester University Press, 1971).

——, *A Ragged Schooling – Growing up in the Classic Slum* (Manchester:

Manchester University Press, 1976).

Schumpeter, Joseph A., *Imperialism and Social Classes* (1st German edn 1919), P. M. Sweezy (ed.) (New York: A. M. Kelly, 1951).

Scott, J. F., *The Menace of Nationalism in Education* (Allen & Unwin, 1926).

Searle, G. R., *The Quest for National Efficiency: A Study in British Politics and British Political Thought, 1899–1914* (Oxford: Basil Blackwell, 1971).

Selleck, R. J. W., *The New Education, 1870–1914* (Pitman & Sons, 1968).

Semmel, B., *Imperialism and Social Reform: English Social-Imperial Thought, 1895–1914* (Allen & Unwin, 1960).

Shannon, R., *The Crisis of Imperialism, 1865–1915* (Paladin, 1976).

Sherington, Geoffrey, *English Education, Social Change and War, 1911–1920* (Manchester: Manchester University Press, 1981).

Simon, Brian, *Education and the Labour Movement, 1870–1920* (Lawrence & Wishart, 1965).

Simon, Brian and Bradley, Ian (eds), *The Victorian Public School* (Dublin: Gill & Macmillan, 1975).

Skelley, Alan Ramsay, *The Victorian Army at Home: The Recruitment and Terms and Conditions of the British Regular, 1859–1899* (Croom Helm, 1977).

Smith, Tony, *The Pattern of Imperialism: The United States, Great Britain, and the Late-industrializing World since 1815* (Cambridge: Cambridge University Press, 1981).

Snyder, L. L. (ed.), *The Dynamics of Nationalism: Readings in its Meaning and Development* (Princeton, NJ: D. van Nostrand, 1964).

Sommer, Dudley, *Haldane of Cloan* (Allen & Unwin, 1960).

Spring, Howard, *Heaven Lies About Us* (Constable, 1939).

Springhall, J., *Youth, Empire and Society: British Youth Movements, 1883–1940* (Croom Helm, 1977).

Tapper, T. and Salter, B., *Education and the Political Order* (Macmillan, 1978).

Thomson, D., *Europe since Napoleon* (Harmondsworth: Penguin, 1966).

Thornton, A. P., *The Imperial Idea and its Enemies: A Study in British Power* (Macmillan, 1959).

——, *For the File on Empire* (Macmillan, 1968).

——, *Imperialism in the Twentieth Century* (Macmillan, 1978).

Vagts, Alfred, *A History of Militarism* (Allen & Unwin, 1938), cited by Volker R. Berghahn, *Militarism: The History of an International Debate, 1861–1979* (Leamington Spa: Berg, 1981).

Van Dalen, D. B. and Bennett, B. L., *A World History of Physical Education – Cultural, Philosophical, Comparative* (Hemel Hempstead/Englewood Cliffs, NJ: Prentice-Hall, 1971).

194

Vane, Sir Francis, *Agin the Governments: Memories and Adventures, etc.* (Sampson Low & Co., 1929).

Wilkinson, R., *The Prefects: British Leadership and the Public School Tradition: A Comparative Study in the Making of Rulers* (Oxford: Oxford University Press, 1964).

Wingfield-Stratford, E. C., *The History of British Civilization*, 2 vols (Routledge, 1928).

——, *The Foundations of British Patriotism* (Routledge, 1939).

Winks, R. W., *British Imperialism: Gold, God, Glory* (New York: Holt, Rinehart & Winston, 1963).

Journals, Newspapers, etc.

Armytage, W. H. G., 'The 1870 Education Act', *British Journal of Educational Studies* (June 1970): 121–33.

Barker, Rodney, 'The Labour Party and Education for Socialism', *International Review of Social History*, 14, 1 (1969): 22–53.

Barnett, Correlli, 'The Education of Male Elites', *Journal of Contemporary History*, 2, 3 (July 1967): 15–35.

Bourke, Joanna, 'Masculinity, Men's Bodies and the Great War', *History Today*, 46, 2 (February 1996): 8–11.

Brown, K. D., 'Models in History: A Micro-study of Late-Nineteenth-Century Entrepreneurship: William Britain's Family Firm Manufacturing Hollow-Cast Toy Soldiers 1891–1914', *Economic History Review*, 42 (November 1989): 528–37.

Cunningham, Hugh, 'Jingoism in 1877–78', *Victorian Studies*, 14 (June 1971): 429–53.

——, 'The Language of Patriotism, 1750–1914', *History Workshop*, 12 (Autumn 1981): 8–33.

Davin, Anna, 'Imperialism and Motherhood', *History Workshop*, 5 (Spring 1978): 9–65.

Dunae, Patrick A., 'Boys' Literature and the Idea of Empire, 1870–1914', *Victorian Studies*, 24, 1 (Autumn 1980): 105–21.

Fieldhouse, D. K., 'Imperialism: An Historiographical Revision', *Economic History Review*, 14, 2 (1961): 187–209.

Guardian, The (3 January 1991; 24 January 1997).

Harcourt, F., 'Disraeli's Imperialism 1866–1868: A Question of Timing', *Historical Journal*, 23, 1 (March 1980): 87–109.

Huttenback, R. A., 'The British Empire as a "White Man's Country": Racial Attitudes and Immigration Legislation in the Colonies of White Settlement', *Journal of British Studies*, 13, 1 (November 1973): 108–37.

Jacobson, Peter, 'Rosebery and Liberal Imperialism, 1899–1903', *Journal of British Studies*, 13, 1 (November 1973): 83–107.

Kirk, David and Twigg, Karen, 'The Militarization of School Physical Training in Australia: The Rise and Demise of the Junior Cadet Training Scheme, 1911–31', *History of Education*, 22, 4 (1993): 391–414.

Little, John Gordon, 'H. H. Asquith and Britain's Manpower Problem, 1914–1915', *History*, 82, 267 (July 1997): 397–409.

Mangan, J.A., 'Images of Empire in the Late Victorian Public School', *Journal of Educational Administration and History*, 12, 1 (January 1980): 31–9.

——, 'Muscular, Militaristic and Manly: The British Middle-Class Hero as Moral Messenger', *International Journal of the History of Sport*, 13, 1 (March 1996).

Miller, J. D. B., 'The End of Bombast and Pessimism?', *Journal of Contemporary History*, 15, 1 (January 1980): 53–65.

Observer, The (16 April 1995).

Otley, C. B., 'Militarism and Militarization in the Public Schools, 1900–1972', *British Journal of Sociology*, 29, 3 (September 1978): 321–9.

Rees, Roy, 'Physical Education Teacher Training in Liverpool in the Nineteenth Century', *History of Education Bulletin*, 19 (Spring 1977): 40–4.

Simpson, Linda, 'Imperialism, National Efficiency and Education, 1900–1905', *Journal of Educational Administration and History*, 16, 1 (January 1984): 28–36.

Springhall, J. O., 'Lord Meath, Youth, and Empire', *Journal of Contemporary History*, 5, 4 (1970): 97–111.

——, 'The Boy Scouts, Class and Militarism in Relation to British Youth Movements, 1908–1930', *International Review of Social History*, 16, 1 (January 1984): 125–58.

Summers, Anne, 'Militarism in Britain before the Great War', *History Workshop Journal*, 2 (Autumn 1976): 104–23.

Surridge, Keith, '"All You Soldiers Are What We Call Pro-Boer": The Military Critique of the South African War, 1899–1902', *Journal of the Historical Association*, 82, 268 (October 1997): 582–600.

Taylor, Miles, 'Patriotism, History and the Left in Twentieth-Century Britain', *Historical Journal*, 33, 4 (1990): 971–87.

Voeltz, Richard A., '… A Good Jew, and a Good Englishman: The Jewish Lads' Brigade, 1894–1922', *Journal of Contemporary History*, 23 (1988): 119–27.

Waites, B. A., 'The Effect of the First World War on Class and Status in England, 1910–1920', *Journal of Contemporary History*, 11 (1976): 27–48.

Wilkinson, Paul, 'English Youth Movements, 1908–30', *Journal of Contemporary History*, 4, 2 (April 1969): 3–23.

Unpublished Dissertations and Theses

Bradshaw, J. T., 'Curricula under the Bradford School Board: Some Possible Reasons for their Extension', MA Dissertation, Leeds University (1972).

Penn, Alan, 'A Historical Survey of Curricular Development in the Elementary Schools of Dudley, and a Review of Present Provisions in a Group of Eight Secondary Modern Schools', Dissertation, Dip. Ed., Birmingham University (1963).

——, 'Education and the War of 1914–1918', MEd. thesis, Manchester University (1970).

Miscellaneous

History of the Victoria League, pamphlet (n.d.)

Howard, Michael, 'War and the Nation State', an Inaugural Lecture delivered before the University of Oxford, 18 November 1977 (Oxford: Clarendon Press, 1978).

Index